Library of
Davidson College

GK:
150 Years of the General Catalogue of
Printed Books in the British Museum

Working in the Catalogue Room, ca. 1935.
Foreground: R. A. Wilson, A. H. Chaplin, F. C. Francis.
Background (left): C. B. Oldman, consulting catalogue;
(right) F. L. Kent, at Incorporator's desk.

GK:
150 Years of the General Catalogue of Printed Books in the British Museum

A. H. CHAPLIN
Principal Keeper of Printed Books, 1966–70

Scolar Press

First published in 1987 by
SCOLAR PRESS
Gower Publishing Company Limited
Gower House, Croft Road
Aldershot GU11 3HR, England

U.S.A.
Scolar Press
Gower Publishing Company
Old Post Road, Brookfield
Vermont 05036

Copyright © A. H. Chaplin 1987

British Library Cataloguing in Publication Data
Chaplin, A. H.
   GK: 150 years of the General Catalogue
   of printed books in the British Museum.
    1. British Museum, *Department of Printed*
    Books   General Catalogue of printed books
  2. British Museum, *Department of Printed*
    Books   Catalogs—History
I. Title
025.3'1   Z792.B863

Library of Congress Cataloging in Publication Data
Chaplin, Arthur Hugh, 1905–
   GK: 150 years of the General Catalogue
   of printed books in the British Museum.
   1. British Library. Dept. of Printed Books.
   General Catalogue of Printed Books.

   2. British Library. Dept. of Printed Books—History.
   3. Library Catalogs—Great Britain—History.
   4. Cataloging—Great Britain—History.
   5. Bibliography—Great Britain—Methodology—History.
   I. Title
Z792.B863C47   1987   019'.1'0942142   87–13032

Printed in England by Billing & Sons Ltd Worcester

ISBN 0 85967 728 1

Contents

List of illustrations vi
Preface vii
Principal sources ix
Editions of the Catalogue x
1 Origins of the system 1
2 The 91 Rules and the 1841 catalogue 15
3 Consolidation, 1841–56 33
4 Continuation, 1856–75 44
5 The question of printing 47
6 Printing the catalogue, 1880–1905 56
7 Development of cataloguing practice, 1841–1900 67
8 Revision of the Rules 75
9 Character of the new catalogue 85
10 Maintenance and improvement 93
11 'GK II' 101
12 Cataloguing in the 1930s 111
13 The last days of GK II 120
14 GK III: production 131
15 GK III: characteristics 141
16 Supplements to GK III 146
17 Post-war cataloguing developments 151
18 The final phase 157
Index 171

List of illustrations

Working in the Catalogue Room, ca. 1935   *frontispiece*
Sir Henry Ellis; H. H. Baber; G. W. Porter, G. Bullen, R. Martineau, F. E. Blackstone and R. K. Douglas   3
A page from the 1841 catalogue   31
Richard Garnett; A. W. K. Miller; R. F. Sharp   61
A page from GK I   104
A page from GK II   105
A title showing change of heading   118
F. C. Francis; C. B. Oldman; N. F. Sharp   122
A page of laid-down catalogue for photography for GK III   136
A page from GK III   137
A page from GK III: Periodical Publications   144
A title showing the removal of the heading GOD   152
A title written by Panizzi as a young Assistant   165

Preface

This book, written after my retirement from the British Museum's Department of Printed Books, is the product of intermittent spare-time activity over a period of ten years.

My subject is the origin, growth and development of the General Catalogue, seen not only as a piece of internal library apparatus and as a publication but also as the product of an organised collective activity with its own traditions and problems. I have not attempted to reproduce the wider historical background provided for particular periods by Edward Miller's *Prince of Librarians: the life and times of Antonio Panizzi* (André Deutsch, 1967) and Dr Barbara McCrimmon's monograph *Power, Politics and Print: the publication of the British Museum Catalogue, 1881–1900* (Linnet, Hamden, Conn.; Bingley, London, 1981), to both of which I am indebted for some pointers to sources of information. My emphasis has been on the catalogue itself and the processes which determined its character and evolution and which account for some peculiar features which make it something of a bibliographical curiosity and may be puzzling to present-day users.

My treatment of the subject admittedly reflects my own point of view as a participant for forty years in the events described. I do not claim that what is largely a personal account constitutes a final and definitive history of the catalogue. I hope, however, that what I have found interesting will also be of interest to other makers and users of catalogues.

Direct experience between 1930 and 1970 has been supplemented for earlier periods mainly by the official records of the Department and for the final period by more superficial observation of events and by consultation with former colleagues still actively involved.

I wish to record my gratitude to the Trustees of the British Museum and the British Library Board, and particularly to two successive Directors General of the Reference Division of the British Library, Mr

Donovan Richnell and Mr Alex Wilson, and to Mr George Morris, Secretary of the British Museum, for easy access to official records and especially for permission to consult and quote from files not yet publicly accessible; and to a number of former colleagues in the Department of Printed Books, particularly Dr Richard Christophers, Mr Frank Fletcher and Mr James Etherington, for information on post-1970 developments with which they have been particularly concerned.

A. H. CHAPLIN

Principal sources

The documentary evidence for statements made in this book is to be found, for the periods and chapters indicated, in the sources listed below, except where reference is made to other sources in the notes to each chapter.

1834–1847 Chapters 1–3
'Appendix' to *Report of the Commissioners appointed to inquire into the constitution and management of the British Museum, 1850.* (Parliamentary Papers, House of Commons, 1850, vol. 24)

This Appendix contains a comprehensive, chronologically arranged collection of reports, minutes and other documents printed for the use of the Commissioners.

1847–1855 Chapter 3
Panizzi papers: official collection, vols. 8–15 (British Library Archives, DH 1). Documents arranged chronologically.

Most of the relevant papers in vols. 1–7 (1836–46) are included in the Appendix to the *Report of the Commissioners . . .*, above.

1856–1973 Chapters 4–17
Department of Printed Books. Minutes, reports, etc., vols. 1–138 (British Library Archives, DH 2).

The volumes are divided into sections, within which the arrangement is chronological. Normally each volume begins with three sections of Minutes, followed by three sections of Reports. Most of the relevant documents are in the third section of each group, 'Miscellaneous minutes' and 'Miscellaneous reports'.

1875–1882 Chapters 5 and 6
Vol. 62 of the 'Minutes, reports, etc.', entitled 'Supplementary volume', contains special collections of documents on various subjects. Sections I–III refer to discussions on the printing of the Catalogue, 1875–1882, and constitute the principal source for Chapter 5 and for p. 60 and the first part of p. 62 in Chapter 6.

The formula 'P.B. file' in the notes to Chapters 13–17 refers to files in the British Library registry which at the time of writing had not been transferred to the British Library Archives.

Editions of the Catalogue

1. *Librorum impressorum qui in Museo Britannico adservantur catalogus*, 2 vols. Londini, 1787. Fol.
2. *Librorum impressorum qui in Museo Britannico adservantur catalogus*, 7 vols. Londini, 1813–19. 8vo.
   (The 'octavo catalogue'.)
3. *Catalogue of Printed Books in the British Museum*, vol. 1. London, 1841. Fol.
   (No more published.)
4. *Catalogue of the Printed Books in the Library of the British Museum*, 393 parts. Printed by William Clowes and Sons, London, 1881–1900. Fol.
   — Supplement, 1900–05, 44 parts.
5. *The British Museum Catalogue of Printed Books, 1881–1900*, 58 vols. J. W. Edwards, Ann Arbor, 1946.
   — Supplement, 1900–05, 10 vols. 1950.
   (A reduced photographic reproduction of 4.)
6. *British Museum General Catalogue of Printed Books*, vols. 1–51 (*A–DEZ*). Trustees of the British Museum, London, 1931–54.
   ('GK II'. No more published.)
7. *British Museum General Catalogue of Printed Books*, photolithographic edition to 1955, 263 vols. Trustees of the British Museum, London, 1959–66.
   — Ten-Year Supplement, 1956–65, 50 vols. 1968.
   — Five-Year Supplement, 1966–70, 26 vols. 1971–72.
   — Five-Year Supplement, 1971–75, 13 vols. Published for the British Library by British Museum Publications, London, 1978–79.
   ('GK III'.)
8. *British Museum General Catalogue of Printed Books to 1955*, compact edition, 27 vols. Readex Microprint Corporation, New York, 1967.
   —Ten-Year Supplement, 1956–65. 1969.
   — Five-Year Supplement, 1966–70. 1974.
   — Five-Year Supplement, 1971–75. 1980.
   (A reduced photographic reproduction of 7.)
9. *The British Library General Catalogue of Printed Books to 1975*. Clive Bingley, London; K. G. Saur, London, München, New York, 1979– .

1 Origins of the system

Since the end of the nineteenth century the General Catalogue of Printed Books has been known in the libraries of the world as an imposing series of large folio volumes, which in 1905 filled about 15 feet of shelf space and in its latest complete form nearly four times as much. Users of the British Museum Reading Room have known it also in the form of a much more extensive series of still larger volumes in which printed slips representing later additions have been pasted alongside columns of entries from the published catalogue. In both forms it is the product of a cataloguing system of which the essential characteristics were developed between 1834 and 1850 under the guidance of Anthony Panizzi, who in cataloguing, as in almost everything else, shaped the character of the Department of Printed Books as it persisted through the second half of the nineteenth century and the first half of the twentieth.

From the outset the system was designed to produce a catalogue appropriate to, and worthy of, a library that was one of the largest and fastest growing in the world and a great national institution. This objective and the conditions for its fulfilment were conceived with great clarity by one man, Panizzi, and communicated by him to his staff: but the full development of the system was impeded by a struggle lasting 16 years — exacerbated by prejudice and personal animosities and ultimately only partly successful — to get it understood and accepted by Panizzi's employers, the Trustees of the British Museum.

The course of this struggle is amply documented in a series of reports, minutes and letters reproduced as an appendix to the *Report of the Commissioners appointed to inquire into the constitution and management of the British Museum*,[1] published in 1850, and has been well summarised in Edward Miller's biography of Panizzi.[2] It is outlined again here with special attention to factors affecting the character of the catalogue itself.

In April 1834 the Trustees asked H. H. Baber, the Keeper of Printed

Books, to prepare a plan for a new alphabetical catalogue. This would replace two existing catalogues: the catalogue of printed books published in 17 volumes in 1813–19,[3] compiled by Henry Ellis, Keeper of Printed Books from 1806, and H. H. Baber, who succeeded him in this post in 1812; and the printed catalogue of the King's Library – George III's collection, which was added to the British Museum in 1823.[4] In two copies of the former, mounted on larger paper and interleaved, entries for additions were made in manuscript, or, in some cases, taken from other, separately printed catalogues – for example, that of Sir Joseph Banks's collection. By 1834 the catalogue in this form had swollen to 40 folio volumes. Their poor state of repair, the inconvenience resulting from two sequences of entries, one printed and the other manuscript, and the labour involved in maintaining the accession entries in correct alphabetical order had stimulated demand for an entirely new catalogue. Dissatisfaction was increased by the fact that the books in the King's Library, an extremely important part of the total collection, were recorded only in a separate catalogue, and that a large collection of pamphlets forming part of the King's Library was not recorded in either catalogue.

Baber's proposals, worked out in consultation with H. F. Cary, the Assistant Keeper, and with Panizzi, who had joined the Department as an Assistant in 1831, were clear and firm. First, no start could be made on the work until additional staff were appointed: otherwise arrears in other work would accumulate. Because the existing catalogues had been compiled by a number of librarians, of varying degrees of competence and following different principles, the whole would have to be revised and the manuscript slips, which had been preserved, would have to be compared with the books. One person would have to be put in charge of the whole operation. Mr Panizzi was eminently qualified for the position, and would undertake with the help of three suitably qualified 'assistants', to complete the work of revision and arrangement in five or six years. Nothing should be sent to the printer until the whole of the copy was ready, and printing, with proof correction, would take at least three years. The report also contained a detailed statement of the principles to be followed in revising the catalogue entries. These included several refinements of earlier practice, the most important being the inclusion of the titles of works in cross-references from editors, translators, etc. instead of giving only the heading of the work referred to, as in the octavo catalogue.

Panizzi had undoubtedly played a large part in the preparation of this report, and he made it the basis of later arguments with the Trustees. On

Top left: Sir Henry Ellis. *Top right*: H. H. Baber.
Below: G. W. Porter, G. Bullen, R. Martineau, F. E. Blackstone,
R. K. Douglas; detail from staff group ca. 1885.

one point in it, however, he had disagreed. 'My opinion', he wrote later, 'was that for consistency's sake, the first word in the title (except an article or preposition) ought to be taken as the leading one under which to place anonymous publications. Mr Baber and Mr Cary differing from me on this point, my opinion was overruled.' A tortuous and almost meaningless sentence in Baber's report seems to reflect a long and inconclusive discussion: 'in the instance of anonymous publications, there should be prefixed to the title, for want of the surname of the author, some such principal word, selected from the author's title, as would most immediately direct the student to that place in the catalogue in which a production so published would be most likely to be entered'. This conflict between the need for a clear, unambiguous rule and the desire for a useful, acceptable heading was to have important consequences for the future of the catalogue.

Ellis (now Principal Librarian) thought the plan for the new catalogue unnecessarily elaborate and, at the Trustees' meeting at which Baber's report was considered, he put forward a short report of his own in which he described the method by which he and Baber, unaided, had produced the octavo catalogue, which he thought needed only enlargement, not extensive revision. He implied that similar procedures could produce the new catalogue much more quickly and economically than was suggested. Influenced by this intervention by their principal officer, the Trustees declined to enlarge the staff and persuaded Baber to adopt a less satisfactory plan. Three Assistants, Panizzi, Glover and Horne, were to be transferred from other duties to revise titles in Romance languages, in English and in Greek and Latin respectively, while a fourth was to be engaged for 'German, Danish and all the various languages used in the northern half of Europe'. (Baber suggested that the revision should proceed room by room and shelf by shelf, starting with the King's Library.) Baber and Cary were to exercise general supervision, and the titles, after they had all been arranged in alphabetical order would be prepared for the press by 'some one of the librarians' to be designated later. Panizzi lost no time in protesting that, as no individual would have full responsibility for the catalogue while the work was in progress, an expensive and time-consuming general revision would have to be undertaken at the end, and that the catalogue would take longer to compile and would probably cost more than under the original plan. His protest was ignored.

By the end of 1835 about one-sixth of the catalogue entries had been revised by the four Assistants, and the Principal Librarian, advised by Baber, told the Trustees that the completion of this first revision would still take five or six years, with a further three years for final revision and arrangement and the insertion of cross-references. To speed up the work Baber recommended once more that a superintendent should be appointed, who would receive all revised titles as the work proceeded, make final decisions on headings and arrangement and give instructions for cross-references to be made; he also reiterated the demand that all persons working on the catalogue should give their whole time to it. This time his proposals received the support of Sir Henry Ellis, but a decision on them was deferred pending further discussions with Baber and members of his staff, thus affording Panizzi the opportunity to address a report directly to the Trustees. In this report, he insisted on the importance of a catalogue worthy of the Library, at least as good as any other alphabetical catalogue, strongly supported the standards and methods of work proposed in Baber's original 1834 report, and in an outline of the rules to be followed included, without comment or argument, the sentence: 'Anonymous publications should be entered according to the first word of the title.' He also mentioned the desirability of adding to the alphabetical catalogue an 'index of matters' – always a part of his plan, although never fully provided – and suggested the maintenance of copies of the catalogue by 'transcribing titles on half-sheets of an uniform size, kept together by *reliures mobiles*', so foreshadowing, in a rudimentary form, the system more fully developed later.

In February 1836 work on the new catalogue was almost completely suspended so that the Assistants could devote their time to an even more urgent task – direction and revision of the transcription, in two copies, of the whole of the old interleaved catalogue, which was now condemned as unusable in its existing form. This, with other activities, such as the preparation of evidence for the Select Committee of the House of Commons which examined the Museum's affairs in 1835 and 1836, and the production of the regular annual lists of accessions to the Library, prevented resumption of work on the new catalogue until after Panizzi's appointment as Keeper of Printed Books in succession to Baber in July 1837.

Panizzi himself now became the author of his department's reports to the Trustees and the direct recipient of the Trustees' instructions. However, despite frequent communications in which he defended with great force and skill his original concept of the catalogue, from which he never wavered, the answers he received often showed little grasp of the points he had made, and it was not until he had been Keeper for 13 years that he at last achieved full control of the project (and even then only in a form containing features to which he had always objected).

Several factors contributed to this situation. An extraordinarily untidy system of committees and subcommittees, without fixed membership or continuity of attendance by individual Trustees, put the Board very much at the mercy of their regular advisers – the Principal Librarian, Sir Henry Ellis, who had been successively Keeper of both Printed Books and Manuscripts, and Josiah Forshall, the Secretary of the Museum. Panizzi's reports all passed through the hands of these two officers, who were regularly present at Trustees' meetings while Panizzi was not, except when specially summoned. Although he was frequently interviewed, he was not present at subsequent discussions on which decisions were based, nor was he regularly informed of reports by others on the same questions or of items in the minutes which did not directly refer to him or his department. Among the higher officers in the Museum outside the Department of Printed Books there was jealousy of the rapid rise of a foreigner to a position of prominence, and irritation caused by his quickness to take offence, his acerbity in argument, and his firm (and in professional matters usually justified) belief that he was always right.

Since the question of a new catalogue had first been raised, it had been understood that the Trustees had a printed catalogue in mind. One of Panizzi's first suggestions as Keeper was that this idea should be reconsidered, and he put forward four reasons against printing:

1. it would be unreasonable to expect the public to buy a very large catalogue in which most of the entries would be for 'common and comparatively insignificant books' which, if wanted at all, could easily be found elsewhere and could in any case be presumed to be in the British Museum;
2. a printed catalogue of a rapidly growing library would be 'from its origin an incomplete and imperfect work';
3. for use in the Library, a printed catalogue must either have numerous supplements or have entries added in manuscript: both would be inconvenient as they would involve searching in more than one alphabetical sequence.
4. printing the catalogue would cost about £7,000 (not counting staff time employed in proof correcting).

He believed, however, that it would be advantageous to print separate catalogues of the rare books in the Library, of the Thomason Civil War tracts, and of the French Revolution tracts: these would be more saleable than a general catalogue of the whole Library.

Despite these objections the Trustees, on 9 December 1837, resolved not only that they continued 'to be decidedly of opinion that a General Alphabetical Catalogue of the Museum Library should be printed', but also that 'it should be printed at the earliest period which is consistent with the due execution of the work'.

Panizzi's estimates of the magnitude of the task and the staff and time needed to carry it out were once more questioned by Sir Henry Ellis. In a letter dated 11 December 1837 to the Earl of Aberdeen, one of the Trustees, he complained that the octavo catalogue, one half of which he had himself compiled, was being represented as unfit to be the foundation of the new catalogue. He defended the methods used in compiling the earlier catalogue and the accuracy of their results, even offering to pay the expense of a comparison of the entries with the books and to give a reward for every error discovered. This letter was read to the Trustees on 16 December, and then to their subcommittee on the Department of Printed Books on 25 April 1838. It was not communicated to Panizzi by either Ellis or Forshall and did not come to his knowledge until nine years later, in 1847. It was clearly a major influence on the subcommittee's recommendation, confirmed at a general meeting on 12 May 1838, that 'the Trustees adhere to their intention of printing a useful catalogue, *formed upon the general plan and basis of the catalogue now in use*'. It was useless to protest that 'the catalogue now in use' was a combination of elements produced at different times and by different hands, and had no 'general plan'. Panizzi had no alternative but to assume that the plan submitted by Baber in 1834, which involved a systematic comparison of title-slips with the books, was still in force. In his opinion, however, the work already done by himself and others had been largely wasted because of the rejection of the original proposal that the revision of the catalogue should be continuously supervised and co-ordinated by a single editor. In a supreme effort to convince the Trustees of the importance of this point he had, on 12 January 1838, devoted the whole of a lengthy report to it. His argument cannot be better expressed than in his own words:

To compile a good catalogue – a catalogue worthy of this institution – is a work of great, nay, of immense difficulty, which will require a length of time scarcely credible, and which should be under the direction of *one* person, who must himself see in each case that the principles determined upon are actually adhered to, either by watching the work as it proceeds, or by re-examining the whole minutely when considered ready for his inspection. Mr Panizzi does not think there can be any question as to which of these two methods is the shortest, the safest, and consequently the least expensive. In the first case, errors are corrected almost the moment they are committed, and precedents fixed to prevent like ones occurring, and the reviser, as well as those who work under him, have the benefit of each other's mutual advice and assistance. In the other, errors are allowed to accumulate, and are actually received as principles by each individual, according as he interprets the rules laid down for him: persons employed on the same work are isolated and thereby deprived of the advantage of mutual help; and it will take more time, finally, to revise the work in detail, than to prepare it for revision.

In support of his contention, Panizzi quotes long extracts from Hyde's introduction to his catalogue of the Bodleian Library (1674) and from Giovanni Battista Audiffredi's introduction to his catalogue of the Biblioteca Casanatense in Rome (1761–80), which (although it was never finished) Panizzi describes as 'certainly the finest work of the kind ever done'. As further proof he presents the then quite recent case of the catalogue of the Public Library of Geneva (1834). For this classified catalogue, 15 *savants*, working to an agreed plan, had in about two years prepared the titles for the classes in which each was expert. However, when the titles came to be arranged for publication, the editor, Louis Vaucher, found them full of inconsistencies, and had to spend three years putting them in order, with frequent recourse to the books themselves, and seeing them through the press. 'In 1831', comments Panizzi 'the plan was adopted that ought to have been adopted in 1825, and the catalogue would have been published in half the time.'

The Trustees' subcommittee noted the report but made no further comment than to add to their already quoted resolution an instruction to Panizzi 'to offer to the Trustees, from time to time, such suggestions with regard to the direction of his Department, as shall, in his opinion, most effectually tend to accomplish the intention of the Trustees within the shortest possible period'. The alarming extent of the divergence between Panizzi and the Trustees on what was 'the shortest possible period' did not become fully apparent until the end of the same year. On 5 December 1838 Panizzi received a note from Forshall conveying a request from the Trustees that he should 'lay before them, when they meet on Saturday the 15th instant, a plan for the immediate printing of the new Alphabetical Catalogue of the Museum Library'. Panizzi replied that Baber's plan should be proceeded with immediately, and that Assistants should be appointed to replace those originally employed on the work, who were now occupied by other duties. He pointed out that, when their work of revision was completed, the titles would have to be alphabetically arranged and prepared for the press. This done, he thought that printing would proceed at the rate of 48 pages a week.

In this reply he assumed the continued acceptance of the principle, unquestioned since April 1834, that no part of the catalogue would be printed until the whole of the copy had been prepared – an operation that would take at least five years. His assumption now abruptly received its death-blow in a Trustees' minute of 15 December: 'The Secretary was directed to acquaint Mr Panizzi, that it was the fixed determination of the Trustees to commence the printing of the new Alphabetical Catalogue of the Library in the course of the ensuing year.'

The decision had to be accepted, and by 26 December (no prolonged Christmas holiday in those days!) Panizzi was ready with his new plan of action. First, all the existing title-slips, including those for the King's Library, would be arranged in alphabetical order. 'Competent persons' would then examine them and separate those which they thought should be transferred to a different letter; those to be transferred to the letter *A* would next be corrected. Meanwhile, he himself, or another responsible editor if one were appointed, would look through the whole of the letter *A*, and have corrections made where they seem necessary. The titles for the letter *A* could thus be made ready for the press during 1839. Panizzi then warned the Trustees that the catalogue, produced in this way, would inevitably contain many errors that the original plan would have avoided. In addition, he drew attention to a particular problem affecting cross-references. He wished to adhere to the decision that in the new catalogue references from editors etc. would include details identifying the works referred to, but doubted the wisdom of printing references pointing to entries which had been made under letters not yet revised, which might later be moved or materially altered. He therefore proposed to omit cross-references altogether at this stage and to number consecutively the entries printed under each letter, so that a separate volume of cross-references, leading to numbered entries, could be printed at the end of the catalogue. Finally, he repeated his earlier statement that the work could not be done at all without additional staff. On 12 January 1839 the Trustees agreed to the appointment of two extra Assistants and two Attendants. There was no immediate reply to the question about cross-references, but when it came it was accompanied by a further turn of the screw. On 13 July the Trustees resolved that:

without undervaluing the principles suggested by Mr Panizzi for the formation of a Catalogue of Printed Books ... the Trustees, considering the time, labour and expense already devoted to the preparation of a catalogue, and the urgent desire expressed in the House of Commons ... that the work may be completed with the least possible delay ... wish that Mr Panizzi would be pleased to proceed with the work upon the general understanding that their object is to have the best catalogue, cross-references included, which can be delivered to them complete for press on the 31st December 1844; and that, approving generally the rules which he has laid before them, they leave to his own discretion the application of those rules, subject always to the condition that the catalogue be completed as aforesaid.

The extract from the minute forwarded by the Secretary to Panizzi ended at this point. Not only did it contain a subtle but misleading variation, 'complete in press' for 'complete for press', it entirely omitted the final paragraph:

that the preceding resolution be forwarded to the Trustees forming the sub-committee on the Library, not now present; and that, unless they should transmit to the Secretary an intimation of their objection to the same, it be considered as the final determination of the Board: in the other event, such resolution to be again brought under consideration.

Kept in ignorance of this opportunity of explaining to the subcommittee his conviction that the proposed completion date was an impossible one, Panizzi had to accept it as a firm decision and do his best to meet it.
Meanwhile, another important question had been under discussion: the cataloguing rules referred to in the Trustees' resolution. On 5 December 1838 Panizzi sent to Forshall, at the Trustees' request, a copy of the brief set of 16 rules which Baber had given as guidance to his assistants in May 1834, and which the Trustees had not before asked to see or subjected to criticism. In his covering note Panizzi referred to his disagreement with Baber and Cary over the cataloguing of anonymous works, and added: 'I have very lately requested Mr Garnett[5] to prefer the first word for the principal entry of such works, giving, however, as many cross-references as he may deem requisite from any other entry he thinks proper to make.' This elicited a prompt reply, in which the Trustees announced for the first time their intention to control the cataloguing rules in detail: 'in the opinion of the Trustees no alteration should be made in any of the rules established by Mr Baber ... without the express sanction of the Board'. By Baber's rule, entry was to be under 'some prominent or leading word in the title'. Panizzi proposed an addition, based on his instruction to Garnett, requiring entry under the first word (other than an article or preposition) 'whenever any doubt arises as to which may be deemed the leading word'. Before passing this proposal to the Trustees, Sir Henry Ellis appended a note: 'This is not in accordance with the method pursued in the octavo catalogue ... which Sir H. Ellis believes the Trustees consider as the groundwork of the new

one.' The Trustees substituted the words: 'whenever no leading word can be fixed upon'; and Forshall, in communicating this amendment to Panizzi, added in explanation: 'They wish that when two or more words appear to have an equal claim to be considered the leading word, any one of them should be preferred to the first word of the title.' 'It is precisely', observed Panizzi in a later report, 'when more words than one appear to have an equal claim ... that the difficulty chiefly arises and errors and inconsistencies become unavoidable.' In this view he was strongly supported by a letter sent to him, with Garnett's approval, by Edward Edwards (then a newly appointed Assistant) asking for reconsideration of the instruction to select 'the most prominent word', on the ground that 'it will be impossible to make such selection upon any principle or system on which all ... can agree; and that hence there must necessarily arise such great diversity of practice as will deprive the catalogue of that which ought to be its chief characteristic – a clearly ascertainable *system*'. The letter contained a number of convincing examples, and concluded with an appeal for entry under the first word. Panizzi forwarded it to the Trustees with a note saying that Garnett, Jones and Edwards, all having formerly differed, now in the light of experience agreed with him; and that Watts had always agreed. The precise form of the rule remained undecided for the time being.

Having started to examine Baber's rules, the Trustees found another that puzzled them – rule 3:

In the instances in which variations may be found in the surname, peculiar to the same author, it must be transcribed in that form, language, or peculiar orthography, in which it may happen to be expressed in the respective title pages in which it is recorded, as Grange, La Grange, De la Grange ...

Did this mean, they enquired, that works by the same author would be entered in various places, according to the form in which the name appeared on the title pages? Panizzi had to explain that Baber's rules were merely instructions to those making the first revision of titles, and that the exact form of heading for each author would have been determined by the responsible editor who was to have been appointed later. Asked how the problem was being dealt with in current additions to the existing catalogue, he replied that, since he became Keeper, 'Quérard's principles' had been followed for names of the 'La Grange' type which were new to the catalogue, while for those already there the existing form continued to be used: he could not say what principles had been followed earlier. French catalogues did not show any consistent practice.

He now found himself obliged to explain 'Quérard's principles'. (They are stated in the introduction to the first volume of his *La France littéraire*, and deal with French names only.) He then submitted a rule on surnames with prefixes, expanding Quérard's to cover other languages, together with rules for cross-references, which had also been a subject of discussion. Foreseeing an indefinite series of further enquiries and discussions, he wrote to the Trustees on 8 March 1839 suggesting that, to ensure consistency in the rules ultimately decided on, it would be better if a full set of rules were drawn up at once and submitted to them for approval or amendment.

Some progress in formulating instructions supplementary to Baber's rules on other points than those raised by the Trustees had clearly already been made. Edwards's letter quoted above had, for example, included an enquiry whether an anonymous work addressed to, or referring to, a person whose name appeared in its title was *invariably* to have its principal entry under that name; and Panizzi's marginal note ('Certainly; except if the person's name be introduced *merely* to say that the book is dedicated to him') anticipates part of the rule on anonymous works that was finally adopted. Whatever the position may have been on 8 March, Panizzi was able, after the surprisingly short interval of only ten days, to present to the Trustees a general set of rules which, however, he acknowledged were hastily compiled and imperfect. It would still be necessary, he said, to compose special rules for academies, almanacs and calendars, the Bible, liturgies and periodicals.

The Trustees' Committee immediately began discussions with Panizzi, and on 20 March, in a three-hour sitting, examined 34 rules and suggested amendments. At four more meetings, on 6, 13, 20 and 24 April, the rest of the rules, now 87 in number, were considered and amendments proposed. To incorporate the amendments and to cast the rules as a whole, including those for special categories of books, into an appropriate form was still a considerable task. 'Several of my assistants, and myself occasionally', he wrote later, 'worked on them for more than 12 hours a day, not excepting Sundays, for weeks together'. The group of 'assistants' consisted of Winter Jones, Watts and the two Assistants newly appointed to work on the catalogue, Edward Edwards and John Humffreys Parry. The last two have left accounts[6] of this period of intensive work, continued after closing time in Panizzi's apartments, and have testified to Panizzi's willingness to consider all suggestions from members of the team and to accept majority decisions when they did not accord with his own opinions.

On 27 June, Panizzi laid before the Trustees the rules 'as originally proposed, and as altered by the Trustees in Committee, accompanied by the requisite illustrations'. The 'illustrations', or examples, included the whole of the heading HORATIUS, both as it stood in the existing catalogue and as it would appear under the new rules as amended. On 29 June the Committee ordered rule 20 to be struck out and approved the remainder. (The text of the deleted rule 20 has not survived, but it appears to have dealt with the indication of omissions from transcribed titles by a series of dots: the Trustees later ordered the deletion of such dots where they appeared in the examples.) On 13 July, at the meeting which fixed 31 December 1844 as the date for completion of the catalogue, the rules (now 91 in number) were finally approved by the full Board and ordered to be printed.

The decision on the completion date was communicated to Panizzi's staff, with copies of the rules and examples, in a memorandum dated 8 August. It directed that the staff, who were already working on alphabetically arranged title-slips instead of examining the books shelf by shelf, should now correct only obvious errors in the old titles, that they should compare them with the books only when there was cause to suspect some serious mistake, and that even then they should not make alterations that might lead to important changes elsewhere or to misleading inconsistencies in the catalogue. Nothing was to be done that would lead the cataloguers 'to spend in researches that time which must be devoted to the compilation and printing of the best catalogue which can be completed before the end of 1844. All our efforts must be directed to this end'. Panizzi thus accepted, with as good a grace as possible, an instruction he was convinced could not be carried out, providing himself at the same time with a defence against any future charge of not complying with the Trustees' orders. Earlier in the year, Panizzi had suggested that some of the 'very long articles' (that is, long series of entries under particular headings) in the catalogue should be prepared and printed in advance of the rest, as a test of the rules and as a means of putting in order some of the most confused portions of the existing catalogue. The first two would be ACADEMIES and ARISTOTLE. By 9 October he was able to report that ACADEMIES was in proof, and that considerable omissions discovered there were now being made good. By 8 January 1840 the proofs of ACADEMIES were corrected and those of all entries preceding ACADEMIES were in course of correction. By the end of 1840, all titles up to and including ARISTOTLE were ready for the printer, but as early as April Panizzi had reported his conviction 'that the whole of the work, however hastily performed, if done in a tolerable manner, cannot be completed as soon as the Trustees expect'. He asked permission to extend the hours of work of the Assistants involved from six to nine hours a day during the summer months, and that an additional Assistant be appointed. He also offered to postpone his own summer vacation. The Trustees did not accept his offer, or the proposal for longer hours, but offered extra staff. Panizzi tried unsuccessfully to convince them that extra time from experienced Assistants would be much more useful and economical than extra hands who had to be trained, and the request for an additional Assistant, which had been an integral part of his proposal, was dropped. It was not until 8 June 1841 that the whole of the letter A had been prepared for the press. On 22 July 1841 the completed first volume of the catalogue was laid before the Trustees, with a bitter comment on the 'many and grave errors' that it contained on account of its hasty production, and a restatement of the impracticability of the instruction to complete the catalogue by the end of 1844. 'Experience has taught him', he wrote, 'that he was attempting what is impossible; and that, without saving time, he was only hurrying the publication of a work, disfigured by such errors, as would be a just cause of dissatisfaction to the public, and subject him to the imputation of ignorance and carelessness.'

Notes and references
1. Parliamentary Papers, House of Commons, 1850, vol. 24.
2. Miller, E. *Prince of Librarians.* André Deutsch, London, 1967.
3. *Librorum impressorum qui in Museo Britannico adservantur catalogus,* 7 vols. Londini, 1813–19. 8°.
4. *Bibliothecæ Regiæ catalogus,* 5 vols. London, 1820–29. Fol.
5. The Revd. Richard Garnett, father of Richard Garnett, later editor of the catalogue and Keeper of Printed Books.
6. Edwards in his *Lives of the Founders of the British Museum,* vol. 2, pp. 567–8; Parry in *Report of the Commissioners ..., 1850,* Minutes of evidence, Questions 7317, 7319, 7320, 7323.

2 The 91 Rules and the 1841 catalogue

The 91 Rules approved by the Trustees on 13 July 1839 have long been recognised as a landmark in the history of library cataloguing. Because they were published, as an aid to users, in the initial volume of the projected catalogue, they had a wide circulation and could therefore be used as a model in other libraries. They constitute the point of departure from which the later cataloguing codes of the English-speaking world developed, and also gradually diverged, for over a century. Within the British Museum, too, there was development and divergence, but these were slower and more limited, so that in course of time British Museum practice came to differ in important respects from that of most other libraries.

The Rules were not, however, conceived as a code for general use, nor were they based on a thought-out theory of cataloguing. They were hurriedly put together to solve the problems of a particular library at a particular time. The occasion of their production was the need to effect a compromise between Panizzi's clear, professional conception of a bibliographical record and the much vaguer idea entertained by the Trustees – who in this matter were representative of a large and influential body of the Library's users – of a useful catalogue which would follow familiar practices. The lasting importance of the Rules lies in their attempt to give a coherent and precise form to parts of the cataloguing system which had so far been vague and uncertain, so that the combined work of a number of cataloguers would produce consistent results.

In form, the Rules as first presented to the Trustees in March 1839 were an expansion of Baber's 16 very summary rules, which represent broadly, though with some improvements, the practices followed in the octavo catalogue of 1813–19. Twelve of Baber's rules are reproduced exactly, or with only minor alterations. In two rules the order in which data are to be recorded is changed: the real name of an author using a pseudonym is to be given at the end of the heading, not at the end of the title; and the 'form' – that is, bibliographical format (also referred to in the rules as 'size') – is to follow the place and date of publication, instead of preceding them. Only two of Baber's rules disappear, to be replaced by entirely new ones: rule 3, on names appearing in varying forms, and 13, on anonymous books. Both of these had been the subject of exchanges between Panizzi and the Trustees. In a number of other rules additions are made to render them clearer and more precise; and numerous new rules, covering points of detail not mentioned by Baber, bring the total number from 16 to 53.

Both sets of rules deal with a series of major topics in the same order:

(a) the basic structure of the catalogue, defined by reference to the predominant type of entry – entries under authors' surnames in alphabetical order (Baber 2; Panizzi 2);

(b) choice and form of names to be used as headings (Baber 3–6; Panizzi 3–17);

(c) transcription of the title (Baber 7; Panizzi 18–24);

(d) number of parts or volumes, imprint and format (Baber 8–10; Panizzi 25–27);

(e) conventional notes indicating special features of the book catalogued (Baber 11, 12; Panizzi 28–31);

(f) use of headings other than authors' names, for anonyma, pseudonyma, collections, etc. (Baber 13–15; Panizzi 32–49);

(g) translations and commentaries (Baber 16; Panizzi 50–53).

The remainder of the 91 Rules deal with matters not covered by Baber's rules. First there are two groups which were probably included in the draft submitted by Panizzi on 18 March 1839: rules for cross-references (54–68), formulating more precisely principles communicated to the Trustees in February; and rules for the arrangement of entries under a heading (69–78). These are followed by the special rules (79–91) which, on 18 March, Panizzi had told the Trustees would be submitted later. The categories to which they apply are a mixture, not arranged in any logical order, of types of publication and types of corporate body: Bible; academies; periodicals; almanacs and calendars; religious and military orders; anonymous catalogues, dictionaries and encyclopaedias; and, lastly, liturgies.

While some of the additions to Baber's rules are merely explicit statements of practices already followed (for example, entering certain classes of persons under their first or Christian name), a considerable number represent innovations. One of these is the adoption of the

English form of name for sovereigns and princes of sovereign houses (and in practice also for place-names used in headings). For authors who have used more than one linguistic form of their names the vernacular form is prescribed if it has been used in their printed publications. The earlier practice had been to prefer Latin forms. The new rule for names with prefixes puts French names (following Quérard) under an article but not under a preposition, all other foreign names under the part following the prefix, and English names of foreign origin under the whole name including the prefix.

A major innovation is the rule (9) that acts of corporate bodies should be entered under those bodies, but not directly under their names: these are to appear as subheadings under 'the name of the country or place from which they derive their denomination, or, for want of such denomination, under the name of the place whence their acts are issued'. Baber's rules had made no mention of publications issued by corporate bodies and the practice had been to use their names as headings only when, in the absence of a personal author, they were chosen under the rule for anonymous works as a 'prominent or leading' part of the title.

The rule for transcribing titles is expanded by a requirement to observe the original orthography. A rule is supplied for books without title pages, allowing for entry under head title or colophon, preceded by 'begin.' or 'end.' respectively and, when these are lacking, for 'some idea of the work to be given in English, between brackets'. Titles of separate works included in a publication, if not mentioned on the title page, are to be added 'between brackets or parentheses, as the case may be'. This last phrase is unexplained, but can be interpreted in the light of some of the preceding rules, by which various additions made by the cataloguer to headings are to be 'in brackets', while the transposed Christian names following the surname are to be 'in parentheses'. The instruction clearly refers to the establishment of the practice, which became permanent in the British Museum catalogues and was also followed extensively elsewhere, of distinguishing additions to titles by parentheses ('round brackets') when transcribed from another place in the book and by brackets ('square brackets') when supplied by the cataloguer.

There is a rule stating that works in oriental characters or languages (except Hebrew) will be catalogued separately 'in a supplementary volume', but that, as an exception, the Bible and its parts, in whatever language or characters, will be included in the general catalogue.

The rules for physical description and imprint are expanded by an instruction that division into parts or volumes is to be recorded 'in the words of the title', but that, in the absence of such words, the term 'volumes' will be used when the numerical sequence of pages (or, when pages are unnumbered, the register) is interrupted, otherwise the term 'parts' will be used. The position allotted to the format (8vo, 4to, etc.), as already stated, is altered from before the place of publication to after the date. The reason for this change is obscure: it is a departure from all earlier British Museum practice and from the prevailing practice in other catalogues of the period. In T. H. Horne's *Outlines for the Classification of a Library* (1825) and in one contemporary catalogue referred to by Panizzi in his report of 12 January 1828, namely that of the Geneva Public Library (1834), the format appears at the end of the entry, but the customary link with the number of volumes is preserved by inserting the latter immediately before the format. (The separation of these two elements later led to a divergence from general practice in the treatment of the collation.)

Another characteristic feature of British Museum cataloguing is the insertion, between the title and the imprint, of certain notes on the peculiarities of the book catalogued (for example, 'editio princeps', printed on vellum, in Gothic type, with manuscript notes) reduced to a conventional abbreviated form. Baber's rules imply that these notes will follow the imprint and date, and in the octavo catalogue this is the position that they commonly, but not invariably, occupy. Panizzi's rules on the subject (28–31) also come after the rule for the imprint (27). However, two of them direct that the information should be given 'at the end of the title', so introducing another peculiarity into the order of items in a British Museum catalogue entry. The number of such conventional notes has been increased, and their precise form (for example, roman or italic, large or small capitals) is indicated.

In the next group of rules, concerning works for which the heading is not the author's name, Panizzi first provides a rule (32) for entry under initials when the indication of authorship is in this form. Then follow the eight rules (33–40) embodying Panizzi's compromise with the Trustees over anonymous works. There seems to have been no disagreement with the principle, common to Baber and Panizzi, that a book should be treated as anonymous if its author's name, although known to the cataloguer, did not appear in it. The decisive importance of the title page, supplemented when necessary by other information presented in the book, was generally accepted. The Rules are an elaborate attempt to ensure that, while accepting the desire for entry under a 'prominent or leading' part of the title, the choice of headings will be consistent and that a user who is acquainted with the Rules will know where to find the entry he seeks. The solution adopted is, whenever possible, to take a *name* from the title, applying the following order of priority: the name of a person; the name of a corporate body; some other proper name; an adjective derived from a proper name. In the absence of such a name or adjective, the first option is the name of the editor, or failing an editor the translator, if any; the second is the first substantive, and the last resort, if there is no substantive, is the first word. This system concedes something to the previously accepted practice of entry under a subject-word, but only when the subject is a named entity, not a class or concept represented by a common noun. The decision to prefer the first substantive to the first word is in the spirit of the compromise and had been noted by Panizzi[1] as a practice found in German catalogues that might be acceptable as a general rule. The rule for entry under the first substantive is supplemented by the following sentence: 'A substantive, adjectively used, to be taken in conjunction with its following substantive as forming one word; and the same to be done with respect to adjectives incorporated with their following substantive'. The meaning of the last phrase is not immediately obvious: its interpretation in practice will be mentioned later.[2] The general scheme is modified by an additional rule directing that an anonymous work 'purporting to comment or remark on a work of which the title is set forth in that of such publication' is to be catalogued under the heading used for the work commented on.

In dealing with 'pseudonymous publications' the new rules extend the concept 'pseudonym' to cover certain words and expressions that are not names: 'Assumed names, or names used to designate an office, profession, party or qualification of the writer, to be treated as real names ... The works of an author not assuming any name but describing himself by a circumlocution, to be considered anonymous' (rule 42).

Baber's general rule for entering collections under their editors is supplemented by a rule (47) for entering collections of the laws of one country under the name of the state or nation concerned, the same rule providing also for entering single laws or collections confined to 'one reign or period of supreme government by one person' under a subheading consisting of 'the name of the person in whose name or by whose authority they are enacted'.

Cross-references had been an essential part of the octavo catalogue and of cataloguing practice under Baber, but Baber's rules make no reference to them. In the new rules (55–64) they are divided into three classes: 'from name to name, from name to work, and from work to work'. An improvement to which Panizzi attached great importance was the inclusion, in references to a particular work, of enough of the work's title to identify it, together with the date and size. In the octavo catalogue only the headings of works referred to had been given. In cross-references 'from work to work' the title of the work referred *from* is also to be given, immediately after the heading. Such references are, however, subject to the general rule (69) that, under each heading, cross-references are to be placed first and arranged in the alphabetical order of the entries referred to. The result is that entries for works catalogued by means of a cross-reference (usually because they were published as part of a collection) are entirely divorced from the main alphabetical series under their authors' names, where entries for other editions of the same works may appear. (This practice, in spite of its obvious inconvenience, persisted until the 1880s.)

The rules for arrangement of entries under a heading are quite new. In the octavo catalogue, works entered under an author were arranged chronologically by the date of first publication of each work or, when the original edition was not in the Library, by the date of the earliest edition catalogued. Evidence that this practice was still observed while Baber was Keeper is provided by the fact that it is followed in the lists of additions to the printed books in 1836–38.[3] The new rule is that entries for individual works are to be arranged alphabetically.

The full rules for arrangement under an author's name lay down principles followed with only minor modifications throughout the later history of the catalogue. Cross-references come first, followed by complete works, then by partial collections of two or more works, then by selections or collections of fragments, and then by separate works in alphabetical order. In each category, editions of the same material follow one another chronologically by date of publication, those to which no date can be assigned being placed first. Editions in the original language are followed first by editions of the original text accompanied by a translation, then by translations into other languages, in the order Latin, English, other languages in alphabetical order of their English names. Editions of 'entire portions' of a separate work follow those of the whole work or, if the whole work does not occur in the catalogue, are placed after all the separate works. Entries for works not written by the author, but required by the rules to be entered under his name, come last 'as an appendix'. The same rules are to be followed, where appropriate, under headings other than authors' names. The scheme includes two complications that were later abandoned. The first of these appears in rule 70, as follows: 'Editions by the same editor, or such as are expressly stated to follow a specific text or edition, and editions with the same notes or commentary, to succeed each other immediately in their chronological order'. At a very late stage in the consideration of the Rules, just before the submission of the complete text to the full board of Trustees, Panizzi attempted unsuccessfully to have this clause removed. It has the effect of introducing subsidiary chronological series into the main chronological arrangement of the editions of a work. The second such complication refers to the arrangement of 'collections of two or more works' (rule 73): 'such partial collections to precede, as are known or are supposed to contain the largest number of an author's works'.

The first of the special headings for which rules are provided is BIBLE. Following a principle suggested by Panizzi in February 1839 for general application in the catalogue and adopted, without specific mention in the Rules, for place-names in headings, this is in the English form, not, as in earlier practice, in the Latin (BIBLIA). On the same principle, English replaces Latin in the titles of the books of the Bible and their authors' names when used in subheadings or in headings of cross-references: in both cases the form found in the Authorised Version is used. The main arrangement of entries under BIBLE follows already established practice: complete Bibles first, followed by the Old Testament and its parts, then by 'the Apocrypha as declared by the Church of England', and then by the New Testament and its parts. Within each of these sections, groups of books (for example, Pentateuch, Gospels) and individual books are arranged in the order of their appearance in the Authorised Version. The arrangement of editions and translations follows the general principles laid down for the catalogue as a whole, but with one provision (later abandoned) applying solely to the Bible: 'editions with comments to follow those having the text only'.

The creation of a special heading, ACADEMIES, for the publications of learned societies is a clear departure from the practice followed in the octavo catalogue, where the heading ACADEMIÆ is used for anonymous works whose titles include the word 'academies' or 'academy', or their equivalent in other languages. The new heading has, however, a precedent in the printed catalogue of the King's Library. On 7 February 1839 Panizzi had reported that he had entrusted Mr Horne with the task of arranging on a uniform plan 'the article *Academiæ et Societates*', and the heading appears in this form in the King's Library catalogue. The transactions of academies and other learned bodies are arranged there under the names of countries: Great Britain and Ireland first (divided into three sections for England, Scotland and Ireland – no Welsh societies are mentioned), followed by other European countries in the order France, Italy, Spain, Portugal, Germany, Belgium, Switzerland, Denmark, Norway, Iceland, Sweden, Russia. Under each country, national organisations and those in the capital usually come first followed by those in other towns, named in alphabetical sequence. Names of countries are in Latin, in the genitive case. Names of towns in the British Isles, France, Italy, Spain and Portugal are given in the vernacular form, the rest in Latin, also in the genitive case. European countries are followed by short sections on Asia (with the one subheading *Bengal*) and America. The last, surprisingly, has local names in Latin, for example 'Massachusettensis Reipublicæ' for the State of Massachusetts. The arrangement under each town puts academies and societies with broad general functions first (for example, Royal Society of London, Académie Française) with others in alphabetical order not of their names but of words indicating their character or scope: for example, *Athenian* Society, Society of *Dilettanti*, *Horticultural* Society, Royal *Institution* of Great Britain, *Linnean* Society, *Medical* Society.

Panizzi's reference in his report of 7 February to '*Academiæ et Societates*' implies that this heading was already in use, but needed reorganisation. It may be that this feature of the King's Library catalogue had for some time been extended to the cataloguing of additions generally, or at least had been adopted in the revision begun under Baber's direction.

The naming of Horne as the reviser is significant. The Revd. Thomas Hartwell Horne, who had already compiled a classified index to the Harleian MSS and a classified catalogue of the library of Queen's College, Cambridge, was engaged by the British Museum as a special assistant in 1824 for the particular task of making a classified catalogue of the Library. He worked on this project until 1834, when it was suspended (but not completely abandoned) in favour of the proposed new alphabetical catalogue. The influence of his experience in, and zeal for, classification may be seen in the form given to the new heading ACADEMIES in the 91 Rules.

The scope of the heading is defined as including 'all acts, memoirs, transactions, journals, minutes, &c. of academies, institutes, associations, universities, or societies learned, scientific, or literary, by whatever name known or designated, as well as works by various hands, forming part of a series of volumes edited by any such society'. The whole of this body of material is to be arranged in a classified order, combining geographical and alphabetical features. The first division is by continents ('the four parts of the world ... Australia and Polynesia being considered as appendixes of Asia'), then by 'the various empires, kingdoms or other independent governments into which any part of the world is divided'; then by the cities or towns 'in which any society of this description meets', and finally by the names of individual academies. At each level the order is alphabetical (thus Africa, America and Asia precede Europe). Only at the level of individual titles is alphabetical arrangement (prescribed elsewhere as normal for the catalogue as a whole) modified: the 'acts, memoirs, &c. of each society' are to be entered chronologically.

The next of the special rules (81) applies the same system of arrangement – that is, by continents, countries and towns – to the heading PERIODICAL PUBLICATIONS, under which are to be catalogued 'reviews, magazines, newspapers, journals, gazettes, annuals, and all works of a similar nature'. The exclusion of the transactions and journals of academies and learned societies, dealt with in the preceding rule, is implicit, not stated. The periodicals are to be entered under their place of publication, 'in alphabetical order according to the first substantive occurring in the title'. This form of alphabetical arrangement is also prescribed in the next rule (82), for 'Ephemerides', that is, almanacs and calendars. (The rule for entry of single works under an author (75) is that they are 'to succeed each other alphabetically', with no mention of the first substantive.) Religious and military orders are to be entered under 'the English name under which they are generally known'.

Two types of publication are to be entered under class-headings, but only if they are anonymous – that is, without the name of an author or compiler. These headings are CATALOGUES and DICTIONARIES: there is also to be a class-heading ENCYCLOPÆDIAS, but for this the qualification is not anonymity in the full sense but only that the editor's name 'does not appear in the title'. The entries under CATALOGUES are to be divided into six groups:

1st. Catalogues of public establishments (including those of societies, although not strictly *public*);
2d. Catalogues of private collections, drawn up either for sale or otherwise;
3d. Catalogues of collections not for sale, the possessors of which are not known;
4th. General as well as special catalogues of objects, without any reference to their possessor;
5th. Dealers' catalogues;
6th. Sale catalogues not included in any of the preceding sections.

The arrangement of entries within the groups varies: under the name of an owner or dealer (1, 2 and 5); alphabetically by title (here again by the first substantive) (3 and 4); chronologically (6).

The last special heading is again a class-heading, LITURGIES. Here entries are to be arranged alphabetically 'according to the English denomination of the communion, sect, or religious order for whom they are specially intended' or, in appropriate cases, under the English name of 'a particular church, congregation, or place of worship'.

In presenting his first draft of the Rules to the Trustees on 18 March, Panizzi wrote: 'he is well aware that such rules must necessarily be affected by the haste with which they have been compiled' and 'he is also aware that many cases may arise unprovided for.' Neither of these deficiencies was entirely removed by the ensuing discussions with the Trustees or the further drafting exercises of Panizzi and his staff. The Rules as published contain many ambiguities, even contradictions, and certainly do not constitute a complete set of instructions for cataloguers.

They survive in two different forms. Fifty copies of the approved text, with examples, were printed by order of the Trustees after their meeting of 13 July 1839 and distributed by Panizzi to his staff on 8 August. Several copies of this document are preserved in the Department of Printed Books, and it was reproduced in full (with a few typographical errors)[4] in the Appendix to the Report of the Royal Commission of 1850.[5] When the Rules were printed again, at the beginning of the 1841 volume, a few small alterations had been made to the main text, and a number of additions to individual rules, printed in italics, recorded decisions made during the preparation of the volume.

An examination of these two editions of the Rules and of the entries in the catalogue volume itself shows how the system developed while work was proceeding, how obscure or ambiguous rules were interpreted, and what practice was adopted in many details not covered by the written rules.

Only three of the textual alterations in the second printing are changes of substance. In rule 3, dealing with works in which more than one author is mentioned in the title, 'the first name to be taken as that of the author' is changed to 'the first to be taken as the leading name'. This amendment permits, without explicitly mentioning it, the practice actually adopted of entering joint works by two authors under a heading consisting of both their names. Earlier uncertainty on this point is demonstrated by two inconsistent examples in the 1839 document: rule 3 is illustrated by an example beginning 'BEAUMONT (Francis) *and* FLETCHER (John) Comedies and tragedies', while an example to rule 42, illustrating cross-references from (*inter alia*) joint authors, has been left in the form 'FLETCHER (John) *See* BEAUMONT (F.) Comedies and tragedies'. Rule 32, which states that, when the cataloguer can complete the words represented by initials under which a work is entered this is to be done in brackets, is revised by the addition of the words 'in the body of the title', so removing an ambiguity which might have been taken to allow completion in the heading, and doubtless representing the original intention of the rule. The third change, in rule 38, deals with the arrangement of entries for anonymous works under a word taken from the title. The instruction to arrange them 'in strict alphabetical order of the words which come after that used as a heading' is reduced to 'in strict alphabetical order.' This change is probably related to an anomaly in the Rules which was *not* removed in the 1841 edition. Rules 81 (for periodicals), 82 (for ephemerides), 86 (for anonymous catalogues) and 88 (for anonymous dictionaries) all require alphabetical arrangement under 'the first substantive occurring in the title'. Rule 75, on separate works of an author, states only that they are to 'succeed each other alphabetically'. The change in rule 38 appears to record a decision to arrange by the first word rather than the first substantive, the text of rules 81, 82, 86 and 88 being inadvertently left unaltered. The decision itself may have been determined by the formulation of rule 38 in such a way that it permits an adjective, in combination with its following substantive – or any kind of word where no substantive was present – to be the entry word. No entries under the special headings mentioned in rules 81 to 88 appear in the 1841 volume, and there is no evidence in later forms of the catalogue that arrangement under the first substantive was ever used.

The italic additions to the Rules record a number of decisions affecting headings: names of sovereigns and princes of sovereign houses are to be given in their English form; a person who is clearly identified by a description on a title page is to be treated as if he were named there; reports of civil actions are to be entered under the party named first on the title pages, of criminal proceedings under the defendant, and of 'trials relating to any vessel' under the name of the vessel; collections without a collective title are to be entered under the name of the first author, not under that of the editor. There is also a note that the rule requiring the setting out under the entry for a collection of all the titles of the works contained in it has not been acted on, 'in order to accelerate the printing of the catalogue'. In fact it was carried out in one case only, a collection of voyages in 137 volumes entered under AA (Pieter vander), which occurs in the first sheet of the catalogue.

Even with these additions, the Rules fall far short of a complete account of the cataloguing system embodied in the 1841 volume. For instance, the rules for anonymous books, complicated as they are, do not cover all cases. Rule 34 directs that, in default of the name of a person in the title, an anonymous book is to be entered under 'that of any assembly, corporate body, society, board, party, sect, or denomination appearing on the title ... subject to the arrangement of Rule IX'. But rule 9 provides only for 'assemblies, boards or corporate bodies (with the exception of academies, universities, learned societies, and religious orders, respecting which special rules are to be followed)'. They are to be entered 'under the name of the country or place from which they derive their denomination, or ... under the name of the place whence their acts are issued'. There is no mention of parties, sects or denominations, which are diffused bodies normally having neither a fixed headquarters nor a name derived from the name of a country or place; nor is there any 'special rule' for such bodies. The practice adopted in the catalogue was to apply the special rule for 'religious and military orders' (84): that is, to enter them under 'the English name under which they are generally known'. Thus we find entries under 'Albigenses', 'Anabaptists', 'Antinomians', 'Arians' and 'Arminians', and even under 'Atheists', all treated as proper names having precedence over other substantives in the title, and all in English regardless of the language of the works catalogued. (As an exception, ARISTOCRATES, occurring only in French titles, appears in its French form but is still given precedence over other substantives. The headings APOTHECARIES and APOTICAIRES are *both* used in this way.)

Entries in the catalogue also reveal the rather complicated interpretation put on the brief but obscure rule 36: 'Adjectives formed from the name of a person, party, place or denomination, to be treated as the names from which they are formed.' This is not normally taken to mean that the name itself is used as the heading, rather that the adjective is given the same priority in the choice of heading that the name would have if it occurred in the title. However, it is combined in the heading with the substantive it qualifies, so giving an example of what is meant in rule 38 by 'adjectives incorporated with their following substantive'. Following the practice of giving place-names in headings in their English form, and the application of the same convention to names of 'parties, sects and denominations', the combination of adjective and substantive is translated into English. When the adjectival form is used as a substantive (as in words denoting nationality) it constitutes a heading by itself. We thus have such headings as AMERICAN LETTERS for 'Le lettere americane'; AFRICANS for 'Scripture evidence of the sinfulness of injustice and oppression in behalf of the much-injured Africans'; and, as a forerunner of many strange headings to appear later in the catalogue, ARMINIAN DUNG-CART for a controversial pamphlet of 1636 entitled 'Den Arminiaenschen-dreck-waghen, ghevoert by de societeyt'. Under ANGLAIS there is a cross-reference: 'See ENGLISH and ENGLISHMAN.' An exceptional practice is found when the adjective derived from the name of a person can be taken to imply authorship: thus entries for 'the Athanasian creed' appear under ATHANASIUS, *Saint, Archbishop of Alexandria.*

The use of headings made up of an adjective derived from a proper name and its associated substantive still does not fully clarify the phrase 'adjectives incorporated with their following substantive'. The not very illuminating example attached to rule 38 is GREAT BRITAIN. Examples of such combined headings occurring in the 1841 volume do not remove the obscurity. There are entries under ACCOMPLISHED MAID and ABDICATED PRINCE for anonymous works whose titles consist of these words preceded by the definite article, but 'Rejected addresses' is entered under ADDRESSES and 'The practising attorney' under ATTORNEY. Attempts to clarify the rule will be mentioned in later chapters.[6]

Numerous examples could be given of unwritten rules implied by entries in the catalogue but not expressed in the Rules themselves. For instance, the Rules direct that English forms of names should be used for names of sovereigns and princes of sovereign houses, and a similar practice for biblical names is conveyed by the instruction to use the forms found in the Authorised Version. The catalogue extends the practice to ancient Greek authors, who are not mentioned in the Rules: we thus find the headings ÆSOP and ARISTOTLE, while Greek authors for whom a specifically English form does not exist are entered in their Latin form. The rule that a person identified in the title by a description is to be treated as if named there is extended in practice to cover corporate bodies. Thus 'The case between the African company and the people of England' is entered under AFRICA, *Company of Royal Adventurers in England trading to Africa.* The generous interpretation given to this rule is illustrated by the entry under the same heading of 'The African trade in no danger of being lost otherwise than by the designs of the company'. The ten rules (69–78) for the order of entries under a heading do not mention subheadings, and in general the 1841 volume follows the prescribed order without using them. Under the most important authors, however, subheadings are introduced, the most usual being *Works* (for complete collections only), *Separate works* (for partial collections as well as individual works) and *Appendix*. In detail, however, the treatment of individual authors varies. In the headings for Æsop and Apuleius, for example, the rule that cross-references are placed at the beginning is followed literally, all cross-references being collected together and preceding the subheading *Works*. Under ÆSCHYLUS and ARISTOPHANES, cross-references for works of a general character are put under the subheading *Works*, while those relating to particular works are at the beginning of *Separate works*. A development in the direction of later catalogue usage appears under ARIOSTO: there are no cross-references under *Works*, and those of a general character all appear at the beginning of *Appendix*, which surprisingly also includes references for publications dealing with a separate work – 'Orlando furioso'. A number of cross-references appear at the beginning of *Separate works*, but these are all entries in cross-reference form for editions of works by Ariosto occurring in collections entered under other headings. The fullest development of the practice of devising special schemes for particular large headings (exemplified in the Rules only by the heading BIBLE but much used in later periods) is seen in the heading ARISTOTLE. Here the subheading *Works* (starting with cross-references to works by other authors relating to Aristotle's writings generally) is followed by *Two or more separate works*. Then follow individual works, not under a general subheading 'Separate works', but each under a subheading consisting of its own title, in English. The titles are not arranged in alphabetical order, but in the traditional order adopted in Immanuel Bekker's standard complete edition published by the Prussian Academy of Sciences in 1831. Under each subheading the entries for editions of the text of the work are preceded by cross-references.

Two further important characteristics of the catalogue are not touched on in the Rules: the system of alphabetical arrangement of headings and the typography and layout of the entries.

It is clear that a complete system of alphabetisation had not been worked out before printing of the volume began. In the sequence of headings, alphabetical arrangement is to a considerable extent applied mechanically, without reference to the division of the heading into distinct functional parts. Thus we find transposed forenames (in round brackets), epithets (in italics) and words continuing the main heading (in capitals) mixed together in such sequences as:

ALEXANDER *ab Alexandro*

ALEXANDER (Alexander), *Optician*
ALEXANDER, *Aphrodisæus*
ALEXANDER BALAS, *King of Syria*
ALEXANDER (Benjamin)
ALEXANDER, *Bishop of Lycopolis*
ALEXANDER (Samuel)
ALEXANDER SEVERUS
ALEXANDER *the Great, King of Macedon.*

It is noteworthy that prepositions and the definite article are both taken into account in the arrangement: in earlier practice (for example in the octavo catalogue) both had been ignored.

Frequently, but not always, headings consisting of two words are arranged as single words, for example:

AMERICA
AMERICAN LOYALISTS
AMERICA, *North*
AMERICAN REVOLUTION
AMERICANS
AMERICAN SKETCHES
AMERICANUS
AMERICAN WAR
AMERICA, *South*

But the surname, ALEXANDERSSON comes after ALEXANDER (William), not between ALEXANDER SEVERUS and ALEXANDER *the Great*. In general, the practice of word-by-word rather than letter-by-letter arrangement becomes more prevalent towards the end of the volume, as in the sequences:

AUGUSTA VINDELICORUM
AUGUSTAN HISTORY

and

ASTRONOMI VETERES
ASTRONOMICA SCRIPTA
ASTRONOMICAL SOCIETY

There are also signs of a developing distinction between forenames and surnames of the same form and between epithets and other additions to the single-word heading as in:

ARTHUR, *King of Britain*
ARTHUR CONINGSBY
ARTHUR (Archibald)

Earlier practice is consistently followed in the treatment as one letter of *I* and *J* and also of *U* and *V*. (This continued as a peculiarity of the British Museum catalogue until 1930.)

In the arrangement of titles under a heading, strict alphabetical order is usually followed in the sense that prepositions (though not the definite or indefinite article) coming at the beginning of a title are taken into account. There are, however, exceptions in the early part of the volume where the order is controlled by the word following the preposition (or combination of preposition and article), for example, under ABATI-OLIVIERI-GIORDANI, the sequence:

Di alcune ...
Dell'antico ...
Esame ...
Delle figline ...
Della fondazione ...

In contrast to the practice in headings, word-by-word, not letter-by-letter, arrangement is almost always adopted as, for example, under AMSTERDAM:

Amsterdams dam-praetje ...
Amsterdamsche vermakelyke tuyn-vrugten

although with occasional exceptions, for example, under ALBERTI (Leandro) we find the sequence:

Descrittione ...
De viris illustribus ...
Isole ...

Here, under word-by-word arrangement the second item would come first.

Alphabetical order is occasionally abandoned, as when several similar works are distinguished by numbers. Thus, under ALTHAM (Roger) 'A charge delivered to the clergy of the archdeaconry of Middlesex' is followed without regard for their main titles by works described in their subtitles as 'a second charge', 'a third charge', and so on. Under the heading ACADEMIES the specific instruction in rule 80: 'the acts, memoirs, &c. of each society to be entered chronologically' is in practice applied only to formal series of proceedings and similar publications. Separate works issued by a society or academy are entered in alphabetical order, and come after the chronological sequence of proceedings, etc.

AITON—AKENSIDE

AITON (WILLIAM TOWNSEND).
    See AITON (W.). Hortus Kewensis .... Second edition. 1810, *etc.* 8°

    See BAUER (F.). Delineations of exotick plants, *etc.* 1796. fol.

An epitome of the second edition of Hortus Kewensis ... To which is added, a selection of esculent vegetables and fruits cultivated in the Royal Gardens at Kew. *London*, 1814. 8°

AITSINGERUS (MICHAEL). *See* EYTZINGER.

AITSMA (LIEUWE VAN). *See* AITZEMA.

AITZEMA (LIEUWE VAN). *See* A., L. V.

L. ab A. Historia pacis a fœderatis Belgis, ab anno cIↃ IↃCXXI ad hoc usque tempus, tractatæ. *Lugduni Batavorum*, 1654. 4°

✠ Vermeerdert verhael van de vreede-handelingh der Vereenighde Nederlanden, sedert den jare 1621 tot 1626 door L. V. A. Deel 1. (Historie; of, verhael van saken van staet en oorlogh, in ende omtrent de Vereenighde Nederlanden, beginnende met den jaere 1626 tot ... 1630 [and continued to 1669]. Deel 2–14.) The 11th vol. in two pt.
's Graven-Hage, 1655, 1657–71. 4°

AIX.
Academies and learned societies at A. *See* ACADEMIES—*Europe*—*France*—*Aix*.

Procession de la fête-Dieu d'Aix. *See* LEBER (C.). Collection des meilleurs dissertations, *etc.* Tom. 10. 1826, *etc.* 8°

Événemens qui se sont passés du 25 au 29 Mars, 1789. *See* M. Lettre à M****, *etc.*
1789. 8°

See RIQUET (V. M. DE), *Count of Caraman*. Récit de ce qui s'est passé à Aix, *etc.*
[1788.] 8°

(Adresse de l'administration du district d'Aix, département des Bouches du Rhône, à la Convention Nationale.) *Aix*, an II. (1794.) 8°

(Détail de l'infâme complot qu'on avoit commencé à exécuter à Aix en Provence. Événemens qui l'ont suivi.) *Grenoble*, [1791.] 8°

Mémoire historique des événemens arrivés à Aix, le 12 Déc. 1790, publié par les officiers du régiment de Lyonnois. [*Paris*, 1791.] 8°

Another copy.

Hospital of Nôtre Dame.
Institution et réglemens de l'Hôpital Nôtre Dame de Misericorde établi dans la ville d'Aix. *Aix*, 1688. 8°

Parliament.
Protestation des officiers du parlement d'Aix.
[1788.] 8°

AIX (ALBERT D'). *See* ALBERTUS, *Aquensis*.

AIX, JEAN-DE-DIEU RAYMOND DE BOISGELIN, *Archbishop of*. *See* BOISGELIN.

AIX-LA-CHAPELLE.
Abgekürztes Tagebuch einer Reise von Aachen über Frankfurth am M. und viele deutsche Höfe, nach Thüringen, 1769, 1770. *See* BERNOUILLY (J.). J. B.'s Sammlung kurzer Reisebeschreibungen, *etc.* Band 16.
1781, *etc.* 8°

Treaty of. *See* GREAT BRITAIN—*George II., King of Great Britain, etc.* A letter concerning the treaty, *etc.* 1748. 8°

1749. 4°

AIX-LA-CHAPELLE—*continued*.
Treaty of. *See* GERMAN EMPIRE—*Maria Theresa, Empress of Germany, etc.* Intérêts de l'impératrice reine, *etc.* 1748. 8°

Amusemens des eaux d'Aix-la-Chapelle. [By Charles Louis Baron de Pöllnitz, or —— Hecquet, junior.] 3 tom. *Amsterdam*, 1736. 12°

Beschryving van de stad Aken, mitsgaders van alle desselfs fonteinen en minerale wateren en baden. [By J. du Vivie?] *Leiden*, 1727. 4°

Another copy.

Description de la ville d'Aix-la-Chapelle, de Malmedi, de Stavelo et du Bourg de Spa. *Bruxelles*. 8°

Observations on the probable issue of the congress at Aix-la-Chapelle. In a letter to a friend.
London, 1748. 8°

Burgomasters of.
Placcaet van borghemeesteren ende raet der stadt Aken ... waerin alle predicanten, lesers ende leerders, ooc alle wederdoopers de stadt verboden wardt. *Aken*, 1614. 4°

Another copy.

AKAKIA (M.). *See* ACACIA.

AKBAR JILALLEDDIN, *Mahommed, Emperor of Hindoostan*. *See* MUHAMMAD.

AKBER JILALEDDIN, *Mahommed, Emperor of Hindoostan*. *See* MUHAMMAD.

AKEN. *See* AIX-LA-CHAPELLE.

AKEN (CORNELIUS AB).
See BIBLE. Versio Hebraica, *etc.* [Polyglott.] 1683. 4°

Introductionis historicæ ad Cartesii philosophiam pars quinta quam ... sub præsidio G. de Vries ... publice ventilandam proponit C. ab A.
Trajecti ad Rhenum, 1684. 4°

AKEN (F. VAN).
Aan de muitzugt na het oproer in Leyden den 9 Juny 1784. *Leyden*. 8°

AKEN (ROLAND AB).
Exercitatio de creatione. *Ultrajecti*, 1682. 4°

AKENSIDE (MARK).
WORKS.
[*Life.*] *See* ALDINE EDITION of the British poets. Vol. 32. 1830, *etc.* 8°

Poetical works. *See* ALDINE EDITION of the British poets. Vol. 32. 1830, *etc.* 8°

——— *See* BELL (J.). Bell's edition of the poets, *etc.* Vol. 85 and 86. 1783, *etc.* 12°

Life and poems. *See* CHALMERS (A.). The works of the English poets, *etc.* Vol. 14.
1810. 8°

Life and poetical works. *See* JOHNSON (S.). The works of the English poets, *etc.* Vol. 6, 63 and 64. 1790. 8°

See MONRO (A.). Notes [by M. A.] on the postscript to a pamphlet, entitled, observations anatomical, *etc.* by A. M. 1758. 8°

Poems. 2 vol. *See* PARK (T.). The works of the British poets, *etc.* Vol. 25. 1808. 16°

Poems omitted in his works. *See* PARK (T.). Supplement to the British poets. Vol. 6.
1809. 16°

✠ The poems of M. A. [edited by the Rt. Hon. J. Dyson. To which is prefixed an account of his life.] *London*, 1772. 4°

✠ Another copy. *L. P.*

VOL. I.   2 P

A page from the 1841 catalogue.

In typography and layout, the catalogue sets a number of precedents which had an important influence on later cataloguing. The printing of the heading in capitals, with transposed forenames following in round brackets and in small capitals, and with distinguishing epithets added in italics, follows the octavo catalogue. (The King's Library catalogue, taken as a model in some other respects, separates forenames from surnames by a comma.) The 1841 volume follows the King's Library catalogue in keeping the heading on a separate line. In most of the volume only simple references from one name to another are run on, although in the first few pages (preceding ACADEMIES) the first reference of any kind under a heading is treated this way. The titles in main entries are aligned throughout to a left-hand margin indented one em from the margin for headings (here following both the King's Library catalogue and the octavo catalogue). Cross-references for particular works (which do not occur in the King's Library catalogue) have a substantially larger indentation of three ems. The long dash used in the octavo catalogue to indicate repetition of the heading is omitted. The final items of each main entry (place, date and size) are treated as a separate unit and aligned to the *right*-hand margin. When a printer or publisher is named, his name is treated as part of this unit, and precedes the place of publication. (Both are printed in italics.) This feature has the practical use of throwing the date into relief and so facilitating the consultation of a chronological series of entries. A similar feature appears also in the almost contemporary catalogue of the Bodleian Library (1843), but with the elements in the more traditional order – size, place, printer, date – used in the British Museum's octavo catalogue.

Typographically, the volume with its folio-size pages printed in double columns is elegant and clear, and the layout and spacing of the entries make it easy to consult. It set a high standard for the visual appearance of later editions of the catalogue.

Notes and References
1. In a note appended to Edward Edwards's letter of 18 February 1839 (see p. 11).
2. See p. 27.
3. *List of additions to the Printed Books in the British Museum in the years MDCCCXXXVI–MDCCCXXXVIII.* Printed by order of the Trustees, London, 1843.
4. Including the introduction in rule 7 of the solecism 'unequivocably' for 'unequivocally'.
5. 'Alphabetical Catalogue of Printed Books. Rules to be observed in preparing and entering titles', *Report of the Commissioners . . ., 1850*, Appendix, pp. 185–218.
6. In Chapter 8 (p. 80) and Chapter 10 (p. 99).

3 Consolidation, 1841–56

The publication in 1841 of the volume covering the letter *A* and containing about 18,200 entries (including cross-references) was a considerable feat of organisation and the result of much hard work. But it satisfied neither the Trustees, who wished for a complete catalogue within five years, nor Panizzi, whose aim was a catalogue that would meet the needs of scholars pursuing serious research. Of the five years allowed by the Trustees, almost two had passed, but only one-seventh of the estimated 400,000 title-slips had been revised, and the volume itself contained only one-twentieth of them, another 40,000 or so having been produced in advance work on headings later in the alphabet, which had to be linked by cross-references with headings under the letter *A*. While the entries printed conformed closely to the rules Panizzi had agreed with the Trustees and also to his own standards of bibliographical accuracy, it was clear to him that many thousands that should have appeared under that letter were missing and would have to be added as the work proceeded. On presenting the volume to the Trustees in July 1841, he had emphatically declared that completion of the catalogue by the end of 1844 was impossible. In January 1843, however, the Trustees again drew his attention to the date fixed for completion and received the reply that, supposing that the whole catalogue were to consist of 400,000 titles and that these were ready in manuscript, it would still take four years to print it. His estimate of the total number of titles was now, however, 800,000, of which only 140,000 had been prepared. In reply to a further enquiry, in July 1844, he gave his opinion that, with the staff then available, the titles for all the works in the Library at the end of 1838 could not be 'written out in conformity with the rules now adopted' before the end of 1854, and that this did not take account of their arrangement in proper order for the press.

Meanwhile, the work continued, and revision had reached the end of the letter *B* by December 1844 and *CHE* by December 1845, providing enough material for two further volumes equal in size to the first. On 10 January 1846, the Trustees therefore requested Panizzi to state 'the reasons which have induced him to suspend the printing of the new catalogue'. Part of his reply, repeating his former arguments against printing before revision was complete, was included in the Trustees' annual report to Parliament, dated 24 January 1846, with the addition of the words: 'Upon these representations the Trustees have consented for the present to suspend the printing of the catalogue'.[1] However, although Panizzi's contention that the copy must all be prepared before any more was printed was thus conceded, the Trustees were far from satisfied by the estimated rate of progress. Criticism from users of the Library had been directed far less at the incompleteness and inaccuracy of the new volume, of which Panizzi was so conscious, than at the whole concept of the new catalogue, which was held to be too ambitious and complicated, and unnecessarily time-consuming. A good example is the attack by Sir Harris Nicolas, a historian with long experience of using the Reading Room, in three articles which appeared anonymously in *The Spectator* in May 1846 and were reprinted with the author's name a few weeks later as part of an acrimonious exchange with Panizzi over a relatively trivial issue, the failure of the Reading Room staff to deliver to Nicolas a book the details of which he had filled in wrongly on his application form.

His attack on the catalogue[2] first emphasises the need for a new catalogue 'at the earliest possible moment'. It should be 'a *practical* catalogue, having the titles or authors' names placed in alphabetical order, and not a catalogue formed upon so abstruse a plan as to require *ninety-one* rules for its construction'. Of his particular objections to the Rules, the first is to the creation of large class-headings such as ACADEMIES and PERIODICAL PUBLICATIONS, which remove the entries for particular publications from the place in the alphabetical sequence where they will naturally be looked for. He complains, for instance, that no entry for the *Annual Register* appears under the letter A, but only a cross-reference, ANNUALS: *See* Periodical Publications; and that to find the proceedings of a society the reader must look not just under the heading ACADEMIES and a subheading for the country, but then also under the name of the town where the society is located, which he may not know. He also deplores the need created by this system of cataloguing for numerous cross-references which increase the bulk of the catalogue and are a major cause of delay in its production.

The next object of his attack is the use, as headings for some anonymous works, of 'many words, not merely insignificant, but under which no sane man would think of seeking for a book' – for example, ACCOUNT, ABSTRACT, ANSWER. It seems obvious to him that works whose titles begin with these words will be looked for under their subjects. He complains, incidentally (apparently without having studied the rules for anonymous works whose titles contain the name of a person or institution or which are replies to or comments on other named works), that there are so few titles under the words in question that many that begin with them must have been omitted, and that, with eight entries under APPEAL, there is no reference to 'Appeals in the House of Lords'.[3] However, he concludes (rightly) from cross-references under ADMIRALTY that 'all the Departments of the Public Service' will be entered under such large general headings as 'Great Britain', 'divided and subdivided, and filling very many pages, like "Academies" and "Periodical Publications"'. Finally, Sir Harris maintains that authors' names should be in the form occurring on the title pages of the books, and complains that a reader looking for 'a work by Voltaire (by which name he took the liberty of describing himself in the title-pages of his own books)' will be referred back to the heading 'Arouet de Voltaire (François Marie)'. If exaggeration or oversimplification in the heat of debate is allowed for, some at least of Sir Harris's arguments will appear reasonable to modern readers and, as will be seen later, they ultimately won acceptance in the British Museum itself. These include the objections to large class-headings like ACADEMIES, to the absence of full entries under the titles of periodicals, and to the choice of Voltaire's full name instead of the one usually appearing on title pages. The uneasy compromise between subject entry and first-word entry for anonymous works was clearly confusing to readers and was a permanent source of difficulty. It is important to remember that, in Panizzi's plan, the dilemma was intended to be solved by an 'index of matters', but this was never provided, except for the part of the catalogue written after 1880.

Similar arguments in favour of the rapid production of a concise, 'useful' catalogue were reaching the Trustees from other quarters as well, and it is not surprising that in July 1846 they once more appealed over Panizzi's head to Sir Henry Ellis, asking him to report on the impediments to the completion and printing of the catalogue and how he would propose to overcome them.

Ellis sent a brief note to Panizzi asking for his help in making his report, but received the reply that Panizzi could add nothing to what he had already said to the Trustees on the subject and that he knew of no means of further expediting the completion of the catalogue if the plan adopted by the Trustees and the rules agreed by them were to be followed.

Sir Henry was thus driven to formulate his own opinions, which still favoured a catalogue closely resembling the one for which he had himself been responsible 30 years earlier, and his report dated 14 November 1846 supports Panizzi's critics on several points. He lists as impediments first, 'the broad principle on which the catalogue was framed' which was 'too extensive to be carried to the end of the alphabet by any one officer within a prescribed time'; second, the unforeseen quantity of cross-references; third, 'the multiplication of rules', some of which required research or allowed different interpretations which had to be settled by conferences; fourth, the requirement that one man's work should be revised by another. He does not dispute Panizzi's arguments for suspension of printing until the copy is complete. His suggestion for accelerating the work is what he calls 'absolute division of labour' as formerly operated, according to him, between himself and Baber. Each cataloguer should be made fully responsible for his portion of the catalogue, with Panizzi giving only general guidance and 'occasional glances at the sheets'. As the catalogue was to include only books acquired to the end of 1838, it was urgent that it should be finished quickly. By the end of 1846, nearly half the titles would have been prepared. The implication was that, if Ellis's suggestions were heeded, the catalogue could be completed much sooner than Panizzi had estimated.

Panizzi's reaction was to provide the longest and most detailed defence he had so far produced of his own position. It included a recapitulation of all communications about the catalogue between the Trustees and either Baber or himself from April 1834 onward, and also an analysis of Ellis's report of the 30th of that month, which had not been seen by Baber at the time and had come to Panizzi's notice only in October 1846. 'The authority of Sir. H. Ellis', he wrote, 'the great and unfortunate effect which seems to have been produced by his statements, and, above all the recent renewal of the former suggestions in his last report, have made it absolutely necessary for me to subject it to a careful and minute examination.' He was able to point out inaccuracies in almost every sentence in the report, and challenged Ellis's statement that all the entries in the octavo catalogue had been compared with the books by producing, from the parts for which Ellis himself had been responsible, a number of gross errors repeated unchanged from the still earlier catalogue of 1787, even though some of these had been corrected in manuscript in the copy of that catalogue used in the Library at the time. A month later he submitted to the Trustees a comprehensive statement of errors in Ellis's part of the octavo catalogue, filling 14 folio pages in the printed version. Ellis defended himself by stating that his work had been done single-handed and that, out of over 50,000 entries he had prepared, the errors found 'after so many months of exertion in the search', were really very few and did not seriously damage 'the character of the catalogue, for the purposes of use'. No more was heard of his offer, made ten years earlier, to reward from his own pocket anyone who could discover errors in the work.

Meanwhile, Panizzi was not entirely without support. On 19 January 1847 Augustus de Morgan, a distinguished mathematician with an interest in bibliography and, like Panizzi, one of the first professors at University College, London, wrote him a long letter condemning the widespread opinion that the printing of a short 'finding' catalogue without bibliographical detail could be useful and describing as 'insufficient' the entries in the octavo catalogue. 'I feel certain', he wrote, 'that no catalogue would be of any use to me *out of the Museum* which was not a real aid to history, independently of the existence of the Museum', and 'I am every day more and more in possession of proof that persons who cite books do not know how to do it, in the large majority of cases; and that nothing but the opportunity of consulting a really good catalogue will teach them how to do it.' These views doubtless also reached at least some of the Trustees.

The outcome, in the first instance, was no more than a mild reproof of Panizzi by the Trustees for having 'thought it necessary to enter so minutely into the alleged defects of the printed octavo catalogue'. In further discussions, opposing positions were taken up by two of the Trustees who attended meetings most regularly. Sir Robert Inglis (Conservative MP for Oxford University and a strong opponent of Catholic Emancipation and Parliamentary Reform) took the part of Panizzi's critics, and proposed that the printing of the catalogue should be resumed. On the other hand, William R. Hamilton (who, as secretary to Lord Elgin, had assisted him in collecting the Greek marbles, and who had published material on Egyptian antiquities) wholeheartedly supported Panizzi. Finally, Hamilton won the day, and at a General Meeting of the Trustees on 11 December 1847, the following resolution, proposed by him, was adopted:

1. That Mr. Panizzi be directed to proceed with the utmost despatch in the compilation of a full and complete catalogue in manuscript of the books in his custody, in such manner as may appear to him most consistent with correctness and accuracy, and adhering as closely, as circumstances will permit him, to the rules laid down and approved by the Trustees on 13th July 1839, and,

2. That, should any opportunity present itself, by which Mr. Panizzi should think that the completion of the manuscript catalogue might be accelerated, without injury to its accuracy and completeness, he forthwith suggest such means of improvement to the consideration of the Trustees.

The question of printing had now been suspended indefinitely, and Panizzi was in a position to proceed undisturbed with the compilation of a complete catalogue. But the battle was not yet quite over.

On 17 July 1847 a Royal Commission was set up, under the chairmanship of the Earl of Ellesemere, to enquire into the constitution and government of the British Museum, 'with the view of ascertaining in what manner that National Institution may be made most effective for the advancement of Literature, Science and the Arts'.

The Catalogue of Printed Books was one of the subjects to which it gave particular attention, and it heard copious evidence not only from Panizzi himself but from many of his critics and supporters. The critics included Thomas Carlyle, three officers of the Museum (Forshall, the Secretary; Madden, the Keeper of Manuscripts; and Gray, the Keeper of the Zoological Collection), at least two of the Trustees (Sir Robert Inglis and Viscount Mahon) and John Payne Collier, who, besides being a scholar of note, was Secretary to the Commission. The supporters included Augustus de Morgan, John Wilson Croker, Dr S. R. Maitland (who had been librarian to the Archbishop of Canterbury), one Trustee (W. R. Hamilton) and, on some but not all points, Edward Edwards.

The Commission's conclusions, published in 1850, were entirely favourable to Panizzi. The Trustees were criticised both for the general irregularity of their proceedings and for their ill-advised interference with the professional responsibilities of an officer, and the Commission particularly recommended that the shelf-by-shelf method of cataloguing should be adopted. On this last point Panizzi had hesitated to act, in spite of having been authorised to complete the catalogue in manuscript, because the possibility of a renewal of printing before it was completed had not been formally removed. The Commission also deplored the rules for anonymous books as an unsatisfactory compromise which had 'seriously delayed the progress of the work without contributing to its better execution', and recommended that Panizzi should have unfettered discretion to apply them or not. Here too he hesitated, and appealed to the Trustees for a decision. He reminded them that he had thought in 1841 that it would save time to undo what had been done and adopt the first word or first substantive as the heading throughout the catalogue. Now, nine years later, he still believed that the remainder of the catalogue would be compiled more quickly if the rules were changed, but doubted the expediency of doing this now that the work had progressed so much further. Finally, on 7 December 1850, the Trustees approved shelf-by-shelf cataloguing but decided that no change should be made in the rules for anonymous works. The protracted struggle was concluded in Panizzi's favour, except on one point – and here too it was now officially recognised that, although overruled, he had probably been right all along.

Meanwhile, the work of cataloguing had to proceed from 1841 onward in a new situation, complicated by the existence of a new catalogue for the letter *A* side by side with the old catalogues covering the whole library. The cataloguing staff had three tasks: to press on with the preparation of the rest of the new catalogue; to maintain the existing volumes for *B* to *Z* by adding entries for new accessions; and to keep the newly printed volume up to date by adding not only entries for accessions but also entries under the letter *A* resulting from the continued revision of the old title-slips.

When the 1841 catalogue was printed, 15 copies were produced on larger paper, with a single column printed on the recto of each leaf, and three of these copies, interleaved and each bound in five parts, were used for adding manuscript entries. The old catalogue had been maintained in two copies only, one for readers, the other for the staff. The use of three interleaved copies of the new volume instead of two marks the beginning of a system, later extended to the whole catalogue and continued permanently, by which a spare copy of the updated catalogue was used to replace volumes of the Reading Room copy while these were removed for the insertion of additions. By 25 December 1841, 2,788 entries had been added in each of the three copies. Additions continued at the average rate of 1,300 titles a year.

The task of transcribing new titles in the two copies of the old catalogue was much larger and also more difficult. Between 1841 and 1846 the average annual number of entries added in each copy was 12,500. To find room for them, while preserving the correct order, it was necessary each year to retranscribe an increasing number of the existing entries: the annual average of retranscriptions in the six years was 6,400, an addition of over 50 per cent to the work; and in the last year it was 8,584, an addition of 77 per cent. During the same period the number of titles transcribed into the catalogue fell short of the number written by over 40,000.

The accumulation of arrears had become a serious problem. In

January 1845[4] Panizzi had estimated that 25,000 'uninserted titles' had accumulated because of the necessary diversion of several Attendants from transcribing to stamping the books in the King's Library. In October of the same year he reported that a large number of titles arising from special cataloguing tasks outside the normal cataloguing of accessions – 24,000 for music, 12,000 for the geographical collection, and 20,000 for the King's pamphlets – were now ready for transcription. He proposed the addition of a new category of staff – 'Transcribers' – who, though graded as Attendants, would not be employed also, like the existing Attendants, on miscellaneous duties. Five were required in the first instance, with one 'extra-Assistant' to supervise them and ensure the insertion of entries in their proper place. (Here we may see the origin of the officer known later in the Department as the 'Incorporator'. The first occupant of the post was L. J. Lardner.)

A further element in the arrears had now emerged. Despite the transfer of three Assistants from work on the new catalogue to the cataloguing of accessions, a considerable increase in the number of books acquired had led to a large number of books awaiting cataloguing: this was estimated in July 1846 at 10,000, possibly increasing to 20,000 by the end of the year. Panizzi's request for four more 'extra-Assistants' was agreed to by the Trustees, but it was not approved by the Treasury until November. Meanwhile, the purchase of books with the £10,000 grant obtained from the Treasury in 1846 by the Trustees at Panizzi's instigation[5] had made the situation worse, and Panizzi wrote in a report dated 18 September of 'heaps of books amassed on the tables unarranged' and of the Secretary's office 'crammed to inconvenience with books for which there is no place in the library'. (Here we see looming, besides insufficiency of cataloguing staff, the severe shortage of space which was to lead within a few years to the building of the new Reading Room and its surrounding iron book-stacks.)

Additions to the staff did not solve the problem. In June 1848 Lardner reported 50,000 unentered titles, and did not expect to be able to reduce the number with the staff at his disposal. By this time the number of retranscriptions required exceeded the number of new entries. The four additional Assistants were writing titles for accessions much more quickly than they could be entered, and by January 1849 the situation was critical. Arrears alone would occupy the available transcribers for ten years, without reckoning the new titles being created. To make matters worse, the state of the two working copies of the old catalogue was such that their complete retranscription had become an urgent necessity. The Trustees secured authority from the Treasury to appoint ten additional Transcribers and two extra-Assistants to supervise them, their salaries being paid by transferring money already provided for the completion of the new catalogue.

Panizzi then proposed that the retranscribed old catalogue should be in a new form. The inlaid printed leaves of the old catalogue would be replaced by two new sets of inlaid printed leaves, on which the press-marks and cross-references written in the margins of the old leaves would be transcribed. To save labour, a retranscription of the entries on the additional leaves of the old catalogue would be made in copying ink, so that the second copy could be mechanically reproduced from it. Only three entries would be transcribed on each page, to leave ample room for further additions. The solution actually adopted was, however, a different one. Within a few days of writing his report Panizzi received a suggestion from E. A. Roy, a Transcriber whom he had warmly commended, in his evidence to the Royal Commission, for his knowledge of languages and general ability.[6] This suggestion was 'to form the catalogue from moveable titles, that may be fixed when in use but taken to pieces to allow other titles to be inserted when required'. Roy's letter does not explain how the slips were to be attached, but he submitted a specimen (which has not survived). However, the same suggestion had been made two months earlier in a more detailed form by Charles Tuckett junior, of C. Tuckett & Sons, the binders to the Museum. His letter is preserved in the official file, but was ignored in Panizzi's own proposal for mechanically copied pages. Tuckett suggests that the slips be 'fastened *round the edges* by a preparation I have discovered from Gutta Percha which can at any time be taken off (without in any way injuring the slips)'. He also describes a kind of loose-leaf binder to hold the sheets.

Another suggestion with some similar features was made only a month later, on 29 March, by J. W. Croker in his evidence to the Royal Commission.[7] He asked whether 'printing, instead of writing, the slips and then pasting in all your additions also in print might be convenient'. Apart from greater legibility and saving of space, this, he added, would 'have the advantage too, that when you became crowded in any particular place you need not tear your old catalogue to pieces – you could easily, by a warm moist preparation, remove those slips to different distances and make room for your new slips'. 'I have done it on a small scale myself,' he said, 'and have found it useful.'

Whatever the relation between the proposals of Tuckett, Roy and Croker, the suggestion of movable slips was now adopted and a method of reproducing them was found. Additional Transcribers were quickly appointed, and on 11 May 1849 Panizzi was able to report that 'transcription of the arrears of titles has begun and eight transcribers are engaged on it' and that 'the transcript is executed by the "manifold writer" invented by Mr Wedgwood and three copies of each title are made at once'.[8]

The work proceeded at a good pace. By September 44,000 entries had been transcribed, and in January 1850 Panizzi asked for £500 to be included in the estimates 'for arranging, pasting on leaves, and binding these leaves in volumes for three copies of the transcripts of the entries of the new series of the catalogue'. At the same time he sounded a warning that something must be done about providing space in the Reading Room for the new volumes, of which 153 had been laid down and bound by the end of 1850. By October he saw the possibility of entering all the accumulated titles by the end of January 1851 and also of completing two copies of the separate catalogues of maps and music, which had been compiled by two Assistants employed specially for these tasks – Major for maps and Oliphant for music. But to achieve this it would be necessary for the staff involved to work three additional hours at night, which he assured the Trustees they would be willing to do 'on being remunerated in about the same proportion, or perhaps a very small trifle more than they are at present'. He would set apart a room in his own house for the purpose. The Trustees agreed, and on 8 February 1851 they were asked for and gave their approval to the next step: the transcription by the same method of the many thousands of titles that had been revised for the new General Catalogue. The way was now clear for the compilation, in three copies, of a manuscript catalogue of the whole library that would eventually entirely supersede the old mixture of print and manuscript.

However, before this goal could be reached there was a formidable and complex task to be done. This involved the creation of a new set of laid-down volumes to hold the transcribed slips and the gradual amalgamation of these with the volumes in which the transcribed accession-entries were already being inserted. This work could be begun immediately by transcribing the slips, from *A* to *G*, already written and revised under the alphabetical system since 1839. This operation, including the formation of the amalgamated volumes, had progressed as far as *F* when Panizzi left the Department in 1856 to become Principal Librarian.

A further use for carbon copies of the transcripts was found in 1851, when the number of copies made was increased to four. The additional copies were pasted on stout cartridge paper and arranged by pressmarks. The resulting card file, always known in the Department as the 'fourth copies', constituted both a shelf-list and a record of all entries made for any particular book. It replaced an earlier 'hand-catalogue' begun in 1840, in which books had been listed under pressmarks, one leaf being used for each shelf. By the end of 1852, 166,000 titles had been mounted on cards.

Panizzi's 1844 estimate that the preparation, for the new catalogue, of titles for all books that were in the Library before 1839 might be completed by the end of 1854 was based on an output of at least 50,000 titles per annum. However, because of the continually increasing demands made on the staff by the cataloguing of new accessions, this number was hardly ever reached. The total number of titles prepared by the end of 1854, including those written before July 1844, did not reach 600,000, leaving at least a quarter of the work still to be done, and it remained unfinished when, in 1856, Panizzi on his promotion left the catalogue, with the other cares of his department, to his trusted lieutenant and friend John Winter Jones. The cataloguing system he had devised remained in force (with some important modifications in the 1880s) for the next 75 years.

Notes and References

1. Parliamentary Papers, House of Commons, 1846, vol. 25, p. 217.
2. Nicolas, Sir Harris. *Animadversions on the Library and Catalogues of the British Museum: a reply to Mr Panizzi's statement*. Richard Bentley, London, 1846.
3. A manuscript note by Panizzi in his own copy of the pamphlet remarks that these were not in the Library at the time covered by the catalogue.
4. 'On the collection of printed books in the British Museum, its increase and arrangement', Parliamentary Papers, House of Commons, 1846, vol. 25.
5. Ibid.
6. *Report of the Commissioners...*, *1850*, Minutes of evidence, Questions 2865 and 2867. (Roy was the translator of the travels of Ambrosio Contarini published by the Hakluyt Society in 1873.)
7. *Report of the Commissioners...*, *1850*, Minutes of evidence, Question 8718.
8. Report, 11 May 1849, Panizzi Official Papers, 1849, fol. 4. The essential feature of Ralph Wedgwood's invention was 'carbonated paper', sheets of which were laid, alternately with sheets of plain thin paper made semi-transparent by oiling, on a smooth metal plate. When the top sheet was written on with an agate-pointed stylus, the writing immediately became visible on the upper surface and was also transferred to the other sheets. See Patent Specification A.D. 1806, no. 2972, 'Producing Duplicates of Writings'.

4 Continuation, 1856–75

For almost 20 years after Panizzi left the Department, his cataloguing system continued in operation with little change. He was followed by three Keepers who had long worked under his direction and had the greatest respect for him: John Winter Jones (1856–66), Thomas Watts (1866–69) and W. B. Rye (1869–75). Jones had been one of Panizzi's collaborators in the original drafting of the Rules. Watts had been responsible for the arrangement of the books on the shelves of the new 'iron library' surrounding the Reading Room and was later Superintendent of the Room. He was famous for his vast and accurate memory of the books he had placed, and their location in the Library. Rye, who succeeded him both as Superintendent and later as Keeper, had arranged the collection of reference books placed in the new Reading Room in 1857 and had compiled the first catalogue of them, issued in 1859.

The need, to which Panizzi had drawn attention on first presenting the Rules, for additions to settle doubtful points and to cover cases not provided for still persisted, and was met by discussions among cataloguers and revisers leading to decisions which, in each case, had to be approved by the Keeper.

Examples of the questions that arose are provided by two documents surviving from the time in office of Panizzi and the next three Keepers. The earlier one, preserved among Panizzi's official papers and dated 3 May 1847, is a single sheet bearing the title 'Abstract of additions to rules'. It lists 22 subjects in alphabetical order, each accompanied by a brief statement of the relevant rule. Two of these items – on the cataloguing of collections and on reports of civil and criminal cases – had already appeared as additions to the original rules in the 1841 catalogue volume, and one – entry of saints in the English form – had been adopted in that volume without being mentioned in the Rules. The more important later additions are: a definition of a calendar as any publication, other than a directory, containing 'information connected with a year to come, whether accompanied by an almanack or not'; rules for entering cathedral churches ('under city to which they are attached'); continuations and supplements (under the original work when published with it, otherwise under the author of the continuation, with a cross-reference); indexes and concordances (as original works); and treaties ('under the first contracting power, with preference for England if a party').

The second document is a copy of the 1841 volume in which notes have been written on blank leaves inserted in the section containing the Rules. The cover is stamped with the name 'Mr Porter', that is, G. W. Porter, who was promoted from Assistant to Assistant Keeper in 1870. The original set of manuscript additions in the volume appears to have been made soon after 1860. In addition to repetition of some of the points in the 1847 'Abstract', it includes one more, of which an example occurs in the 1841 volume (the entry of institutions 'deriving their title from a proper name' under their names rather than under a place), and one (that 'the names of writs, as Habeas Corpus', may be used as headings for anonymous works) which can be dated to 1856 or earlier, as Panizzi is named as approving it. Some of the later notes are not written on the leaves but are separately inserted carbon copies of transcribed slips. Six of these carry dates, ranging from 1864 to 1873. The decisions recorded in this document may be divided into three groups, affecting respectively choice of heading, problems connected with anonymous and pseudonymous works, and preference for the English language in headings. In the first group, documents issued in their official capacity by Popes and by 'Bishops who as such are sovereign princes' are assimilated to the provision in rule 67 for laws and acts of sovereigns: they are entered under the official heading (in the case of the Pope, ROME, *Church of* or STATES OF THE CHURCH as appropriate, and for Bishops the name of the See), with the individual name as a subheading. Periodicals issued by an academy are to be entered under ACADEMIES, not under PERIODICAL PUBLICATIONS. In the second group are rulings that the points of the compass are to be treated as proper names when occurring in the titles of anonymous works, and that, when a book is entered under initials, a cross-reference is to be made under the heading which would have been chosen if the initials had not been there. The use of the English form in the heading, regardless of the language used in the book, is extended to 'Councils' (that is, Councils of the Church, later entered under CHRISTIAN CHURCH. – *Councils*) and to descriptive words used as pseudonyms (for example, 'Un Français: works so signed are to be entered under FRENCHMAN').

Only one substantial change in the Rules was made before 1875, and this is not recorded in the volume just referred to. In June 1873 Rye asked the Trustees to approve the reorganisation of the heading ACADEMIES by omitting the subheadings for continents and countries, so that the primary arrangement would be by names of towns in one alphabetical sequence. This was the first step in a long process of dismantling some of the complications of doubtful utility embodied in the 1839 Rules.

The writing and revision of titles for the new General Catalogue of books in the Library before 1839 continued throughout Winter Jones's period as Keeper, but constituted a steadily diminishing proportion of the total cataloguing output. The abandonment in 1851 of the plan to print the catalogue had indeed diminished the urgency for its completion. Chief priority now had to be given to the cataloguing of new accessions. Asked in February 1860 to report progress Jones stated that he expected the shelf-by-shelf revision to be completed by the end of the year. In this, like other Keepers both before and after him, he showed himself over-sanguine. His next report on the subject, dated January 1861, says that 'the cataloguing of the books by presses for the New General Catalogue is drawing towards completion, and in a few months the titles will most probably be in a fit state for final arrangement prior to transcription'. In fact, this position had still not been reached when Jones became Principal Librarian in 1866. By that time the new General Catalogue, in which the entries from the old catalogue were combined with those for the subsequent accessions, had progressed from *F* to *L* and filled 931 volumes, while the 'supplementary catalogue' – that is, the volumes containing the unrevised entries of the old catalogue for the remaining letters of the alphabet, and all additions to them – occupied 305 volumes.

During Watts's short period as Keeper, the laying down of the amalgamated volumes advanced only as far as the middle of the letter *M* and by 1875, when Rye retired, it had reached *S*, and the total number of volumes (including indexes) in the amalgamated and supplementary catalogues was 1,761.

In the new Reading Room, opened in 1857, this rapidly growing series of large folio volumes was accommodated in specially designed bookcases, two shelves high and with sloping desk-tops for volumes being consulted, arranged in two circles round the centre of the Room, where they still serve a similar purpose today.

5 The question of printing

In Rye's last year as Keeper, the great question that had been dormant since 1850 – the printing of the catalogue – resurfaced. The occasion was a question raised during the deliberations of the Civil Service Inquiry Commission presided over by Lyon Playfair. The Commission's main task was to examine the selection of Civil Servants, and the possibility of creating a unified service with a single system of grading and pay, but it was also asked to consider 'the system under which it is desirable to employ Writers or other persons for the discharge of duties of less importance than those usually assigned to established Clerks'; and it was in the application of this question to the work of Junior Assistants (formerly 'Transcribers') in the British Museum, which included the more or less mechanical operation of transcribing catalogue entries, that the Commission suggested that 'if a staff corresponding to the Lower Division of the General Civil Service were introduced into the Museum, and printing instead of transcribing were freely resorted to, a considerable saving of expense would probably be effected'. The idea of using printed slips rather than manuscript transcriptions was not entirely new. As far back as 1849, J. W. Croker in his evidence to the Royal Commission had suggested not only that movable slips should be used but that they should be printed,[1] and within the Library itself Thomas Watts (as revealed in a letter addressed by him to Panizzi in 1855)[2] had favoured printing rather than transcribing in multiple copies when the movable slips were introduced, also in 1849. In 1861 the printing of catalogue slips had been introduced in the Cambridge University Library, a fact well known to the British Museum's staff. When, just before his retirement in July 1875, Rye was consulted by the Principal Librarian on the question raised by the Civil Service Inquiry Commission he revealed that he already had it in mind: about a year earlier, in a conversation with Aldis Wright, the Librarian of Trinity

College, Cambridge, about new cataloguing rules for the Cambridge University Library, he had asked about the printed titles used there and the cost of producing them. Wright had sent him a specimen sheet and a statement showing the cost to be about 4d a title. Rye thought that Museum titles would, on average, be longer, and he obtained from his friend William Blades a further sheet of specimen entries, similar in form to those in Panizzi's 1841 volume but in larger type, for which the average cost of an entry would be 6d. He expressed the opinion (which had no doubt been the reason for not sooner following Cambridge's example) that the mixing of printed with transcribed entries 'would present a very incongruous and unsightly appearance' and advised the postponement of printing until the remainder of the catalogue, from S to Z, had been completed in its existing form.

Three months later Rye's successor, George Bullen, repeated this advice in a formal report to the Trustees. He had consulted the senior Assistant Keeper, Porter, who had ascertained that, while Rye's enquiries indicated a printing cost of between 4d and 6d a title, the cost of transcribing was not more than 2½d; printing therefore could not be recommended on economic grounds.

The official departmental view represented by Rye, Bullen and Porter had, however, been questioned by the other two Assistant Keepers, E. A. Roy (who was in charge of the amalgamation of the old and new catalogues) and Richard Garnett[3] (who had been promoted to Assistant Keeper and made Superintendent of the Reading Room when Bullen became Keeper).

Roy, who had been one of the originators of the idea of movable slips, suggested that printing should be adopted at once, as part of the process of amalgamating the catalogues. He saw no serious objection to the mixing of print with manuscript, and thought that considerable benefits could result from separating the 'intellectual' and 'mechanical' parts of the Assistants' work – a notion also implicit in the report of the Civil Service Inquiry Commission. He also hit on another idea which did not achieve wide acceptance until later: that of the 'unit entry'. His proposal was that, in future, the cataloguing of a book should begin with the purely clerical operation of transcribing the whole of the title page. The transcript would be revised, with the book, by an Assistant, who would abridge the title according to his judgment, would ensure that the author's name was added if it was not already included, and would then add, in the margin or on the back of the slip, all the headings under which entries for the book should appear. The titles so revised would then be printed, but without the headings, space for the heading being allowed above each title. Then would follow the second clerical operation – writing in a bold, clear hand each of the required headings on three copies of each printed slip. All entries for a book would thus be identical apart from the heading, and the distinction between main entries and cross-references would disappear. Under the supervision of an experienced Assistant, the slips would be incorporated in the three copies of the General Catalogue, the original manuscript slips providing a fourth copy to be filed in shelf order. This system would avoid the laborious writing out of full or abridged titles for main entries and cross-references; it would eliminate the retranscription of titles once written and also the need for transcribers familiar with foreign languages and scripts, their work being replaced by proof-reading by Assistants. Because the titles would be printed on stout paper which could withstand the strains of removal and reincorporation, another process – that of mounting the thin, transcribed slips on stronger paper – would also be eliminated. Roy conceded that, as all entries for a book would be equally full, some of the space saved by printing would be lost, but felt this would not be a disadvantage for readers.

Bullen's report and subsequent official discussions of printing made no reference to Roy's scheme. It did not meet the objections felt by Rye, Bullen and Porter to the mingling of print and manuscript; and, later, when the printing of the whole catalogue was considered, the repetition of full entries under several headings was no doubt thought inappropriate and dismissed as wasteful. Assistants therefore continued to write out cross-references, with shortened titles, as well as the whole of each main entry.

Garnett advanced an entirely different argument. In his new position as Superintendent of the Reading Room he had quickly realised that the space available for the catalogue in the Reading Room would be exhausted before the remaining entries of the new General Catalogue from S to Z had been incorporated. He suggested that the only way to limit the bulk of the catalogue was to substitute print for manuscript in all future additions, and to find a way of gradually converting the whole catalogue to printed form.[4] At this stage, his arguments had no more influence than Roy's, but they did have a decisive influence when the question was reconsidered a few years later.

Meanwhile, outside pressure was mounting. The straightforward demand for a printed British Museum catalogue was, however, complicated by other proposals. The first of these was for the production of a Universal Catalogue, which would be based on that of the British Museum but would also include records of all known books not in the

Museum's collection. This had been put forward as far back as 1850 by Charles Wentworth Dilke (the father of the first and grandfather of the second, and more famous, baronet of the same name) in a review of the Royal Commission's report which he contributed anonymously to the *Athenaeum*, of which he was the editor.[5] His suggestion involved the appointment of more Assistants in the Museum to collect, from bibliographies and other catalogues, information about English books not in the Museum, as well as the co-operation of foreign governments in supplying lists of the books published in their own countries. This utopian scheme met with no immediate response, but the idea was revived in a modified form by the Society of Arts in the 1870s, when it discussed the proposal that a Universal Catalogue of Printed Books should be projected, but that it should be produced in chronological instalments, the first stage being limited to books printed in the fifteenth and sixteenth centuries. The British Museum would be asked to help in the production of the English section, and an attempt would be made, through an international convention, to get the corresponding sections for other languages compiled in other countries.[6]

The part of the proposal relating to English books received strong support at the Conference of Librarians held in Edinburgh in 1877, at which the Library Association of Great Britain was founded. The Conference passed a resolution 'recognizing the urgent necessity for a General Catalogue of English Literature' and recommending to the Council of the new Association 'that steps be forthwith taken to prepare such a catalogue'.[7] The Council also had to take into account another project which had meanwhile evolved in the British Museum. Both Rye and Bullen, while agreeing that the question of printing the whole catalogue should be deferred for at least five years and probably longer while the amalgamated manuscript catalogue was being completed, favoured the interim printing of special catalogues of particular parts of the Library. They proposed that the first of these should be a catalogue of English books printed before 1641 (the date being chosen to avoid the great expansion of printing activity during the Civil War). Rye had already prepared the way by having the titles for such books filed separately, and Bullen's formal proposal to produce the catalogue was approved by the Trustees on 9 March 1878. On 5 July the Library Association's Committee on the General Catalogue of English Literature resolved 'that the authorities of the British Museum be urged to make their proposed list of English books to 1640 cover the whole literature of the period', and a letter was sent to the Museum conveying this request and the offer that 'the Council of the Library Association would undertake to use their organisation for the supply of additional slips, prepared by librarians and private collectors on a uniform system'.[8] Bullen doubted the readiness of librarians generally to do the necessary work and of the British Museum cataloguers to add to their existing burdens.[9] Consequently, on 2 August, Winter Jones wrote to the Association that the Trustees felt they must decline to participate in the preparation of the General Catalogue of English Literature.[10] The *Catalogue of Books in the Library of the British Museum printed in England, Scotland and Ireland and of books in English printed abroad, to the year 1640* was published, in three volumes, in 1884. It consists of full entries following the rules for the General Catalogue. The more ambitious scheme favoured by the Library Association had to wait for its fulfilment until the publication, in 1926, of Pollard and Redgrave's *Short-title Catalogue,* based on the holdings of 153 libraries and private collections and covering the same period as the British Museum's list but with shorter entries.

The Library Association's scheme received a further blow from a change in the approach of the Society of Arts. The Society's Committee had been considering the question of the Universal Catalogue during July 1878, and had received evidence from a number of witnesses, including Bullen. In a report published early in 1879[11] it announced its decision that the printing of the whole of the British Museum catalogue would be the best first step towards its objective. In this, it was following a suggestion made by Bullen and supported in the Committee by Sir Henry Cole. The Committee believed that the catalogue could be printed quickly and cheaply, and issued a specimen page in a very cramped style (58 entries to the page) of which it was said by one reviewer that 'anything more repellent and objectionable, in a typographical sense, it would have been difficult for the Council and their printer to have produced'.[12] The Society estimated that if produced in the suggested form by the Stationery Office, the catalogue could be printed in five years and would fill about 45 foolscap folio volumes of 1,000 pages each, which could be sold at 16s or 17s a volume. In the event, the scheme proceeded no further, being overtaken by developments within the Museum.

Early in 1878, Winter Jones was absent for several months because of illness which led to his resignation in August that same year. With an acting Principal Librarian (C. T. Newton, the Keeper of Greek and Roman Antiquities) in charge, Garnett found an opportunity to renew his advocacy of the introduction of printing by stages. The records of the Department of Printed Books contain two documents in Garnett's hand both dated January 1878. The first is the draft of a letter addressed to Newton, pointing out that by the time the unified manuscript catalogue was completed the number of volumes would exceed by over 200 the capacity of the catalogue shelves in the Reading Room, and proposing as a solution the conversion of 'the present MS catalogue first into one of mixed print and MS., and ultimately into a printed one by printing the MS entries of each volume singly, as each, in consequence of accessions, comes to require breaking up'. 'The printed titles', he continues, 'would then be rearranged in double columns, and space for further expansion secured for an indefinite period.' The letter also draws attention to the 200,000 titles written for the new General Catalogue but not yet transcribed for incorporation; they comprised 120,000 entries from the middle of S to Z and 80,000 cross-references relating to these entries but which had to be inserted under earlier letters. 'If', he writes, 'from considerations of space, they must one day be printed, to have them transcribed previously would be sheer waste.' The suggestion that certain large headings, such as BIBLE and SHAKESPEARE, should be printed separately and offered for sale is also repeated, and figures are given showing that the number of volumes occupied in the Reading Room by entries under PERIODICAL PUBLICATIONS could, by printing and remounting with space for additions, be reduced from 50 to 10.

The second document is a memorandum setting out the same points in a more succinct form and with some additions. It is pointed out here that the sale of volumes reprinted to avoid breaking up and re-laying and of the printed lists of new accessions could also produce revenue to set against the cost of printing; and that Assistants, who had to have the necessary qualifications for higher duties, would be spared the wasteful and demoralising task of transcribing titles. Garnett's purpose was to secure, over a period of years, a complete printed catalogue without making a request to the Trustees, which would probably be refused, for a straightforward programme for printing the whole catalogue starting with the letter A. The records preserved by the Trustees do not show whether either of these documents reached the Principal Librarian's office, but Newton was clearly interested in the printing question (Garnett's draft letter starts with a statement that it was written 'agreeably to your instructions'), and he was no doubt fully aware of Garnett's case. However, no official action was taken until after October 1878, when E. A. Bond, the Keeper of Manuscripts, was appointed Principal Librarian, Newton having declined the post. In the meantime, other methods of reducing the cost of the catalogue were considered. Prompted by the Treasury's desire to use the cheapest possible form of labour for each task, the Trustees decided to try the experiment of using 'Copyists' for transcription, and asked Bullen to report on it after six months, a period later extended for a further four months. Various copying devices recommended by the Treasury for multiplying letters and other documents, and also the typewriter (which in the form then available could produce capital letters only), were examined and dismissed as less suitable for cataloguing than the existing method of transcription with carbon copies.

In January 1879 Bullen reported that the Copyists were not proving satisfactory. Their ignorance of foreign languages was resulting in a multitude of transcription errors. He therefore requested, and received, authority to ask the Treasury for permission to employ men with the requisite knowledge at a higher rate of pay. The whole question was, however, soon to become irrelevant. Bond, who was strongly in favour of printing the catalogue, had been impressed by Garnett's arguments, and started his campaign to get them implemented by asking Bullen, on 27 January 1879, to report on the present state of progress towards completion of the manuscript General Catalogue. In reply, Bullen reported the alarming total of 67,025 revised titles waiting to be incorporated (of which 58,820 were still the subject of unsettled queries) and 199,000 titles still awaiting final revision. He estimated that five years were needed for completion. From this point onward Garnett's proposed strategy was put into operation in stages by Bond and Garnett acting in concert, and the official records give the impression that Bullen – the last defender of the Panizzi doctrine that the catalogue must first be finished in manuscript – was carried along with it, perhaps against his own judgment and certainly without making any contribution to the plan himself. In March 1878, when Garnett was discussing his ideas with Newton, Bullen had submitted a report in which one of Garnett's proposals, the printing of certain large headings to save space, is referred to. 'Mr. Bullen', he wrote, 'has already shown that there is still sufficient space for some years for the growth and accommodation of the Catalogue in the Reading Room, and that in any case the relief to be obtained by the printing of such headings would be inconsiderable' (this in spite of Garnett's calculation that space for 40 volumes could be saved by printing the heading PERIODICAL PUBLICATIONS alone). At the same Trustees' meeting that received this report, Bullen obtained authority to go ahead with his own favoured project, the catalogue of English books before 1641, which, because its entries were scattered throughout the alphabet, could not be used to save space in the Reading Room.

On 6 May 1879 Bond received from Garnett a brief official communication on the shortage of space for catalogue volumes in the Reading Room, ending with the words: 'Being aware that the subject has not escaped your attention, I will not at present discuss any of the remedies or palliatives which may have been proposed by myself or others, but confine myself to bringing it officially under your notice.' In fact he had repeated his suggestions of January 1878 in an article which appeared in the April 1879 issue of the *New Quarterly Review*. In a note to a reprint of this article in his later collection of *Essays in Librarianship and Bibliography* he states that Bond had seen this article when it was in type and 'returned it without remark'.[13] Bond's report, made on 9 May, shows his acquaintance with Garnett's proposals and his preference for Garnett's rather than Bullen's advice by suggesting 'the substitution of printed for written copies of new titles and the printing of portions of the General Catalogue already in a sense complete – as the sections of Academies, Bibles, Liturgies, Periodicals'.[14] By October he was ready to advance a definite proposal for the first phase of the conversion to print – the printing of entries for future accessions and of the older entries already revised for the new General Catalogue but not yet transcribed. Estimates had been received from William Clowes & Sons and from Spottiswoode & Co. showing a printing cost of not more than 5d a title. Assuming 60,000 titles a year to be printed, the cost would be £1,250 – about £550 more than the cost of hand-copying. This additional expense would be amply compensated by reductions in binding costs, by sales of copies of printed accession-lists (estimated at £250) and, most important, by dispensing with the services of seven Copyists. On 13 December the Standing Committee of the Trustees approved a report from Bullen recommending acceptance of the tender from Clowes, and the printing of title-slips in seven classes, each to be arranged in alphabetical order. The classes were:

- I New English books
- II New Foreign books
- III Older English books
- IV Older Foreign books
- V Main titles from old catalogue, finally revised
- VI Finally revised cross-references to main titles in present catalogue
- VII Oriental, in languages

Classes I and II were to be sent for printing monthly, III to VI every three months, and VII 'as occasion may require'. Printing was begun in January 1880.

Notes and References

1. *Report of the Commissioners . . ., 1850*, Minutes of evidence, Question 8718.
2. Letter dated 28 May 1855, Panizzi Official Papers. (B.L. Archives DH1/15.)
3. Son of the Revd. Richard Garnett, Assistant Keeper, 1838–50.
4. Garnett, R. 'The Printing of the British Museum Catalogue' (read before the Library Association, Cambridge, 1882), in his *Essays in Librarianship and Bibliography*. George Allen, 1899.
5. *Athenaeum*, 1850, pp. 499–502.
6. *Journal of the Society of Arts*, vol. 26, pp. 227–9.
7. *Transactions and Proceedings of the Conference of Librarians held in London, October 1877*. Printed at the Chiswick Press, London, 1878, p. 181.
8. *Library Journal*, vol. 3, 1878, pp. 188, 225, 226.
9. *Library Journal*, vol. 3, pp. 129 and 296.
10. *Library Journal*, vol. 3, p. 226.
11. *Journal of the Society of Arts*, vol. 27, 1878–79, p. 427.
12. Extract from an unidentified publication, inserted after the specimen in Minutes, reports, etc., supplementary vol. I(16). (B.L. Archives, DH2/62.)
13. Garnett, R. *Essays in Librarianship and Bibliography*, p. 65.
14. British Museum Archives, 'Original Papers', 9 May 1879.

6 Printing the catalogue 1880–1905

The printing of the accessions was warmly welcomed by the Society of Arts and the Library Association, who rightly saw it as the first step towards the production of a complete printed British Museum Catalogue, which would lay the foundation for their own cherished projects of a Universal Catalogue and a General Catalogue of English Literature. This was indeed the end pursued, though not yet officially declared, by Bond and Garnett; but before the second step could be taken, the first had to be firmly established. For the purpose of dividing the accessions into classes, 'English books' were defined as those published in the United Kingdom, the USA and the British colonies, and included 'works in foreign languages printed in England'. 'New books' were those published within the previous five years. The number of copies printed was 250 for classes I and II, 200 for III and IV, 100 for V and VI and 250 for VII. Half the copies of classes I to IV and all of classes V to VII were printed on one side of the paper, to allow for pasting into catalogue volumes. Entries were printed in double columns on large quarto pages and were separated from one another by a space, with a rule across its centre as a guide for cutting into separate slips.

The annual subscription prices for the various sections were fixed at £2 for class I, £1 for class II and 15s for each of the others. The task of 'superintending the printing operation and communicating with the printer' was entrusted to Robert Kennaway Douglas, the senior Assistant. Douglas was primarily an orientalist: he had compiled the catalogue of Chinese printed books and manuscripts published in 1877, and in his spare time was Professor of Chinese at King's College, London. (At the end of 1880, while retaining responsibility for cataloguing Chinese and Japanese accessions, he was made an Assistant Keeper and put in charge of the Sub-Department of Maps, and in 1892 he became Keeper of the separate Department of Oriental Printed Books and Manuscripts.) Garnett was to 'watch over the accuracy of the printed titles'.

In June 1880 Aldrich, who for some years had been superintendent of the transcription process, was able to report that 19,057 title-slips had been printed and were ready for incorporation in double columns in the spaces between the much wider transcribed slips. Incorporation commenced on 21 June with Aldrich leading a team of five Assistants. By the end of the year 60,000 titles had been prepared for printing, 46,000 printed off and over 30,000 incorporated.

One of the benefits expected from printing multiple copies of catalogue entries was the possibility of arranging sets of slips in various ways to form other types of catalogues. The idea that such catalogues could be produced as printed publications without resetting the type, by using stereotype plates, was now revived. It had been suggested as far back as 1849, in evidence to the Royal Commission, by W. D. Cooley, the Secretary of the Hakluyt Society,[1] as part of his suggestion for printing the General Catalogue from the entries then available. The idea resembled that put forward in 1847 by C. C. Jewett, Librarian of the Smithsonian Institution, as the basis of a co-operative cataloguing system for American libraries.[2] It was not then examined further by the Commission or in the British Museum because of the acceptance of Panizzi's objection to any form of printed catalogue at that stage. Now, however, in June 1880, the Trustees approved a proposal that the printed entries for new English and foreign books, for books printed in the fifteenth century and for English books printed before 1641 should be stereotyped. The intention was that the stereotype entries should be accumulated over a period of years and then used to produce a classified catalogue of newly acquired books and a separate catalogue of fifteenth-century books, and for supplementing the catalogue of older English books then in course of production. Although the first two of these projects came to occupy members of the library staff within a few years, it seems that the stereotypes were never used. Their production was discontinued in March 1882[3] – 'because no space for storing the stereotype plates could be found at the printing office or at the Museum'.[4]

By October 1880 Bond was ready to proceed to the second stage of his plan. He proposed to the Trustees that the splitting and re-laying of volumes that had become overfull should be discontinued, and that the contents of such volumes should be printed instead. The additional printing cost was estimated at £1,800 a year. There would be compensatory savings in binding costs, as the volumes to be laid down for Reading Room use would be far fewer and would last much longer; and a further economy could be effected by employing boys to insert the slips at 4d an hour instead of men at 8d an hour. The Trustees accepted the proposal, amended their estimates accordingly, and intimated that the printing of volumes should begin in January 1881.

The printing contract was again given to Clowes. The printed volumes were equal in height to the 1841 volume of the catalogue but were slightly wider, and the entries were printed in the same type as the accessions but with some differences in form and layout. Headings projected one em to the left of an entry, and repeated headings were replaced by a dash, as in the octavo catalogue but unlike the 1841 volume. Each printed part contained between 200 and 300 columns, designed to form the basis of one laid-down volume for the Reading Room. The columns and not the pages were numbered consecutively in each part. The normal print-run was 150 copies, but 250 were to be printed of parts containing important headings for which there might be a separate demand. Ten copies were in a special form: they consisted of separate columns, each printed in the left-hand half of a page on leaves of the strong cartridge paper used in the Reading Room volumes; the right-hand half was left blank for the insertion of new entries. The printed volumes could be purchased at a subscription price of £8 per annum (equivalent to about 10d for a sheet of 16 columns at the expected rate of production); a subscription of £13 secured all accession parts printed in the year as well. The price fixed for important headings issued separately was 1s a sheet.

During 1881 14 parts were printed, totalling 3,012 columns, or about 60,000 entries, the equivalent of a year's accessions. However, this rate of progress was not achieved without some strain on the Department's resources. The necessary work of checking the printer's copy to eliminate mistakes in arrangement, inconsistencies in headings and other obvious defects, followed by proof-reading, was an addition to the duties of the staff. It was found necessary to employ two Assistants on this work in 'non-official time' at the rate of 3s 6d an hour. The Treasury agreed to this expenditure for a period of four years, subject to a limit of £250 a year (representing a maximum of about 12 extra hours a week for each Assistant).

The first part of the catalogue to appear in its new form contained all the entries under the initial *B* (headings 'B.' to 'B.y S.').[5] It was laid before the Trustees on 30 April 1881, with the heavily overcrowded manuscript volumes from which it had been printed exhibited for comparison. The remaining parts produced during the year were six from *A*, one more from *B*, two from *C*, one from *D* and three from *F*.[6]

In January 1882 Bond reported that there were 12 subscribers for the printed parts of the catalogue and 24 subscribers (taking in all 49 copies) for the accessions. He was authorised to increase the impression of the catalogue volumes to 250 and diminish that of the accessions to 150, while reducing the annual subscription rates to £3 10s for the volumes and £3 for the accessions with a discount of ten per cent for agents, single parts being priced at 5s. It was decided at the same time 'that copies of both series be presented to public libraries in the United Kingdom'. During the year, 3,030 columns were printed, in 13 parts. Nine of these were in the early letters *A*, *D* and *G*, but there were also three running from *STE* to *SUE*, for which the old titles had just been finally revised. By printing these at this stage the transcription of the revised titles and the laying down of new manuscript volumes to accommodate them were avoided. The thirteenth was the first heading to be issued as a separate part – VIRGILIUS MARO, in 74 columns, also just finalised and provided with a system of subheadings.

Now that the Treasury was committed to a printing programme that would continue indefinitely, Bond and Garnett were anxious to press on with a plan for printing the whole catalogue in alphabetical order. They were deterred by what they felt to be the unreasonable slowness of the final revision of the older titles – which had still not passed the letter *T* – and by the large collection of still unsettled queries affecting other parts of the alphabet. In October 1882 Bullen reported, at Bond's request, on the time needed to complete the revision. At the current rate of progress, he estimated this at three years, but thought it could be halved by the allocation of a further Assistant, A. W. K. Miller, to help Roy, who was working through the 24,000 titles still remaining under the letter *W*. *U/V* and *X*, *Y*, *Z*, comprising 12,000 titles in all, were in the hands of Blackstone and could be completed within the same period. The addition of more Assistants to the staff would not help, as the work required considerable experience. There were already two vacancies, which should first be filled. He still thought that printing from *A* to *Z* should not be started until the revision was completed.

Bond was dissatisfied with this reply: he thought the printing of the catalogue was of overriding importance, and that more Assistants with the required experience could be released by appointing new men for the easier duties. On 11 November he persuaded the Trustees to agree that printing in alphabetical order should go ahead and that Bullen should be asked to find ways of doing it. Within a fortnight Bullen had found another Assistant – Graves –, who could be transferred from the examination of invoices, his place being taken by Evans, who would combine this work with his responsibility for music cataloguing, while Aldrich would be asked to join the two Assistants who were reading proofs in non-official time.

Bond's impatience was not allayed. He had calculated that Bullen's estimate of the time needed to complete the revision implied that each Assistant would dispose of only 40 titles a day. In consultation with Garnett he carried out a test and reported that Miller, in his presence, had examined in one hour 103 titles 'of which 58 had been finally disposed of, 35 contained cross-references which were to be verified, and 10 were to be compared with the printed works'; also that 'an independent test made in the same manner by Mr Garnett gave a still higher number of titles examined and disposed of, viz. 120'. This time, however, the hard-pressed Bullen had no difficulty in showing that haste had led Bond and Garnett to false conclusions. Before making his reply, Bullen secured from Miller, Roy and Blackstone written statements on the nature of their work. Miller pointed out that in Garnett's test the examination of the titles had been 'of the slightest possible character', sufficient to divide them into classes, certainly not to 'dispose' of them; they had all had to be gone through again later to cancel, alter or revise them. He had not known at the time that a calculation of the rate of revision was intended. The subsequent examination of the cross-references and other titles put aside during the test represented at least a whole day's work, and 'an entire heading ... was unsettled at the last moment by the appearance of a cross-reference to a totally different form of the author's name'. Roy, in a full description of the final revision process, of which he had been in charge for years, pointed out that making the revised titles available for incorporation was only part – and a steadily diminishing part – of the work. The number of laid-down volumes was now 15 times as great as when the work had begun 30 years earlier, and the final reviser, besides passing the unincorporated titles, had to check a much larger number already in the catalogue for errors and discrepancies. A reviser could not be expected to dispose of more than 1,000 titles in a month – and this was a maximum, not an average. Blackstone's statement, while covering much of the same ground, emphasised the work involved in dealing with large headings where a system of subheadings had to be worked out: in three weeks' work on the heading UNITED STATES OF AMERICA he had had to examine and alter 600 transcribed titles and send for 200 books, but had passed only 85 untranscribed titles. All these statements were supported by another Assistant, Russell Martineau, who was not engaged in final revision, but was responsible for much of the cataloguing of older and more difficult

Top: Richard Garnett.
Below left: A. W. K. Miller.
Below right: R. F. Sharp.

books. He had recently been rearranging the heading HORATIUS and reported that in 15 days, while examining titles and looking at books as a preparation for dealing with the heading, he had written one title, revised 42 and cancelled 18 – an average of four titles a day. Once the decisions had been made, he had been able to dispose of 333 titles in three days. Thus, it was absurd to make a judgment on the basis of a small sample taken on a single day.

Bullen, after establishing the inadequacy of the tests, accepted a suggestion from Garnett that part of the work – the checking of cross-references with the headings to which they referred – should be done by a Junior Assistant instead of a reviser, and also made yet one more Assistant – G. W. Eccles – available for revision on a part-time basis.

Garnett was now able to press on with the work. Without waiting to ensure that all cross-references written under *A* for entries under *U/V* and *W* had been made available, he had all the remaining volumes of *A* prepared for press. Except for one part (*ANT–ARC*) and two major headings requiring special attention, ACADEMIES and ARISTOTLE, the whole of *A* was in print by the end of 1883. During the same year the two remaining parts of *S* (*SUE–SWE* and *SWE–SZY*) were also printed, and printing of the volumes from *U* and *V* onwards, for which the old titles had been revised but not yet transcribed, was also begun. (At this point, the practice of printing some copies, in single columns, on sheets of the paper used to form volumes on which accessions were to be mounted was abandoned. Thenceforward, a few copies were printed on the ordinary paper on one side only and the accession volumes were prepared with columns cut from these and pasted in.)

The next portion to be ready for the press was *X* and *Y*, which together formed one printed volume of 258 columns. In addition, the policy of printing overfull volumes from all parts of the alphabet was continued with volumes from *B* and *S* and some taken out of turn from *U* and *W*. This resulted in the completion, in 1883, of 17 printed parts, replacing 70 manuscript volumes and comprising 4,326 columns, an increase of 42 per cent over the previous year's output. In 1884 there was a further increase of over 50 per cent: 6,638 columns were printed, in 29 parts. The final revision of *U* and *V* (still treated as one letter) and of *W* and *Z* was finished early in that year, and the publication of *A* (apart from ACADEMIES) was completed by the separate issue of ARISTOTLE, carefully revised by Blackstone and exhibiting for the first time in its full development the system of subdivision of large author-headings which became a characteristic of the catalogue.

From the outset Garnett emphasised that speed of production was vital to the success of the project, since each volume was printed from the manuscript slips as they stood at the time of preparation for the press and therefore included entries for accessions catalogued after the printing of the earlier volumes. This was a new departure which would certainly have been abhorrent to Panizzi and was probably not even contemplated by Bullen in 1879 when, following Panizzi's example, he advised against any printing before revision was complete. It was, however, inherent in the method by which the printing of the catalogue had been initiated – taking the volumes not in alphabetical order, but as each became too full to allow the insertion of further entries. The result was that, as the work progressed, more and more main entries appeared in the catalogue without the related cross-references, and vice versa. (This inconvenience did not apply, of course, to the large folio volumes in use in the Reading Room, which were constantly kept up to date with slips from the printed accessions.) Garnett cheerfully accepted this defect, along with others that resulted from the inclusion of vast numbers of earlier, unrevised entries which, while not obviously erroneous, did not conform to current cataloguing practices, such as the inclusion of the publisher's name, obligatory in English books since 1880.

A communication from Garnett to the American Library Association's conference in September 1885[7] shows his appreciation of the importance of speed. He estimated that, when printing began, the catalogue contained about three million entries, to which at least 40,000 were added every year. The extent of the catalogue when completed would thus depend on the rate of printing. After describing the work of the Assistants in preparing copy for the printer, which included the elimination of inconsistencies and bibliographical errors as well as careful checking of the arrangement of entries and the reorganisation of such large headings as ACADEMIES and ARISTOTLE, he described his own function as 'to provide for the regular delivery of copy to the printer, and the speedy return of proofs and revises', while doing such 'literary' revision as he could at the stage of passing revises for the press. 'One principle', he continued, 'has always governed my work: to prefer rapidity and regularity to minute accuracy, and to take the risk of error rather than encounter the certainty of accumulation and arrear.' His aim was to have the catalogue completed by the end of the century. In November 1884, following the death of E. A. Roy, his senior in the grade of Assistant Keeper, Garnett was relieved of the post of Superintendent of the Reading Room (where he was succeeded by Fortescue) and was able to give more of his time to the catalogue.

The year 1885 saw another substantial advance – about 30 per cent – in the rate of printing: 8,688 columns were issued, in 38 parts, including four of the five parts of the heading ACADEMIES (revised by A. W. K. Miller), HORATIUS FLACCUS (by Martineau) in 90 columns, and the first half, in three parts, of the heading PERIODICAL PUBLICATIONS (on which another Assistant had been working for several years). By the beginning of 1890, when Garnett became Keeper and was succeeded as editor of the catalogue by A. W. K. Miller, progress through the alphabet had almost reached the end of the combined letters I/J (like U/V, still treated as one), with IRELAND outstanding and the large headings BIBLE, CATALOGUES, ENGLAND, FRANCE and GERMANY, and the parts containing HOLLAND and HOMER, still under revision. Altogether, in nine years, over a million entries had been printed and almost half the work had been done. With Miller as editor and Garnett, as Keeper, still taking a close interest in progress, the production of the catalogue continued steadily, and by the end of 1897 the final parts of the letter T, completing the alphabetical series, were in the printer's hands and only the last of these (*TURK–TZWIVEL*) was issued after the beginning of 1898. Some larger headings which had been held back for thorough revision – HOMER, VICTORIA, IRELAND and CATALOGUES and the first two parts of BIBLE (edited by Martineau) – appeared between 1890 and 1897. The rhythm of production, although never again reaching Garnett's 1885 peak of 8,688 columns, was maintained, with an average of nearly 6,000 columns a year. The new editor, a meticulous scholar, was later described by A. W. Pollard (who had joined the Department in 1883) as 'the life and soul of the revision, to which he devoted himself with every ounce of energy a not very strong body allowed him to muster'. 'Garnett', he continued, 'supplied the driving power and Miller the polish.'[8]

All that was needed to complete the catalogue were the large and complicated headings ENGLAND, FRANCE, GERMANY and LITURGIES, and part of BIBLE. Although Garnett retired early in 1899, with FRANCE, LITURGIES, the last two parts of BIBLE and the whole of ENGLAND still to come, these were all issued in 1899 and 1900, so accomplishing his declared purpose of finishing the work by the end of the century. The years 1899 and 1900 also saw the publication of a complete revised edition of PERIODICAL PUBLICATIONS, first issued in 1885 and 1886. The largest heading of all and the only one to be published entirely in 1900 was ENGLAND. This was formed by combining the entries under the earlier headings ENGLAND, GREAT BRITAIN and GREAT BRITAIN AND IRELAND, and fills 1,582 columns. The decision to merge the three headings was taken at a very late stage: as late as June 1899, Fortescue, who had succeeded Garnett as Keeper, was reporting on progress in the preparation of the three separate headings, and under the heading FRANCE, issued in 1899, cross-references to GREAT BRITAIN AND IRELAND are to be found. At the place in the catalogue where GREAT BRITAIN and GREAT BRITAIN AND IRELAND would have appeared the only entry is for an anonymous work under GREAT BRITAIN, *Steamship.*

This was only the most conspicuous of the many anomalies which arose from the printing of the entries under each heading as they stood when the volume containing them was sent to the press—anomalies of which Garnett and his colleagues were well aware. What seemed to them to be the most regrettable was the fact that by 1900 the earlier parts were seriously out of date and that the catalogue as it then existed outside the Museum was far from being a complete record of the contents of the Library. In several published articles and in official reports Garnett refers to this deficiency, but makes no reference to the inconvenience and frustration caused to users by the presence in the later volumes of numerous cross-references pointing to main entries that were not in the catalogue and of numerous main entries for which cross-references that would have helped to find them were absent. Awareness of this inconvenience was probably dimmed for those working in the Museum by the fact that the missing entries had all been provided, from accession parts, in the working copies of the catalogue.

The question of bringing the published catalogue up to date was already under discussion in 1895. Garnett's proposal was that a new edition of the whole catalogue, incorporating the missing accession-entries, should be printed as soon as possible. He deprecated the alternative of printing a supplement containing the accession entries only, on the ground that this would be useful only to those who already possessed the catalogue, the further sales of which would be severely limited by the smallness of the remaining stock of the earliest parts. The publication of a complete and coherent catalogue would, however, he argued, be 'a great and magnificent undertaking which would confer great advantages upon literature and great honour upon the Trustees'. He believed that, in the reprint, economies could be effected by abridgment of entries and the omission of some types of matter. The Thomason Civil War tracts, 'as far as they are political', and the French Revolution tracts (only partly covered in the printed catalogue) could be listed in separate catalogues; single-sheet items bound together in volumes could in many cases be 'grouped together under one heading';

entries for Acts of Parliament and cross-references from authors of prefaces could be omitted.

In spite of Garnett's representations, however, the Trustees decided on 14 December 1895 'that the Parts issued in 1881 be reprinted in sufficient numbers to raise the stock of those Parts to an equality with the rest', and 'that an Appendix of Accessions, to date, be printed'.[9] This decision was followed by a discussion on the application to the supplement of the suggestion that some material of minor importance should be omitted, and in December 1898 the Trustees approved the preparation of the supplement 'with reduction of the number of main titles and cross-references, and omission of trivial matter, as proposed by the Keeper'. Garnett's final proposals were for a more modest set of exclusions: the main-titles of duplicate copies; entries for 'children's toy books', school test-cards and blank forms; cross-references from preface-writers and the majority of illustrators; and many 'cross-references of form' which could be replaced by general cross-references. By December 1899 Fortescue, the new Keeper, was ready with estimates for printing the supplement. He proposed to use the manuscript title-slips as copy rather than cutting up copies of the printed accessions: although this would increase the cost of printing, it would save the staff much time and trouble. He was authorised to start the printing in January 1900 and, over-sanguine like other Keepers before and after him, forecast its completion by the end of 1901. The price of the complete supplement was fixed at £10.[10] The printing, in 43 parts containing 16,014 columns (about 330,000 entries) and including all accessions to the end of 1899, was in fact completed in 1905. Garnett, who died on 13 April 1906, had lived to see the completion of the job he had initiated 25 years before.

Notes and References

1. *Report of the Commissioners . . ., 1850*, Minutes of evidence, Questions 4713 *et seq.*
2. See below, p. 68.
3. Report of Principal Librarian, 25 March 1882. (B.M. Archives.)
4. According to an article in *Quarterly Review*, October 1898.
5. According to a note in *Journal of the Society of Arts*, vol. 29, 27 May 1881, p. 594.
6. Francis, F. C. 'The Catalogues of the British Museum. I. Printed Books', *Journal of Documentation*, vol. 4, no. 1, June 1948, pp. 14–40.
7. *Library Journal*, vol. 10, 1885, pp. 200–6.
8. *The Library*, 4th series, vol. 12, no. 1, June 1931, p. 113.
9. Standing Committee Minute, 14 December 1895. (B.M. Archives.)
10. Trustees' Minute, 9 December 1899, and draft report by Fortescue dated 'December 1899'. (B.M. Archives.)

7 Development of cataloguing practice, 1841–1900

The way in which the printing of the catalogue had been initiated precluded any reconsideration of the Rules before it was begun. It was thus essentially a reproduction of the manuscript General Catalogue begun by Panizzi in 1839 and was deemed to be complete when the last of the titles written before that date had been revised – a process not completed until 1884, after printing had begun. The catalogue was therefore hardly influenced by developments since 1839 in general cataloguing practice elsewhere, which had rejected some important parts of the British Museum system.

None of the major catalogues produced in Great Britain in the twenty years following the publication of the 91 Rules appears to have been substantially influenced by them. Bandinel's Bodleian catalogue (1843–51) follows the older tradition, preferring Latin headings, such as 'Anglia', 'Biblia Sacra' and 'Museum Britannicum', entering anonymous works under subject or class-headings, and arranging the works of an author in chronological order of first publication. J. H. Todd, the Librarian of Trinity College, Dublin, who had started a new manuscript slip catalogue of his library in 1835 and began printing it in 1848, wrote to Panizzi on 23 February 1849 enclosing a specimen sheet and asking for advice. He had, however, already adopted the Bodleian catalogue as his chief model, and his catalogue appears to have been uninfluenced by the British Museum Rules, except perhaps in its inclusion under one heading ('Biblia Sacra') of all editions of separate books of the Bible, which Bandinel had catalogued individually under the Latin form of their titles or authors' names. The internal arrangement of the heading, however, follows Bandinel in making language the primary factor, so that editions of the Bible and all its parts in the original languages stand first and are followed by polyglot editions and then by versions in strict

(Latin) alphabetical order of languages, each language section comprising both complete and partial editions. The principle established in the British Museum Rules that editions and translations of any given work or part are found together is disregarded. The catalogue of the Advocates' Library, Edinburgh, which began to be printed in 1860, shows the influence of the British Museum Rules in the use of class-headings for anonymous almanacs, directories and encyclopaedias, while retaining the older customs in the cataloguing of anonymous books and in its chronological arrangement of works under an author. It does not use the heading PERIODICAL PUBLICATIONS, but has an analogous heading for newspapers, and assembles under the headings 'Journal', 'Magazine' and 'Review' those periodicals whose titles include one of these words. Other periodicals are entered under their titles, and societies and institutions under their names. These three catalogues all make the main entry for an anonymous book under its author's name, when known, with a reference or a short additional entry under the heading based on the title.

The first and most important deliberate use of the British Museum Rules as the basis of a new system was not made in the United Kingdom, but on the other side of the Atlantic. During a tour of European libraries in 1845 Charles Coffin Jewett, the Librarian of Brown University at Providence, Rhode Island, visited the British Museum and met Panizzi, whose administration of the Library greatly impressed him. Jewett had himself compiled a much-admired catalogue of the library of Brown University and was particularly interested in cataloguing systems. In 1847, in the words of his biographer, he 'conceived the idea of printing catalogues by means of separate stereotyped plates of individual titles'.[1] (The communication of this idea to the British Museum through Henry Stevens in the autumn of 1847 may have been the unacknowledged source of the similar suggestion made to the Royal Commission by W. D. Cooley.) Jewett's appointment soon afterwards as Librarian of the Smithsonian Institution led him to investigate the practical possibilities of the idea, and to propose that stereotyped titles should be set at the Smithsonian to create and keep up to date a union catalogue of the major libraries of the United States while at the same time providing those libraries with printed catalogues of their own collections. Such a project logically required the adoption of a common system of cataloguing, and when Jewett's scheme had been matured to the point of being embodied in an official report, this included a set of catalogue rules.[2]

'The rules', Jewett states in his report, 'are founded upon those adopted for the compilation of the catalogue of the British Museum;

some of them are, *verbatim*, the same. Others conform more to rules advocated by Mr Panizzi, than to those finally sanctioned by the Trustees of the Museum.' This last sentence refers to the rule for anonymous works. Jewett's rule is to enter them under 'the first word of the title, not an article or preposition', as proposed by Panizzi and rejected by the Trustees. (Although Panizzi's rule 38 does not exclude prepositions as entry words for anonymous works with no substantive in the title, this does not necessarily imply that Panizzi accepted entry under prepositions, for they would not be expected to occur in the absence of a substantive.) Jewett allows one exception: the British Museum's use of a proper name as the preferred heading is followed in the case of anonymous biographies, which are entered under the name of the subject. Panizzi's rule that the main entry for a book is not made under its author's name unless this appears in the book itself is modified by the provision that, if the author has issued any edition, continuation or supplement under his name, all editions will be entered under it, including those issued anonymously or under a pseudonym.

Jewett follows Panizzi closely in the rules for entry of authors under surname or first name (including entry of noblemen under surname, not title); for compound names and names with prefixes; for entry of collections under the editor; for exact transcription of title pages (including observance of the original orthography); for insertion of the number of volumes or parts after the title; and for the recording of place of publication, date and size. (For the last item Jewett regards the bibliographical format as necessary but insufficient and requires, in addition, the dimensions of the type-page in inches. He also adds, after the size, the number of pages 'in books of one volume, the body of which does not contain more than one hundred pages'.) For the arrangement of titles under an author, he adopts Panizzi's rules, but places cross-references at the end instead of at the beginning.

It is in his treatment of what later came to be known as corporate authorship that Jewett makes his most important contribution to the development of cataloguing rules. While accepting the principle implied in Panizzi's two rules for 'corporate bodies' in general (rule 8) and for academies as a special class (80), he gives it a far more precise expression in a single rule (his rule 22), the essence of which is expressed in the following words:

... bodies of men, under whatever name, and of whatever character, issuing publications, whether as separate works, or in a continuous series under a general title, are to be considered and treated as the authors of all works issued by them, and in their name alone.

The distinction between academies and other corporate bodies disappears, and the word 'author', not used by Panizzi in this context, is applied to such bodies for the first time. The inclusion of the phrase 'in their name alone' excludes from the rule's operation separate works bearing the name of a personal author. The practice established in Panizzi's 1841 volume, and subsequently followed by the Museum, was to make the main entry for such works under the publishing body if this was classified as an 'academy', although the text of rule 80 required this only when the work formed part of a series. The entry of societies under place-names is also rejected: the second sentence of Jewett's rule reads: 'The heading is to be the name of the body, the principal word to be the first word, not an article.'

Together with ACADEMIES, the other class-headings created by Panizzi – CATALOGUES, DICTIONARIES, ENCYCLOPÆDIAS, EPHEMERIDES, LITURGIES and PERIODICAL PUBLICATIONS – are abandoned: the general rules for anonymous works and corporate authors are applied to all these categories, liturgies being treated as corporate works of the religious bodies 'under whose authority they are prepared and published'. In headings for personal authors who have changed their names, the latest name used in the author's publications is chosen, not the earliest; periodicals are to be entered under the latest title; and exceptions are allowed to Panizzi's rule that foreign compound surnames are entered under the first part, when another part is universally used: 'Voltaire' is preferred to 'Arouet de Voltaire', and 'Fénelon' to 'Salignac de la Mothe Fénelon'.

Jewett's rules were necessarily adapted to usages that were generally acceptable to American libraries at the time. They were the first set of rules designed not for a particular library but for common use by many libraries and were widely accepted as the dominant authority in the United States until the appearance, in 1876, of Charles Ammi Cutter's *Rules for a printed dictionary catalogue*.[3]

Almost everything that Jewett took from the British Museum is also adopted by Cutter. There are a few minor variations. In entering anonymous works under their titles, only articles are disregarded, not prepositions; in the rule that foreign compound surnames are entered under the first part, the exception for Dutch names is omitted; the rule that noblemen are to be entered under the family name is applied to British noblemen only – others are to be entered under their titles; the number of volumes is placed in the imprint, between the date and the format, instead of immediately after the title; the publisher's name is to be given after the place of publication, whereas Panizzi, in the exceptional cases where he included this item (not mentioned by Jewett), adopted the reverse order; cataloguers' additions to titles, in square brackets, are to be given 'in the language of the title', not (as in Panizzi's practice, followed by Jewett) always in English.

On the entry of corporate bodies, Cutter writes: 'No satisfactory usage has as yet been established' – a statement that may be thought to hold true today. He could not accept entry under either name or place as a general rule, and suggests a compromise by which – besides national and local governments, for which the place-name is itself treated as a corporate heading – 'local societies', churches, the royal academies of countries on the continent of Europe, municipal institutions and American state historical societies will be entered under geographical headings, while all other bodies are to be entered under their names. In the internal arrangement of headings Cutter introduces two innovations: when the same word is a heading for different kinds of entry these are arranged not in strict alphabetical order but according to categories, in the order person, place, title, subject (other than a person or place); and where numerous persons are entered under the same personal name (for example, 'John') the arrangement is not, as in the British Museum practice, in the alphabetical order of the distinguishing epithets used, but in a conventional order: 'Saints, Popes, Emperors, Kings, Princes and Noblemen, others'.

The publication of Cutter's rules was quickly followed by a development which started a collaboration between American and British librarians that has continued to the present day. In two conferences of librarians, at Philadelphia in October 1876 and at Edinburgh in September 1877, the Library Associations of the United States and of Great Britain were formed. One of the first tasks undertaken by each association was the establishment of a set of cataloguing rules to facilitate co-operation.

The rules produced by the American 'Committee on Co-operation' were considerably simplified compared with those of Jewett and Cutter, on which they were based. Like Jewett's, and unlike Cutter's, they were rules for an alphabetical author catalogue and were not concerned with subject entries. They followed Jewett in giving rules for titles before rules for headings. Cutter, however, was a member of the Committee, and took a major part in drafting the rules, which embodied almost all the elements that Cutter had derived from the British Museum Rules through Jewett. For 'noblemen', however, after first recommending entry under the surname, the Committee finally decided in favour of entry under the title, 'unless the family name is decidedly better known'. A new principle, suggested by Cutter in a note to his rules, is introduced in relation to pseudonyms: 'In a few cases (selected by a committee of the Association) noted pseudonyms are to be used instead of the surname, and only a reference made under the surname.' The German modified vowels *ä, ö, ü* are to be arranged as *a, o, u* not as *ae, oe, ue*. Among the items associated with the imprint, the number of pages in a single volume, which both Jewett and Cutter had placed last, is placed, like the number of volumes when more than one, before the size.

The American rules quickly became known to British librarians through their publication in March 1878 in the *Library Journal*, a new periodical which had been started in 1876 by the organisers of the Philadelphia Conference. (It was adopted by the American Library Association as its official journal in February 1877 and, from November of the same year, became the 'official organ of the Library Associations of America and the United Kingdom', with a London as well as a New York imprint.)

The Library Association's 'Committee on title entries', appointed in December 1878, decided at its first meeting 'that it would be more expedient to follow lines already laid down than to add another code to those already in existence, and chose as the most recent and authoritative example for critical examination the condensed rules for cataloguing issued by the American Library Association'.

The Committee's first draft of rules differed only slightly from its American model. It observed rather more closely the principle of uniform application to all cases by omitting the provisions for entering anonymous biographies under their subject and for using the pseudonyms of certain authors as headings for main entries, rather than their real names. It introduced a new variant into the recording of bibliographical details by moving the number of volumes back to its original position between title and place of publication and placing with it not only pagination, but also the size.

When the Committee's report, including the draft, was put before the second Annual Meeting of the Library Association on 25 September 1879, Garnett (who had been a member of the Committee) and Bullen declined to vote for it, and 'other members following the British Museum officials, it was agreed that the report should be resubmitted to the Committee, and that Messrs. Bullen and Garnett should be requested to confer with the Committee in the matter'.[4]

The rules, when resubmitted at the next Annual Meeting, showed several important changes.[5] The new rule for anonymous books was, surprisingly, neither the American nor the Museum rule, but reverted to a version of the old practice Panizzi had fought against: they were to be entered 'under the chief subject-word of the titles . . . and, where advisable, with a cross-reference under any other noticeable word'. This at least preserved the title page as the source of the heading, and was presumably accepted as a compromise by the British Museum men because it would produce the same heading as the British Museum rule in those numerous cases where the subject was a person, place or institution named in the title, or where the first substantive indicated the subject. The rule for 'Bible' was expanded to indicate an arrangement of entries similar to that adopted in the Museum and several additional rules also reflected British Museum practice: a class-heading 'Liturgies' was introduced, and rules based on those of the Museum were included for academic theses, trials and civil actions. On the other hand, the trend towards headings based on general usage rather than strict uniformity was taken a step further by an instruction to enter married women and other persons who have changed their names under 'the name best known, with a cross-reference from the last authorized name'. By the time the Library Association rules, with a few more amendments (including a change to arranging German ä, ö and ü as ae, oe and ue, and an instruction to disregard a preposition 'having the meaning of "concerning"' in the arrangement of titles), had been approved at the fourth Annual Meeting (September 1881), the decision to start printing the British Museum Catalogue in its existing form had been taken, and any new move to reconcile its rules with those of the Library Association was impossible.

The Museum's influence had, however, been greater in another direction. Just before the British Committee started its work – in October 1878 – the Cambridge University Library had adopted a set of rules modelled on those of the British Museum and carrying even further the use of class- and form headings. ACADEMIES, PERIODICAL PUBLICATIONS (with titles arranged alphabetically by the first word, not under places of publication), CATALOGUES and ENCYCLOPÆDIAS all appear. 'Almanacks' replaces the British Museum's EPHEMERIDES, and DICTIONARIES is used in the singular. For grammars there is a heading 'Grammar', and other large conglomerations of entries are created under 'Official Publications' and 'Dissertations'. The rule for anonymous books, while following the Museum in choosing as heading a proper name occurring in the title, prefers a word denoting the subject or, failing that, the first word in the title, to the Museum's 'first substantive'.[6] An unfavourable review of these rules, by C. A. Cutter, appeared in the same issue of the *Library Journal* as the first draft of the rules of the British Library Association.[7]

In two small points the British Museum's practice itself was modified in the printed volumes to accord with current ideas about the catalogue of a large library. From 1880 onwards, in all new entries, the pagination of single-volume works was included, and the publisher's name was added for all English books and for foreign books printed before 1700. However, the placing of these items within the entry followed traditions established by Panizzi, not the new Library Association rules. Pagination, like the number of volumes, came between the title and the imprint, and the publisher's name came before the place of publication. Thus a further permanent divergence had been established between British Museum practice and general Anglo-American practice, in the arrangement of collation and imprint data.

Notes and References

1. Borome, J. A. *Charles Coffin Jewitt*. ALA, Chicago, 1951, p. 43.
2. Jewett, C. C. *On the construction of catalogues of libraries*. Smithsonian Report. 2nd ed., Washington, 1853.
3. USA Bureau of Education. *Public Libraries in the United States of America . . . Special Report*, Part II. Washington, 1876.
4. *Library Journal*, vol. 4, no. 11, November 1879, p. 417.
5. *Library Journal*, vol. 5, nos 9–10, September–October 1880, pp. 271–3.
6. *Cambridge University Reporter*, 20 June 1879.
7. *Library Journal*, vol. 4, no. 11, November 1879, p. 422.

8 Revision of the Rules

Although Panizzi's rules remained in force, discussions about their application and extension continued as the work of making the printer's copy coherent and consistent proceeded. One long-overdue reform was introduced during 1884. The rule that cross-references must stand first under each heading was modified to allow those which begin with the title of a work by the author named in the heading to be included among main entries in the alphabetical sequence of his works. This removed the two anomalies of incomplete alphabetical lists of authors' works and of entries in different places for editions of the same work.[1] The change was first made in some large headings printed in 1884 (for example, ARISTOTLE and BACON) without being extended to smaller headings printed at the same time. By the end of 1884 it was being applied consistently to all headings.

In two ways, however, this simple change in the order of entries was not sufficient in itself. First, although it brought entries for works which had been published as part of a collection or series into the desired order, it failed to do so for works published anonymously. These were, and for a time continued to be, entered under their authors by means of cross-references in the form used also for editors and translators, as in this example, printed in 1883:

SWIFT (Jonathan) *Dean of St. Patrick's.*
See TALE. A Tale of a Tub, *etc.* [By J.S.] 1704. 8°.

This entry is widely separated from those for editions published with the author's name. The change to a new form of entry was made in two stages. First, the title of the work was inserted at the beginning of the entry, the rest of the reference remaining unchanged except for the removal of unnecessary repetition, as, for instance under DEFOE (printed in 1886):

DEFOE (Daniel)
– The Fortunes and Misfortunes of Moll Flanders, *etc.* [By D.D.]
  See FLANDERS (Moll) The Fortunes, *etc.* [1721] 8°.

It was not until after 1890 that the second step was taken by transferring the date and size and, in newly written entries, the pagination to join the title, so producing what came to be known as a 'main-title cross-reference'.

The second difficulty concerned cross-references for works *about* an author when these were parts of a collection and therefore entered, under their own authors, by means of cross-references to the entry for the collection. To avoid making a cross-reference to another cross-reference, the entry under the person who was the subject of the work was not a reference to the author but to the collection in which the work was contained, and began with the title of the work and the name of its author. The result is best made clear by an example. Under BUNYAN (John), in one of the last parts printed in 1884, this reference appears:

BUNYAN (John) [*Biographies.*]
– Bunyan. [A biography.] By J. A. Froude. *See* MORLEY (John) *of Lincoln College, Oxford.* English Men of Letters, *etc.* 1878, *etc.* 8°.

The entry under FROUDE, printed in 1887 and showing a change in the form of Morley's heading, reads as follows:

FROUDE (James Anthony)
– Bunyan. [Biography.] pp. vi. 181. 1880. *See* MORLEY (*Right Hon.* John) English Men of Letters, *etc.* 1878, *etc.* 8°.

The Bunyan entry could not be put among the entries for his own works, and is therefore assigned to a special subheading for biographies. But, by a partial application of the new rule, because it starts with a title it is placed in its alphabetical order among the titles of *anonymous* lives of Bunyan, not among the references to authors of lives, where a reference to Froude might be expected. A solution to this problem was not found until 1892, when entries began to appear in which the reference was made directly to the author, and the title (or editor and title) of the collection or series was added in brackets and in italics. An early example is:

POPE (Alexander) *the Poet.* [*Appendix.*]
– *See* STEPHEN (Leslie) Alexander Pope. [An account of his life and writings.] 1880. 8°. [*English Men of Letters.*]

While some modifications and additions to the Rules had been recorded and formally approved, there had also grown up a body of accepted practice which was transmitted orally by revisers to new cataloguers. One of those who felt most acutely the need to commit this tradition to writing was Russell Martineau, and when, at the end of 1884, he was promoted to the rank of Assistant Keeper in succession to Roy, Bullen entrusted him with the task of codifying both the written and the unwritten rules. He worked at this, as he reported later to Bullen, 'in all the time that could be spared from urgent work, and also to a large extent in leisure hours at home, during the year 1885'. His draft (to quote again his own words) was 'examined and generally approved by several of the most experienced men in the Department, and rewritten with many improvements and additions'. It was submitted to the Keeper in August 1886, with a request that it should immediately be printed, in about 20 copies, and then considered by the Keeper, assisted by a committee of Assistant Keepers and experienced Assistants, before being formally approved. It was in fact so printed, and survives in a single copy,[2] discovered in about 1950 by the Principal Keeper, C.B. Oldman, on a shelf in his office, when its authorship and indeed its very existence were unknown to the Department's staff. It is printed on one side only of oblong half-foolscap sheets (8 by 12½ inches), the text occupying the left-hand half of each printed side, the other half being left blank for notes. While most of the 91 Rules, so far as they were still in force, are incorporated in the text (usually in a revised form intended to be more precise and unambiguous), the whole body of rules is rearranged in a systematic order under headings and subheadings thus:

Introduction: Terminology.
  I. Main Titles.
    A. Heading.
      Aa. Choice of Heading.
      Bb. Form of Heading.
        1. Personal Names.
        2. Place-names.
        3. Orthography of ordinary words.
    B. Body of Title.
    C. Post-title.
    D. Imprint.
    E. Note.
  II. Cross-References.
    A. Formal Cross-References.
    B. Editorial and other Special Cross-References.

> C. Analytical Cross-References.
> D. Biographical Cross-References.

Against each paragraph which reproduces or modifies the substance of one of the original rules, the number of that rule is printed in the margin. There is no section dealing with the arrangement of entries: Panizzi's rules 69 to 78 are consequently not represented.

The text, which occupies 70 pages, is voluminous and discursive, and discusses many questions not touched on in the earlier rules. The marginal note 'MS' against some paragraphs indicates the prior existence of written instructions, of which, in several cases, no earlier record has survived. (Evidence that Martineau was working with a copy of the Rules as first printed for staff use and not as they appeared in the 1841 volume is provided by the presence of the marginal 'MS' against instructions which appeared as italicised additions in the latter version.) The style of the work is appropriate to a handbook for cataloguers rather than to a formal code of rules. This may be illustrated by a quotation from the opening of the section on 'Choice of Heading':

> This is the most important of all the subjects connected with alphabetical cataloguing, because upon the correct choice of the heading depends the possibility to the reader of finding the book at all in the catalogue.

or of the rules on corporate authorship:

> But a large proportion of existing books are not the product of an individual author, but of a corporation acting together.

The minuteness of the detail examined is shown by the extent of the sections on the form of an author's name in headings (nine pages); on the use of place-names as headings (five pages); on imprints (five pages); and on the title (also five pages, with one whole page devoted to books without title pages).

Several footnotes illustrate the discussions that went on about points which had not been settled when the draft was printed. One of these refers to the rule that place-names in headings are to be given in English 'when a generally acknowledged English form exists':

> For German names it must be determined ... whether in well-known names, like Königsberg, Göttingen ... Zürich ... the dots are simply to be removed on the plea of giving them an English look, or are to be retained, or the vowels to be written in full, as ae, oe, ue. I advise the retention of the dots ... in accordance with the rule in the text about retaining accents, &c. This is in agreement with what we *must* do in Danish, where ö and ø cannot be written oe. (As no special rule has been given, all these forms are widely used in the catalogue.)

Revision of the Rules

Retaining the dots would have been inconsistent with the rule that, in headings, the German modified vowels should be written with the *e*; writing the vowels as *ae, oe, ue*, would have separated the headings from the place where an English reader would probably look for them. The forms actually adopted in the printed catalogue were KONIGSBERG, GOTTINGEN, ZURICH.

Another case is the suggested rule for cathedrals: 'Cathedrals, Minsters and Abbeys, when commonly known by the name of their respective localities, are entered under the latter, as STRASBURG. – *Cathedral*'. The footnote is as follows:

These other forms are found in cat., and a decision must be made:—
2 EXETER, *Cathedral Church of.*
3 CANTERBURY CATHEDRAL.
4 WELLS, *Cathedral Church of St. Andrew at.*
5 CHARTRES, *Cathedral of Notre Dame* [Why not *'of our Lady'*?]

Form 3 is the worst, for it does not even show that the church is at Canterbury, and the title will not be arranged with the institutions belonging to that City, but with Canterbury Hall (a music hall in London); 4 and 5 unnecessarily mention the Saint; in 2 the comma is bad; either Exeter. – *Cathedral church*, or No. 1 are the best, *Cathedral Church* preferable, as *Cathedral* is not properly a substantive.

It will be noted that not only clarity but also correct English usage and the appropriateness of a heading to a particular kind of institution are in question. The examples quoted had already been printed in the catalogue. Parts printed later still show variations: for example, HEREFORD CATHEDRAL (1889), SALISBURY, *Cathedral Church of* (1895), though the form recommended by Martineau predominates (for example, NORWICH. – *Cathedral Church*).

Martineau's section on anonymous books (pages 12–18) shows how far it had been found necessary to supplement and clarify an important group of rules. In the first place it is made clear that the name of a person or corporate body mentioned in the title as the *subject* of the book (or, in the case of a person, as having the work addressed to him) takes precedence in the choice of heading over such a name appearing in the title for some other reason (for example, 'The gardens of Lord Viscount Cobham at Stowe' will be entered under STOWE). Panizzi's rule allowing entry of an anonymous book under the editor or translator when there is no name in the title[3] is ignored; and in relation to entry under the first substantive, Panizzi's somewhat obscure formula:

a substantive adjectively used, to be taken in conjunction with its following substantive as forming one word; and the same to be done with respect to adjectives incorporated with their following substantive.

is revised in the form:

the first substantive in the title must be taken as the heading; which may be a compound substantive (Family Religion), or a permanent union of adjective and substantive (Grand Duchy), or other technical compound term (Sergeant at Arms).

Later (page 31), in the chapter on 'Form of Heading', an exceptional treatment is laid down for certain cases of compounds which include an adjective derived from the name of a person, place or corporate body, and which, under the rules, have the same precedence in choice of heading as the names themselves. The exception is that 'where the compound phrase is identical or analogous in meaning with one sanctioned by the general usage of the catalogue, the latter is preferred'. Among the examples given are: 'British Arms' (or 'Forces') under GREAT BRITAIN AND IRELAND. – *Army*; 'London Theatres' under LONDON. – *Theatres*; and 'the Bath Guide' (which might equally be called 'Guide to Bath') under BATH. There is a section explaining that in books with a 'double title' – that is, having an alternative title or subtitle – a name occurring in the second part of the title will form the heading only if it is the name of a person (real or fictitious) – or, presumably, of an institution, though this is not stated – appearing as the *subject* of the book.

The cataloguing of 'anonymous books of an early age', which 'often appear under various titles' (the works now commonly called 'anonymous classics'), is discussed in a paragraph which makes suggestions for avoiding the entry of different editions or versions under different headings, but does not formulate a precise rule.

In a few cases Martineau describes a practice which was already becoming obsolete. For instance, his example of a reference from the author of an anonymous book is in the old form, and ignores the new form used under DEFOE (printed in 1886). Martineau's example incidentally provides an interesting illustration of the changes occurring during the printing of the catalogue. The example is:

DRAKE ( ) *See* ESSAY. Essay in defence of the female sex. [By – Drake.] 1696. 8°.

In the printed catalogue there is no entry for the book under ESSAY or under DRAKE – headings which were both printed at about the same time as Martineau's draft. The work was in fact stated in its title to be 'By a Lady', and appears under the heading LADY, printed in 1890, where it is attributed to Mary Astell. Unaccountably, there is no entry for it under ASTELL either in the main catalogue or in the supplement. In later editions of the catalogue it is attributed to 'Mary Astell? or Judith Drake? or H. Wyatt?' and the necessary cross-references have been supplied.

Martineau's rule for directories – that they should be entered under the appropriate place-name or, in the case of directories of a trade or occupation not limited to a country or place, under the trade – represented practice prevailing at the time, but was altered soon afterwards, against his advice. In October 1886, while the draft was in the press, he wrote to Bullen protesting against a proposal to make 'Directories' a 'privilege heading', like ENCYCLOPÆDIAS or EPHEMERIDES. Would the heading, he asked, be limited to books with the word 'directory' in the title? The term would have to be defined to exclude its use in a liturgical sense. If its use as a heading were to depend not on the title but on the general character of a book, this would be a dangerous extension of subject headings. 'The word directory', he urged, 'if not in the title might never occur to the reader as a possible heading.' Despite his opposition, it was decided to create the new heading, but too late for it to be included in its place in the printed catalogue, which passed *DIR* in 1886. The new rule was applied in the manuscript copies of the catalogue used in the Library, and was published in December 1887 in a revised edition of the *Explanation of the system of the Catalogue*, compiled by F. E. Blackstone, of which the first edition had appeared in May of the same year. The full list of directories, with subheadings for places and trades appeared only in the Supplement, in 1902.

In connection with the printing of Martineau's work, Bond, the Principal Librarian, discussed with Bullen the question of publishing the revised rules, and expressed the opinion that the draft was too elaborate for this purpose. Martineau, in another letter to Bullen, explained that, in addition to any rules published as a guide for readers, a need had been felt for 'house-lists of rules', to be used internally in preserving unity of form and treatment, and that the mass of detail contained in his draft, though not intended for publication, had been 'found necessary in the experience of revisers ... forced to choose between two different forms to be found in the catalogue ... and in cases that have not occurred before ... to make a new rule'.

Reports written by Martineau in 1888 refer to participation in a committee on the rules, but no record has survived in the Department of the results of its deliberations, and no definitive code of practice appears to have been produced. With few exceptions, however, Martineau's instructions do faithfully represent, in both substance and terminology, the practices passed down from revisers to new cataloguers during the first half of the twentieth century.

The idea of a new published set of rules was revived in 1895,[4] and in 1897 a provisional text was printed in a small number of copies for the use of the staff and marked 'under revision'. The rules for the General Catalogue numbered 39 and were followed by brief summaries of the rules for the catalogues of maps and music, each occupying only one page.[5] The rules are not presented in the order suggested by Martineau, but broadly follow the order of Panizzi's rules, except that the rules for special headings (ACADEMIES, PERIODICAL PUBLICATIONS, etc.), which Panizzi placed at the end because they were drafted later than the others, are put among the rules for headings other than authors' names and, as in Martineau's draft, the rules for arrangement (Panizzi's rules 69–78) are omitted altogether. The text is intended to assist users of the catalogue, not to record the detailed instructions needed by cataloguers in applying general principles to particular cases. In extent it is roughly equivalent to Panizzi's rules and to only about a quarter of Martineau's, although it incorporates a number of Martineau's improvements. It includes the new rule for directories, to which Martineau had objected, and a rule for the cataloguing of incunabula. There is also a much-simplified rule for catalogues, for which Martineau had accepted most of Panizzi's rule but reduced the number of divisions in the heading from six to five; the new rule abolishes the divisions and limits the heading to those catalogues which, besides being anonymous (that is, lacking a named author), do not contain the name of 'any institution or other owner'. The rule for commentaries includes an instruction not mentioned by Martineau: that editions of single Acts of Parliament with a commentary are to be entered under the commentator. Two practices, dating back to the 1841 catalogue, which led to the creation of numerous strange and unexpected headings, were incorporated for the first time into a printed rule: the adoption for oriental names of 'the forms in use in the various Oriental catalogues', and the translation into English, for use in headings, of any 'compound expression formed with an adjective derived from a proper name'. Several other points in the original rules were now expressed in more precise terms – for instance:

> The choice of a Heading for a main entry must be based on the information supplied in print in a perfect copy of the book itself, and on that only. (Rule 4.)

In some respects, however, the revised rules fall short of a complete description of the essential features of the catalogue. While the entry of official publications 'under the name of the authority by which they are issued' and of the publications of learned societies under ACADEMIES is mentioned, there is no rule describing the treatment of the publications of other kinds of corporate bodies; and there is no mention of the elaborate system of subheadings used under the names of countries and in extensive author-headings. By what appears to be an oversight, rule 25, on joint authorship, while it provides for the entry of works written by two or more authors 'without specification of the parts written by each' (under a joint heading for two and under the first-named only for more than two), and for the entry of 'books . . . made up of separate works by more than two authors' (under the editor or a heading taken from the collective title), omits the case of a book consisting of separate contributions by *two* authors, for which the practice was to adopt as heading the name of the first only. Another rule (21) is inconsistent on two points with the practice described by Martineau and regularly followed in the catalogue. In describing differences in the treatment of the imprint in English and foreign books, 'English books' are defined as including 'all books printed in England', instead of 'all books printed in the United Kingdom', and the date of printing before which the publisher's name must be given in *foreign* books is given as 1600, instead of 1700.

On 10 February 1900 the Rules, now further revised, were submitted to the Trustees, who authorised their publication under a new title.[6] In this edition the rule that the heading of the main entry must be based on information appearing in the book is now relaxed for 'reprints of recognized classics', which may be entered under the author even though his name is not given. The rule for entering all the publications of learned societies under ACADEMIES has an additional sentence: 'Institutions other than Learned Societies are to be entered under the name of the town or country where they are situated, followed by the name of the institution as a sub-heading' – but does not contain any statement about which works are to be entered under these 'institutions'. In the rule for LITURGIES, an indication of a scheme of subheadings, which did not correspond to the more complicated scheme actually adopted when the heading was printed in 1899, has been deleted and not replaced. The imperfect rules for joint authorship and for the treatment of imprints in English and foreign books, mentioned above, have not been amended. The 1900 Rules, which in almost all essential points followed the principles adopted by Panizzi in 1839, were issued in revised editions in 1920, 1927, 1936 and 1951. The alterations introduced in these later editions will be noticed in the appropriate places.

Notes and References

1. See p. 20.
2. *Rules to be observed in the compilation of the Catalogue of Printed Books in the British Museum. Embracing the original ninety-one rules, with additions, corrections and explanations.* HMSO, London, 1887.
3. See p. 19. I have found no example of its use.
4. Standing Committee Minute, 14 December 1895. (B.M. Archives.)
5. The British Museum, Department of Printed Books. *Rules of Cataloguing.* Printed by order of the Trustees, London, 1897.
6. *Rules for compiling the Catalogues in the Department of Printed Books in the British Museum.* Printed by order of the Trustees, London, 1900.

9 Character of the new catalogue

Some important characteristics of the General Catalogue cannot be deduced from the Rules as printed in 1897 and 1900. Foremost among these are peculiarities in the arrangement of entries.

The catalogue was by far the largest for which printed publication had so far been undertaken, and its editors were confronted with vast accumulations of entries under certain headings – those for the principal authors of the literatures of all European languages and for many countries and cities, as well as class-headings created by the cataloguing system itself, such as LITURGIES. Some general principles of arrangement of entries under a heading were provided by Panizzi's rules – separate works in alphabetical sequence, preceded by groups of entries for complete and partial collections; extracts from a work entered below entries for the whole work; cross-references at the beginning, and entries at the end for anonymous works about the person named in the heading.

In so far as this scheme involved departure from alphabetical order, it caused difficulties in searching for particular titles, and in 1841 Panizzi had found it necessary to introduce subheadings in the longer 'articles' (to use the term current before the term 'heading' came to denote the whole collection of entries made under it). Examples have been given in chapter 2.[1] In organising the far larger numbers of titles that had accumulated by the 1880s, individual revisers were allowed much discretion, and, taking Panizzi's principles as a general guide, they devised for each major heading the arrangement they thought most appropriate. In some cases (for example, VIRGILIUS MARO, 1882, ADDISON, 1883) minor or 'miscellaneous' works form a separate group following the main alphabetical series. Sometimes categories of works are treated separately: under Dryden, for instance, the initial section *Works* is followed by three major divisions – *Poetical works*, *Dramatic works* and *Prose works* – each including both collections and single pieces, and with separate subheadings under *Poetical works* and *Prose works* for *Translations* (that is, those by Dryden from other authors).

Martineau's idiosyncratic treatment of HORATIUS FLACCUS (1885) arranges collections, other than complete works, according to the different combinations of works they contain in descending order of number from five works to two; and the single works (or traditionally established groups) are arranged, not alphabetically, but (following the precedent of the 1841 ARISTOTLE) 'in the order usually observed in editions of Horace': *Carmina, Epodi, Carmen Sæculare, Satiræ, Epistolæ, Ars Poetica*. (In the new edition of ARISTOTLE, printed in 1884, the traditional order of the works adopted in 1841 was replaced by alphabetical order.) The *Appendix* to Horace is divided by subheadings into no less than 22 subject-sections.

Under one of the last major author-headings to be printed, SHAKESPEARE (1897), although it is the largest of all, a somewhat simpler formula is adopted and alphabetical arrangement is given more weight. *Works* is followed by *Smaller collections of Plays* and *Collected Poems*; separate works, each under its own subheading, then follow in alphabetical order, whether they are plays or not. In the very extensive *Appendix* there are only nine subdivisions. In all the subdivided author-headings (again following a precedent set in 1841) cross-references (except when placed under the subheading for a particular work) occur at the beginning of the *Appendix* or the appropriate section of it, not at the beginning of the whole heading.

Panizzi's rules give no guidance for the internal arrangement of headings for countries and cities in those cases where the rules for authors do not apply. It was some time before a logical and consistent treatment of these headings was established. The minimum of organisation is represented by one of the earliest of these headings to be printed: AUSTRIA (1881). Here entries made under the name itself, without qualification or subheading, stand first. Cross-references, placed at the beginning, are followed by titles of anonymous works, mingled with some entries for collections of laws and public documents, all in alphabetical order. Then follow entries under the name followed by a qualifying or subdividing element, without distinction. The result is a confusing sequence in which the following headings occur in the order shown:

AUSTRIA. – *Ackerbau-Ministerium.*
AUSTRIA, *Archduchy of* (with subheadings for official bodies, etc.)
AUSTRIA. – *Army.*

AUSTRIA, *Evangelical Church in.*
AUSTRIA. – *Hofkammer.*
AUSTRIA, *House of.*
AUSTRIA. – *Kaiserlich-Koenigliche Statistische Central-Commission.*
AUSTRIA, *Lower.* (with subheadings)
AUSTRIA. – *Ministerium des Innern.*
AUSTRIA. – *Reichstag.*
AUSTRIA, *Ship.*
AUSTRIA. – *Südbahn.*
AUSTRIA, *Upper.* (with subheadings)
AUSTRIA. – *Zollverband.*

These are followed by entries for single acts, treaties and so on, under the names of Emperors, in *alphabetical* order, interrupted by references from other personal names, such as 'AUSTRIA, John of' and 'AUSTRIA, Juan de' (both references to JUAN, *of Austria*), which occur respectively before and after the entries for the official acts of Emperors named 'Joseph'. This type of arrangement follows precedents found in the 1841 volume and was probably common in the manuscript catalogue.

By 1884 the general lines of the new system had emerged. The heading BAVARIA begins with two major subheadings: *Collections of Laws, Public Documents, etc.* and *Publications by Official Departments and Works relating to them*, the latter having the names of the 'departments' (which include *Abgeordneten, Kammer der* and *Army*) as subheadings. These are followed, without a classifying subheading, by a chronological sequence of the names of the ruling Dukes, used as headings for their official acts, and then by an alphabetical sequence of miscellaneous subheadings for societies and institutions, interspersed with groups or classes of persons (for example, *Bishops, Catholics, Lutherans*) named in the titles of anonymous books. Finally, there is an *Appendix* for anonymous works about Bavaria. Separate headings follow for BAVARIA, *Lower*, and BAVARIA, *Upper*. By 1890, when ITALY was printed, the mixture of subheadings with extensions of the heading in the form of epithets or inversions following a comma had been eliminated, so that the form exemplified by DENMARK, *Women of* (1886) is replaced by entries in the form ITALY. – *Merchants trading to Italy*. IRELAND (1891) shows a further development: the separation of *Parliament* as a distinct subheading preceding the general 'official' group, here headed *Departments of State and Courts of Law*. The large heading FRANCE, finally revised in 1899, multiplies the main divisions by adding *Constitutions* (preceding *Laws and other Public Documents*), *Acts of Sovereigns, Legislative Bodies* (preceding *Departments of State and other Official Bodies*), and *Religious Bodies* (preceding *Miscellaneous subheadings*). GERMANY, which, in the sections for collections of laws and acts of sovereigns, covers both the Holy Roman Empire and the nineteenth-century German Empire, fills the period between these two with subheadings for various *Leagues, confederations, etc.* and for the *Zollverein*. ENGLAND, the second largest heading in the catalogue (after PERIODICAL PUBLICATIONS) and the last to be completed (in 1900) is also the most highly organised. The first main division, *Laws and Statutes*, is subdivided into I. *Laws of the Anglo-Saxon and Norman Kings*, II. *General Collections of the Statutes for periods beginning with Magna Carta*, III. *General Collections of Statutes for smaller Periods*, IV. *Collections and Abridgements on Particular Subjects* (with 43 subject-subheadings), V. *Miscellaneous Collections*, VI. *General and Miscellaneous Abridgements*, VII. *Calendars and Indexes* and VIII. *Chronological Series*. This is followed by divisions for *Year Books, Proclamations, Treaties and Negotiations with Foreign Powers, Solemn League and Covenant, 1643* and *Miscellaneous Public Documents*. Then follow *Parliament, Departments of State and Official Bodies, Churches and Religious Bodies, Miscellaneous subheadings* and *Colonies*. The *Appendix*, filling 256 columns, has 16 subject subdivisions, including *Miscellaneous*. Similar but less elaborate systems of organisation were applied to the names of important cities. ROME presented a special difficulty in that the name applies to the Republic and the Empire as well as to the City, and was also used in references to the Catholic Church. In the catalogue, the single word 'Rome' is used for the ancient Roman Republic and Empire, and also, under special subheadings at the end, for the *Roman Republic of 1798* and the *Roman Republic of 1848*. This heading is followed by ROME. – *The City* and ROME, *Church of* (with a long chronological series of ecclesiastical documents issued by Popes, headed by their names – which also appear, for documents of the temporal power, as subheadings under the heading STATES OF THE CHURCH). Entries for anonymous works with titles including the word 'Rome' appear in the appendix to each of these headings, according to the sense in which the word is used.

In all cases the major divisions of headings follow one another in a conventional and logical order, not alphabetically. There are also departures from alphabetical order in the arrangement of individual entries. The titles of individual works by an author and of anonymous works entered under any particular heading are always arranged alphabetically, but complete collections and smaller collections of an author's works and all works issued by and entered under a corporate body are arranged chronologically without regard for their individual titles.

The varying classification of entries under extensive headings, while doubtless useful to readers studying particular subjects, clearly created great difficulties for those seeking particular titles. To assist the latter, the large subdivided headings were furnished with synopses headed *Arrangement* and in many cases also with alphabetical indexes of subheadings. (That this practice had long been in use in the manuscript catalogue is proved by references in official reports from 1859 onward to the transcription and incorporation of 'index slips' as well as titles.) For a few headings title indexes were also supplied, the outstanding example being ENGLAND, where the index of titles extends to 154 columns.

The indexes also served another purpose: they enabled cross-references from other headings to be made in an abridged form. Thus, a cross-reference to the heading ENGLAND from the name of an official or unofficial body is in the simple form '*See* ENGLAND'; in a reference from some other heading to a main entry under such a body, '*See* ENGLAND' is followed immediately by the name of the body as subheading. The reader who is uncertain whether the body is official or unofficial, or is subordinate to a larger body such as Parliament or the Church of England, is expected to find it with the help of the index.

The arrangement of the headings themselves in relation to one another, although alphabetical in principle and more systematic than that found in the 1841 catalogue, presents some complications which, in the absence of an explanation, must have caused difficulties for catalogue users. The main part of each heading, distinguished from subsidiary parts by being printed in bold capitals, may be a single word or a group of two or more words. In a sequence of headings consisting of or beginning with a particular word, the single word is placed first if it is not a name or if it is the name of a person or of a place, but not if it is a surname. The single-word heading is followed by headings in which it is the first of several words. Then follow entries in which the same word is used by itself as a surname. Compound surnames are treated as single words, and therefore not only come after the single surname but are mingled in the catalogue with quite unrelated headings which happen to begin with the same letters.

The effect is most conspicuous under the word 'Saint'. The single word, used as a heading for anonymous works such as 'The Saint turn'd Sinner' (a ballad), is followed by 76 columns of names of places and institutions beginning with 'Saint' and 'Sainte'; then comes the single word 'Saint' as a surname, followed, as single words in strict alphabetical order, by surnames beginning with 'Saint', many of which are identical with place-names in the earlier sequence. In their alphabetical order, surnames beginning with 'Sainte' come between SAINT D– and SAINT F– and are mingled with those headings beginning SAINT E– as well as with such headings as SAINTES (a place-name), and SAINTETÉ. The position allotted to place-names beginning with 'Sainte' (after those beginning with 'Saint' but before the surname) is in fact anomalous: if the rule followed elsewhere in the catalogue had been applied to them, they would all have appeared between the surname-headings SAINT DIDIER and SAINTE-AMARANTHE, where indeed they do appear in later revisions.

The apparent inconsistency in the treatment of compound headings seems to be due to a conflict between the principle, generally followed in the catalogue, of word-by-word alphabetisation and the desire not to separate authors with any particular compound surname from those bearing the same surname written as one word.

Some other departures from strict alphabetical order are worth mentioning. Headings for sovereigns, where the name is followed by a roman numeral, are arranged alphabetically by the epithet which follows (*Emperor, King*, etc.), the numeral being taken into account only when the epithets are the same. Thus CHARLES V, *Emperor of Germany* comes before CHARLES IV, *King of France*, which comes before CHARLES I, *King of Great Britain and Ireland*. Surnames added in square brackets between a personal name and an epithet (for example, FRANCIS [Bernardoni], *Saint*) are similarly disregarded in arrangement, as are certain words introducing an epithet, such as 'calling himself' or 'successively'. A heading beginning with a possessive ending in *'S* is not arranged with the same word extended by an *S* without the apostrophe, but immediately follows the word of which it is the possessive case.

Although known in the Department as the 'General Catalogue' – the name used from Panizzi's time to denote the amalgamation of the octavo catalogue, the King's Library catalogue and the entries for new accessions and distinguishing it from such partial catalogues as the catalogue of English books printed before 1641 and the catalogue of reference books kept in the Reading Room – it was not a complete catalogue of the printed publications in the Museum. It excluded all books in oriental languages (except editions of the Bible and its parts), which were the subject of catalogues for separate languages prepared (except for the earliest ones) in the Department of Oriental Printed

Books and Manuscripts, and also excluded maps and printed music in all its forms, for which separate catalogues were maintained. A catalogue of newspapers published in Great Britain and Ireland between 1801 and 1900 was issued, as part of the supplement to the catalogue, in 1905. The entries were summary, consisting only of the title (omitting the initial article) and a note of the Museum's holding, and were arranged under place of publication in four groups: I. London and suburbs (treated as one place); II. English and Welsh provincial newspapers; III. Scottish newspapers; and IV. Irish newspapers. Parts II–IV have alphabetical indexes of titles. Additions to this catalogue were not treated as accessions to the General Catalogue, but were added to a laid-down copy of the newspaper supplement, treated thenceforward as a separate catalogue and later extended by lists of foreign newspapers arranged first by country and then by place of publication. A large and rapidly growing collection of government publications, both British and foreign, remained for the most part uncatalogued.

One of the outstanding virtues of the General Catalogue lies in its typographical style. The main part of each heading, serving as primary arranging factor, is printed in broad-faced bold capitals, which make it very easy to pick out a particular heading while rapidly turning the pages either of the printed catalogue itself or of the interleaved volumes made from it and completed by mounted accession-entries. Parts of a heading serving different functions are carefully distinguished by changes of type. A surname in bold capitals is followed by transposed forenames within round brackets, in small capitals of the fount used for the body of the entry. Distinguishing epithets added to a name, whether of a person, a place or a corporate body, are printed in italics, preceded by a comma if they do not immediately follow a forename in round brackets. In the columns of the published catalogue, subheadings take the form of cross-headings, degrees of subordination of one subheading to another being indicated by the successive use of bold small capitals, small capitals in the typeface used for titles, and italics. In cross-references from other headings and in entries printed as accessions, subheadings are printed in italics and are separated into two classes by a useful typographical device: classificatory subheadings used to divide large accumulations of entries into convenient groups are enclosed in square brackets; names of subordinate bodies when used as subheadings are preceded by a dash, following a full stop at the end of the superior heading. The full stop and dash are also used between subdivisions of a classificatory subheading – for example, between the title of a work and the language of a translation, or between the word '*Appendix*' and a subject subdivision. Within the entries, the imprint is distinguished from the title by being printed in italics. Each entry, printed compactly within a rectangle about 3½ inches wide, preceded by a marginal dash and ending with the pressmark, with numerals in bold type, aligned with the right-hand margin, is readily distinguishable from its neighbours and may be quickly scanned by the eye.

While some inconsistencies in the form and content of entries were the inevitable consequence of the method by which it was produced, the typography and layout of the catalogue, decided on at the outset, can be said to be admirably functional.

The catalogue was universally welcomed as a major aid to scholarship, but it was not without its critics. An article in the *Edinburgh Review* for January 1906, attributed to W. P. Courtney, may be taken as an example. While strongly approving the subdivision of large authorheadings, the author criticises several survivals from the Panizzi period. He complains that 'the authorities still continue the pedantic practice of writing in one sequence the entries under I and J, and under U and V', and condemns the entry under unexpected names of many famous French authors, mentioning Voltaire, Montesquieu and Fénelon as instances. He suggests that it would be better if the main entries for anonymous works whose authorship had been established were made under the authors, and questions the usefulness of the collective headings PERIODICAL PUBLICATIONS and ACADEMIES. In a footnote he acknowledges that 'since these lines were in type, the entries have been transferred from Arouet to Voltaire' (they had in fact been reprinted under the latter heading in 1905 as part of the supplement); but many years were to pass before any action was taken on the rest of his criticisms, which undoubtedly reflected the feelings of very many users of the catalogue.

Notes and References
1. See pp. 27, 28.

10 Maintenance and improvement

From 1881 to 1900 new 'laid-down' volumes were formed from each printed part as it appeared, initially with one column of printed entries to a page and about 100 leaves or 200 printed columns to a volume. Each volume was bound with numerous guards to which additional blank leaves could be attached, so that the number of entries could be multiplied several times before a volume needed to be split and re-bound.

As before, three copies of the catalogue in this form were maintained: one (bound in blue) for the Reading Room; one (bound in red) for the staff and to provide a replacement in the Reading Room for volumes removed for the addition of new entries; and one (bound in green) as the working copy for the process of incorporation. As each printed column contained about 20 entries and each blank page could carry between 20 and 30 printed accession-slips in place of the average of six transcribed entries in the old catalogue, considerable space was saved and the growth of the catalogue by the creation of new volumes was much slower than before.

The work of inserting new entries was shared between the Incorporator, an experienced cataloguer, and men drawn from the bindery staff. The functions of the latter group were to cut four copies of each accession part into individual entries, to place three copies of each entry so that they projected from the top of the inner margin of the appropriate page of the corresponding volume of the green catalogue, and to deliver the volumes to the Catalogue Room; then, after the Incorporator had marked the volumes to show the correct placing of the entries, to take the volumes back to the Catalogue Shop and there first to attach one copy of each entry, by a thin line of paste at the upper and lower edges, in the green copy (moving existing entries or inserting new leaves when necessary) and then with this copy before them to repeat the operation in the blue and red copies, replacing each blue volume taken from the Reading Room with the corresponding red volume during its absence.

Slips which became worn at the edges through repeated moving were pasted to fresh slips of blank paper. The Catalogue Shop staff also mounted the fourth copies on cards exactly half the size of the slips used for writing manuscript entries and arranged them in pressmark order. The cards were filed two abreast in boxes designed to hold the manuscript title-slips with the old transcribed fourth copies placed at the front of each box. These were kept in an area known as the Title Room, where a complete file of the original slips was also kept. The incorporation process, which was established in its essentials before the end of the nineteenth century, is described below as it became known to me as a member of the staff in the early 1930s.

All volumes of the green copy to which additions were to be made from one issue of the accessions passed through the hands of the Incorporator while the next issue was being prepared – a period, at first, of a fortnight, and later (from 1916) of a month. The correct position for the first additional entry on a page was indicated by writing the figure 1 in pencil in the appropriate space and the figure 2 on the back of the printed slip, the position of the second similarly by the figures 3 and 4, and so on. If a slip had to be inserted where there was no space between two entries, the first figure was written in the margin of the slip that was to precede the new one. When several entries had to be inserted in one place, the slips were numbered consecutively without adding further numbers on the page. If a rearrangement of already mounted slips was required, the Incorporator himself would lift them from the page with a specially designed thin ivory paperknife, jocularly known as the 'excorporator', and mark their new position. Additions to a printed column were as a rule inserted in blank spaces between that column and the following one. Where several leaves had been inserted between two columns, the presence of two alphabetical sequences, columns and accessions, was not obvious and could be overlooked by an uninstructed reader.

The Incorporator's work was highly skilled because the rules of arrangement (which were not recorded and printed until 1940) included many departures from strict alphabetical order not indicated by subheadings or (until a much later period) by devices such as 'filing titles'. The Incorporator had beside him the box containing the manuscript slips from which the accessions part had been printed, and when doubt arose could often get help from pencil notes added to the manuscript by the cataloguer.

Inserting new entries was not the Incorporator's only function. He wrote new index-slips when required for an index of subheadings or titles, and was also concerned with alterations and corrections. Cataloguers often found it necessary to alter existing entries, for which purpose they used the original manuscript slips, making the alterations usually in red ink and initialling them in pencil. The altered slips, known as 'settled queries', were arranged each month in catalogue order in a box placed on the Incorporator's desk. As he worked through the alphabet he compared these with the printed entries and, where possible, made the alterations in manuscript on the slips in the green copy. These alterations were later copied by a clerk into the other two copies. Where the alterations were too extensive for this treatment the title-slips were sent for reprinting, together with additional or 'supplementary' titles for books already entered in the catalogue. The incorporation of additions was thus associated with a continuous process of correcting and improving the whole catalogue. The Incorporator's intimate acquaintance with the catalogue and the close attention to detail required by his function often enabled him to detect and rectify mistakes in cataloguing or printer's errors overlooked by the proof-reader – both of which, if his vigilance flagged, might occasionally be caught by one of the older hands in the Catalogue Shop.

In addition to the cataloguing of accessions and the routine updating and correction of the catalogue, the practice of revising and rearranging material under important headings, started while the catalogue was being printed, was continued under the direction of A. W. K. Miller. Between 1905 and 1912 about 20 headings, including AUSTRIA, BYRON, CERVANTES, KEATS, DISRAELI and BURKE, were reprinted in a form consistent with the latest catalogue practice, and the new columns so produced (including accessions catalogued after 1899) took the place of the old. The heading CERVANTES, substantially increased by numerous editions of 'Don Quixote' received in 1900 as part of H. S. Ashbee's bequest, was published as a special supplement in 1908.

In this way a gradual renewal of the catalogue was begun; and it was not long before the idea of a complete new edition (which Garnett had hoped would quickly follow the printing of the first) was revived. In 1909 Fortescue, who as Keeper since 1899 had been responsible for the publication of the supplement, discussed with the Trustees the desirability of separating *I* from *J* and *U* from *V* and so removing what he described as the cause of 'a great deal of confusion and trouble to all who use the catalogue', and was authorised to rearrange and reprint the headings concerned 'at an early opportunity'. The opportunity did not present itself immediately, but at the beginning of 1911 Fortescue, in his annual report, remarked that this rearrangement would probably be merged in the larger task of reprinting the entire catalogue, which in its published form was 'now practically out of print': the Trustees agreed that the question of a new edition 'should be taken into consideration in the near future'. Another 17 years were to pass, however, before any decisive step was taken.

Fortescue retired in 1912, and his successor, Miller, was asked in March 1913 to report on the General Catalogue. He made a suggestion which was accepted in principle by the Trustees and remained official policy for many years, but was never implemented:

> If the size of the catalogue is to be kept within manageable proportions it appears to be imperative that the quickly growing sections of it, in which provision has to be made for a great influx of accessions, should be separated from the slowly growing portions in which a smaller provision for growth is amply sufficient. Mr Miller therefore recommends that the central feature of the Museum's policy in the matter should be the preparation of a separate Twentieth Century Catalogue as soon as the century is sufficiently advanced for this to be large enough to form an adequate basis to receive additions, i.e. about 1920 or 1925. In this catalogue the old-fashioned treatment of I and J and U and V as in each case a single letter should be abandoned, and advantage could be taken of the experience gained since 1880, when printing was first adopted.

He thought that the older part of the catalogue, containing entries for books published in earlier centuries, while it could be rearranged with a great economy of space, was unsatisfactory because of the treatment of *I* and *J* and *U* and *V* and because of its out-of-date cross-referencing system and should also be reprinted in an improved form if possible. He made the further suggestion that if entries for current accessions were made available on cards there might be a demand for them from other libraries. In March 1914 the Trustees, giving their general approval, directed that steps should be taken to 'ascertain what amount of support would be forthcoming from other libraries, either for the Catalogue itself or for card-descriptions of accessions'. These enquiries were cut short by the outbreak of the First World War, and the scheme was suspended, but not forgotten.

During the war, with staff reduced by absence on military service, the frequency of the accession parts was changed from fortnightly to monthly, and a strict timetable was established: copy to the printer between the 10th and the 17th of the month; proofs to be received between the 13th and the 22nd; last proofs to be returned by the 24th and finished copies to be delivered on the 27th. (This arrangement continued unaltered, except for a temporary change to issue every two months during the Second World War, as long as lists of accessions continued to be published – that is, until 1955.)

As soon as the war was over, the Keeper (now G. F. Barwick, appointed in 1914) turned his attention again to the future of the catalogue. In a general report on the state of the Department, dated 4 April 1919, he referred to Miller's proposals of six years earlier. He thought that the revised reprint of the older part of the catalogue would have to be postponed for many years because of 'the effect of the war on the national finances', but that, 'to relieve the congestion of the present catalogue', a catalogue of twentieth-century books would soon be needed. The production of this separate catalogue of new and recent books would offer, he suggested, an opportunity to join with other important libraries in a move towards a uniform cataloguing system and so towards some form of central or co-operative cataloguing. He proposed, therefore, that a revision of the 1900 Rules should be undertaken in consultation with the University Libraries of Oxford and Cambridge. An agreement with them might be a step towards a uniform set of rules for the English-speaking world, and the possibility that the British Museum might become a cataloguing centre for the British Empire as the Library of Congress already was for the United States.

A revision of the 1900 Rules, embodying only minor changes, was quickly produced by a committee presided over by R. F. Sharp, and was sent in proof to the copyright libraries and the Library Association. Barwick's successor, A. W. Pollard, in submitting the revision to the Trustees, informed them that 'there is just now an urgent demand for a new edition ... in connection with a proposed revision of the Anglo-American Rules'. Three months later, however, he had to report that neither Oxford nor Cambridge was prepared to consider even 'minor changes such as might be adjusted to the existing catalogues', and that co-operation would have to be postponed 'until a start can be made with a catalogue of Twentieth Century Books', which (in a passage deleted from the draft of his earlier report) he had noted was 'likely to be held up for some years by considerations of finance'. (In fact, the revision of the Anglo-American Rules was not started until 1936 and was completed in 1967.)

The failure of the offer of co-operation removed both the Twentieth Century Catalogue and the radical revision of the Rules from the agenda. The revised Rules, published in June 1920, therefore embody few innovations. They record the introduction of two new class-headings: CONGRESSES, under which international conferences had been entered since about 1906, and HYMNALS, which in 1903, when the relevant part of the supplement was printed, had already superseded the heading PSALMS AND HYMNS prescribed in the 1900 Rules. A new rule for cataloguing books published as parts of series was inserted, rather awkwardly, as an addition to the rule for imprints (30). Instead of being entered by means of a cross-reference to the entry for the series, such books would now have a full main-entry, with the series title added in italics and in square brackets – an extension of the device adopted in 1892 to avoid cross-references leading to another cross-reference.[1] There were additional rules on abbreviations and transliteration, and a number of rules were amended without introducing any new principle. It was made clear, for instance, that an official organ of a society was to be entered under the society, not under PERIODICAL PUBLICATIONS. The definition of 'English books' was altered to include 'all books printed in the British Isles in whatever language', and the date before which the publisher's name was to be given for foreign books was corrected to 1700. The absence of a rule for entering a work consisting of separate contributions by two authors was remedied: the heading was to be the name of the first author alone. The entry of publications under a society or institution that was not an academy was provided for in the following addition to the rule on ACADEMIES (17b): 'Works similarly published by Institutions other than Learned Societies are entered under the name of the institution when that is of sufficient importance, and when the institution is not merely a publishing body' – a formulation which gives preference to the institution, if 'important', rather than to the author, but fails to make clear that some kinds of publications, in which no author is named, must have their main entry under an institution, however unimportant. The framework of Panizzi's rules remained untouched, and there is no trace of influence from the Anglo-American Rules,[2] to which Pollard had referred and which, despite Fortescue's membership of the British Committee, differed more widely from the Museum rules than had those adopted by the Library Association in 1881. No further steps towards the reprinting either of the old catalogue or of the twentieth-century accessions were taken during Pollard's time as Keeper, and the question did not again become a central interest of the Department until two or three years after the appointment in 1924 of his successor, R. Farquharson Sharp. Meanwhile, a further revised edition of the cataloguing rules had been produced.

Ever since the production of Panizzi's 91 Rules there had been discussions among cataloguers about details of practice and the interpretation of the Rules, leading often to decisions submitted to the

Keeper for approval but only occasionally to the formal amendment of a rule. Martineau's draft of 1887 attempted to codify oral tradition as well as written rules, and is a fairly complete account of the accepted practice of his time, but for the period from 1873 to 1920 no continuous contemporary record of approved decisions has survived. From 1920 onward, however, a number of such records are available. The first of them, known in its day as the 'Black Book', is a stout exercise-book with a black cover, bearing the title, in manuscript, 'Notes respecting the General Catalogue, 1920– '.[3] Most of the book is blank, but the first 13 pages contain notes, pages 1 to 10 in Sharp's handwriting and 11 to 13 in Marsden's. Only a few of these are dated – the earliest date being 26 February 1920 and the latest 21 January 1925. The majority deal with minor points of practice not mentioned in the Rules – punctuation and use of accents, the method of indicating that a work is in progress, etc. – but several are amendments to rules. Panizzi's rule that 'a substantive, adjectively used [is] to be taken in conjunction with its following substantive as forming one word', unaccountably omitted from the rule on anonymous books in 1897, 1900 and 1920 (although the practice described continued), is now restored but in a new form. After the instruction to include in the heading 'an adjective which gives the noun a special significance' the following words are inserted: 'The same applies to any combination of substantives forming an inseparable expression.' There is an amendment to the rule on translations, excluding the use of the translator's name as the main heading for a translation in which the author of the original is not named; and the use of an insertion at the beginning of a title as an aid to arrangement is mentioned for the first time in a British Museum rule in the instruction that 'in the case of a translation of which no edition of the original is in the Library, the description should be headed by the original title (when ascertainable) in square brackets'. There are two amendments to rule 20 on pseudonyms: one providing that 'in the case of an author who has written exclusively or almost exclusively under one pseudonym ... all editions of works originally published under the pseudonym are entered under it, even though the author's real name occur in the book'; and the other adding to the expressions which may be treated as pseudonyms 'a combination (such as "Red Heather") which is not descriptive of the author but is obviously intended as a pseudonym'. Two changes recorded are of some importance, although not embodied in the amendments to rules. One of these implies a recognition of the inconveniences arising from the use as headings of translations into English of certain expressions occurring in the titles of anonymous works. The rule that in cross-references from the titles of series to the names of their editors the heading must follow the rule for anonymous books meant that such references must in many cases be made under an English translation of a foreign expression, from which a cross-reference also had to be made. The change recorded in the Black Book is that the reference for a *series* should be direct from an expression in its title to the name of its editor, so avoiding a reference leading the reader only to another reference. A further difficulty arose from the fact that references from the titles of *periodicals* had always been from the first word and that a title could often equally well be that of a series or of a periodical. A further decision is therefore recorded, allowing an additional cross-reference to be made from the first word of the title of a series. Thus, a series entitled 'Beiträge zur Englischen Philologie' has two cross-references to its editor: one under ENGLISCHE PHILOLOGIE and one under BEITRAEGE, but none under ENGLISH PHILOLOGY, the heading required by the rule for anonymous books. The other change is an exception to the rule that English and Dutch compound surnames are to be entered under the last part: Dutch married women who use a compound surname in which their husband's surname precedes their own are to be entered under the whole compound name.[4]

With the exception of the rule for translations of anonymous works, which in its published form continued to allow for entry under the translator when neither the author nor the title of the original can be ascertained, the amendments in the Black Book were incorporated in a new edition of the Rules published in February 1927. There were no other significant alterations to the 1920 Rules. The publication was a response to outside demand, not to any internal pressure for substantial revision.

Notes and References

1. See p. 76.
2. The American Library Association and the Library Association. *Cataloguing rules: author and title entries.* Library Association, London, 1908.
3. In B.L. Archives (Printed Books).
4. Incorporated in rule 11 in the 1936 edition.

11 'Gk II'

The revision and reprinting of the Rules in 1927 were not accompanied by any renewal of the discussions on a Twentieth Century Catalogue or on the co-ordination of cataloguing rules with other important libraries. The suggestion that the British Museum should provide a central cataloguing service by printing its accession entries on cards was indeed revived in 1927 by the Committee on Public Libraries set up by the Board of Education,[1] in association with a proposal that the Central Library for Students, reconstituted as a national lending library, should become a department of the Museum. The Trustees, however, declined to accept responsibility for the Central Library[2] and took no action on the cataloguing proposal, which would have involved an attempt to reconcile the Museum's cataloguing rules with those followed by the majority of public libraries.

Meanwhile, the question of reprinting the whole catalogue had once more become a major concern of the Department of Printed Books. This time the impetus came not from the need to restrict the growth of the Reading Room catalogue, which still occupied less space than the transcribed catalogue of 1880, but from the growing demand, chiefly from libraries in America, for copies of the published catalogue, which had been out of print since 1918. This demand led the President of the Bibliographical Society of America, Dr H. H. B. Meyer, to discuss with the Director[3] of the Museum in the autumn of 1927 the possibility of financial aid from America to encourage the production of a new edition. By August 1928 Sharp was ready to put forward a definite proposal.

In the proposed new edition the catalogue would be 'revised throughout to bring its method uniformly into line with the present British Museum Cataloguing Rules'. There would be no change in the general arrangement except the long-overdue separation of *I* from *J* and *U* from *V*. Accessions since the first printing of the catalogue would increase its size by about half, and it would fill 160 to 165 volumes of 500 pages. Assuming that they could be issued at the rate of two a month, the publication would be completed in seven or eight years. The approximate cost of printing and binding was estimated at £175,150; the sale price would depend on the number of subscribers.

The proposal was repeated, with additional detail, in a report by Sharp to the Trustees dated 22 September 1928. This stated that incorporation of accessions into the Reading Room catalogue would continue as usual, so implying that each new volume would contain accessions to the time of its printing. The financing of the project was discussed on the assumption that the cost of production was to be covered by sales. With the encouragement of 'grants in aid', the possibility of which had been indicated by Dr Meyer, a large number of subscriptions could probably be obtained from America. If enough subscriptions were promised the printer would be willing to bear the initial cost and receive payment after the subscriptions for each batch of volumes had been collected. In the Keeper's opinion, the preparation of copy could be done by the existing staff of his department, subject to the addition of two Attendants to fetch the large number of pre-1880 books that would need to be seen so that pagination and publishers' names could be inserted. His draft of the report suggested that four senior members of the staff would be involved – a figure later altered to six. The plan involved the suspension of a projected catalogue of English books published between 1640 and 1700, for which preparation had been made but which, in the event, was never produced.

The Trustees accepted the proposal in principle, fixed the required number of subscribers at 400, and authorised the Director to communicate the details of the project to 'the American scholars interested in the subject'.

In May 1929 the promised American support materialised in the form of a grant from the Rockefeller Foundation of £16,000 to reimburse the Museum for a 20 per cent discount to American and Canadian libraries and £1,920 to pay for 'additional service' – that is, the employment of two Attendants at £120 a year each for eight years.[4] With this encouragement the Trustees issued a preliminary prospectus inviting subscriptions and embodying the Keeper's proposals unaltered except for a cautious reduction of the number of volumes offered each year from 24 to 15. The subscription price, on the basis of 400 subscribers, was fixed at £3 a volume, or £400 in advance for the whole catalogue. The price to non-subscribers would be £4 a volume. Copies of the prospectus, with specimen pages, were sent to between 500 and 600 libraries in the

United Kingdom, the British Colonies and Dominions, and the United States of America.[5] By the end of 1929 enough subscription offers had been received to justify proceeding, and a further prospectus was issued, repeating the subscription terms unchanged except for a statement still further modifying the expected rate of production: 'It is not proposed to issue more than twelve volumes annually.' A further change in the catalogue itself was also announced: the heading ACADEMIES would be abolished and the entries distributed under the names of places.[6]

It was natural that the librarians of public libraries, remembering the free distribution of copies of the earlier catalogue, should hope for similar special treatment on this occasion. In October 1929, before the final prospectus had been issued, the Director reported that he had been asked by the heads of eight of the largest municipal libraries to support a request to the Treasury for the supply of copies of the new catalogue either free or at a reduced price to 'selected public libraries'. The Trustees readily lent their support, but the initial reaction was unfavourable. In reply to questions in the House of Commons, Mr Pethick-Lawrence, then Financial Secretary to the Treasury, rejected the request on the grounds that the publication of the catalogue could not be undertaken unless it were self-supporting and that it depended on a large measure of support from public libraries. However, after a further application from the public libraries, asking not only for free copies for 20 named libraries but also for the application to the catalogue of the 50 per cent discount allowed to public and university libraries on government publications in general, the Financial Secretary announced on 7 May 1930 that the Government had now decided to make a grant of 25 per cent towards the cost of the catalogue to 'public libraries in this country supported by the rates and libraries of Universities or University Colleges receiving support from public funds'.

By the end of 1931 the hoped-for 200 subscriptions from America had been secured, and the prospect of sales was good enough to justify increasing the number of copies printed from 500 to 600, beginning with volume 3, printed in March 1932. One hundred additional copies of volumes 1 and 2 were printed by photolithography to make up the number of complete sets.

In April a new series of the accessions was begun, printed in 400 copies instead of only 100 and offered to the new catalogue's subscribers at the reduced price of £1.10s per annum, to enable them to keep their copies of the catalogue up to date. At the same time they were provided with a supplement to volumes 1–3, containing the accession entries printed between the completion of these volumes and the commence-

193 AKE	AKE 194
AKEHURST (G.) Imposture instanced in the life of Mahomet. [London, 1859.] 12°. 4504. a.	AKENSIDE (MARK) Poetical works. To which is prefixed the life of the author. See ANDERSON (Robert) M.D. A complete edition of the poets of Great Britain. Vol. 9. 1793, etc. 8°. 2046. f.
— [Another edition.] London, 1859. 12°. 4504. a.	— Poetical works and life. See BELL (John) Bookseller. Bell's edition. The poets of Great Britain, etc. Vol. 85, 86. 1782, etc. 12°. 1066. c. 1.
— The Prayer Book, and its history. A lecture. London, 1859 [1858]. 12°. 3477. b.	— Poems. See BRITISH POETS. The British Poets. Vol. XL. 1773. 8°. 11604. a.
A KEIL (ANDREAS) See KEIL (A. von) called CUNÆUS.	
A KEMPIS, THOMAS. See HAEMMERLEIN.	— The Poems of M. A. The life of M. A. by Dr. Johnson. 2 vol. See BRITISH POETS. The British Poets, etc. Vol. 52, 53. 1822. 12°. 11603. aa.
AKEN. See AIX-LA-CHAPELLE.	
AKEN (AD. FR.) Griechische Schulgrammatik. Berlin, 1858. 8°. 12923. bb.	— Poetical Works. See BRITISH POETS. Cabinet Edition of the British Poets. Vol. I. 1851. 8°. 11603. d.
— Die Grundzüge der Lehre von Tempus und Modus in Griechischen historisch und vergleichend aufgestellt. Rostock, 1861. 8°. 12924. f.	— Life, etc. See BUCKE (C.) On the life, writings and genius of Akenside.
— Die Hauptdata der griechischen Tempus- und Moduslehre historisch und vergleichend. Berlin, 1865. 8°. 12924. bb. 34. (5.)	— Life and poems. See CHALMERS (A.) F.S.A. The works of the English poets, etc. Vol. 14. 1810. 8°. 2047. g.
AKEN (CORNELIUS AB) Resp. See BIBLE.—Old Testament. —Ezra. Disputatio octava, continens Versionem Hebraicam capitis quinti Chaldaici Esdræ, etc. 1683, etc. 4°. 1014. b. 10. (19, 18, 17.)	— See CURIO, pseud. An epistle to Curio. [By M. A.] 1744. 4°. 644. k. 16. (1.)
	— See HASTINGS (F.) Earl of Huntingdon. (Ode to F. H., etc. [by M. A.]) [1748?] 4°. 11630. c. 9. (13.)
— Resp. Introductionis historicæ ad Cartesii philosophiam pars quinta. Præs. G. de Vries. Trajecti ad Rhenum, 1684. 4°. 536. c. 18. (12.)	— Poems. See JOHNSON (S.) LL.D. The Works of the English Poets, etc. Vol. 55. 1779, etc. 8°. 11601. d. 26.
AKEN (F. VAN) Aan de muitzugt na het oproer in Leyden den 9 Junij 1784. [In verse.] Leyden, [1784.] 8°. 934. g. 16. (15.)	— Life and poetical Works. See JOHNSON (S.) LL.D. The Works of the English Poets, etc. Vols. 6, 63 & 64. 1790, etc. 8°. 237. d. 6; 238. d. 24, 25.
AKEN (FRANZ JOACHIM VON) The dreadful ... effects of fire in many cases prevented, etc. [London, 1794.] 8°. B. 676. (3.)	— See MONRO (A.) M.D., Second of the Name. Notes [by M. A.] on the postscript to a pamphlet, intitled, Observations anatomical ... by A. Monro. 1758. 8°. 781. b. 20.
— Korrt Afhandling om det bästa Eldsläckniųgs sätt med därtil lämpad Brandredskap och nödig Brand-Ordning. Stockholm, 1797. 8°. 8715. aa.	— The Poetical Works of M. A. 2 vol. See PARK (T.) F.S.A. The Works of the British Poets, etc. Vol. 25. 1808, etc. 16°. 1066. c. 37.
AKEN (HEIN VAN) See HEIN, van Aken.	
AKEN (J. M. VAN) Bezint eer gij begint, blijspel in een bedrijf, etc. [In verse.] Helder, 1867. 8°. 11754. f.	— Poems omitted in the works of A. See PARK (T.) F.S.A. The Works of the British Poets, etc. (Supplement, etc. Vol. 6.) 1808, etc. 16°. 1066. d. 16.
— Recht door Zee. Dramatische Schets in één bedrijf [and in prose], etc. Enkhuizen, 1871. 8°. 11754. bb.	— See PLEASURES. The Pleasures of Imagination, etc. [By M. A.] 1744. 4°. 11630. d. 6. (6.)
— Zoo gaat het! Blijspel in twee bedrijven, etc. [In verse.] Helder, 1867. 8°. 11754. f.	— Odes on several subjects. See POEMS. Select Poems, etc. 1783. 12°. 11601. a.
AKEN (P. A. VAN) See BOURNE (J.) Civil Engineer. Leeren Handboek der Stoomwerktuigkunde, ... vermeerderd ... door P. A. van A., etc. 1868. 12°. 8765. bb.	— The Pleasures of Imagination.—Ode ... to Cheerfulness.—Ode to the Muse [and other poems]. See PRATT (S. J.) The Cabinet of Poetry, etc. Vol. 4. 1808. 12°. 11604. f.
AKENSIDE (MARK) The Poetical Works of M. A. See ALDINE EDITION OF THE BRITISH POETS. The Aldine Edition of the British Poets. 1830, etc. 8°. 1066. c. 15.	— The poetical works of M. A., and J. Dyer. Edited, [with memoirs] by R. A. Willmott ... Illustrated by B. Foster. See ROUTLEDGE (G.) Routledge's British Poets. 1853, etc. 8°. 11603. c.
— The Poetical Works of M. A. (The Life of A., by ... A. Dyce.) See ALDINE EDITION OF THE BRITISH POETS. The Aldine Edition of the British Poets. 1857, etc. 8°. 11604. bbb.	— Life and select poems. See SANFORD (E.) The works of the British Poets. Vol. 28. 1819, etc. 12°. 11602. a. 14.
— The Poetical Works of M. A. (The life of A., by A. Dyce.) See ALDINE EDITION OF THE BRITISH POETS. The Aldine Edition of the British Poets. 1866, etc. 8°. 11604. aaa.	— Commentarius de Dysenteria. See SCHLEGEL (J. C. T.) Thesaurus Pathologico-Therapeuticus, etc. Vol. I. 1789, etc. 8°. 773. e. 22.

A page from GK I.

AKEHURST (S. H.) *See* PERIODICAL PUBLICATIONS.—London. The Lantern. Edited by S. H. Akehurst. 1883, *etc.* 8°. P.P. 502. ac.

AKELEY, *East.—Rural Deanery.* The East Akeley Deanery Magazine. vol. 31. no. 1, *etc.* Jan. 1927, *etc. Loughborough*, 1927– . 4°. P.P. 343. fc.

AKELEY (CARL ETHAN) *See* AKELEY (Mary L. J.) Carl Akeley's Africa, *etc.* [With a portrait.] 1929. 8°. 10094. dd. 20.

—— In Brightest Africa . . . Illustrated, *etc.* pp. xvii. 267. *William Heinemann: London; printed in U.S.A.,* 1924. 8°. 07911. g. 41.

AKELEY (DELIA J.) Jungle Portraits . . . With original photographs. pp. x. 251. *Macmillan Co.: New York,* 1930. 8°. 10094. bb. 20.

AKELEY (MARY LEE JOBE) Carl Akeley's Africa. The account of the Akeley-Eastman-Pomeroy African Hall Expedition . . . With illustrations [including a portrait] and maps. pp. xix. 321. *Dodd, Mead & Co.: New York,* 1929. 8°. 10094. dd. 20.

AKEN. *See* AIX-LA-CHAPELLE.

AKEN (AD. FR.) Griechische Schulgrammatik. pp. xx. 345. *Berlin,* 1868. 8°. 12923. bb. 5.

—— Die Grundzüge der Lehre von Tempus und Modus in Griechischen historisch und vergleichend aufgestellt. pp. xxiv. 260. *Rostock,* 1861. 8°. 12924. f. 3.

—— Die Hauptdata der griechischen Tempus- und Moduslehre historisch und vergleichend, *etc.* pp. xvi. 116. *Berlin,* 1865. 8°. 12924. bb. 34. (5.)

AKEN (CORNELIUS AB) *See* BIBLE.—*Ezra.—Selections.* [Polyglott.] Disputatio octava, continens Versionem Hebraicam capitis quinti Chaldaici Esdræ quam . . . proponit C. ab Aken. 1683, *etc.* 4°. 1014. b. 73.

—— Introductionis historicæ ad Cartesii philosophiam, pars quinta ; quam . . . sub præsidio M. Gerardi de Vries . . . publicè ventilandam proponit C. ab Aken. *F. Halma : Trajecti ad Rhenum,* 1684. 4°. 536. f. 28. (2.)

AKEN (F. VAN) Aan de muitzugt na het oproer in Leyden den 9 Junii 1784, *etc.* [In verse.] pp. 4. *Leyden,* [1784.] 8°. 934. g. 16. (15.)

AKEN (FRANZ JOACHIM VON) The Dreadful and Calamitous Effects of Fire in many cases prevented, in all . . . checked and . . . subdued, with much less expense than by any other method known. pp. 8. 7. *W. Phillips: [London,* 1794.] 8°. B. 676. (3.)

—— Korrt Afhandling om det bästa Eldsläcknings sätt med därtil lämpad Brandredskap och nödig Brand-Ordning. pp. 128. pl. 3. *Stockholm,* 1797. 8°. 8715. aa. 23.

AKEN (HEIN VAN) *See* HEIN, *van Aken.*

AKEN (J. M. VAN) Bezint eer gij begint, blijspel in een bedrijf, *etc.* [In verse.] pp. 48. *Helder,* 1867. 8°. 11754. f. 36.

—— Recht door Zee. Dramatische schets in één bedrijf, *etc.* pp. 76. *Enkhuizen,* 1871. 8°. 11754. bb. 46. (7.)

—— Zoo gaat het ! Blijspel in twee bedrijven, *etc.* [In verse.] pp. 48. *Helder,* 1867. 8°. 11754. f. 37.

AKEN (P. A. VAN) *See* BOURNE (John) *Civil Engineer.* Leer- en Handboek der Stoomwerktuigkunde . . . vermeerderd . . . door P. A. van Aken, *etc.* 1868. 12°. 8765. bb. 12.

AKEN (ROLANDUS AB) *Resp.* De creatione pars secunda, *etc* . 1682. *See* VRIES (G. de) *Professor of Theology at Utrecht.* Meditationes philosophicæ de Deo, *etc.* 1682, *etc.* 4°. 480. a. 5.

AKENHEAD (DAVID) Viticultural Research. Memorandum. pp. 70. *London,* 1928. 4°. [*Empire Marketing Board.* Publications. no. 11.] W.P. 2575/11.

AKENS (J.) Ueber die Adjectiva auf αιος, ειος, ηιος, οιος, ωιος. pp. 18. *Emmerich & Cleve,* [1874 ?] 4°. 624. i. 26. (4.)
The titlepage is mutilated.

AKENSIDE (MARK) *See also* BRITANNICUS, *pseud.* [i.e. M. Akenside.]

—— *See* BUCKE (Charles) On the Life, Writings and Genius of Akenside, *etc.* 1832. 8°. 1162. i. 31.

—— *See* WILLIAMS (Iolo A.) Seven XVIIIth Century Bibliographies . . . Mark Akenside, *etc.* 1924. 8°. 011904. aa. 37.

—— The Poems of Mark Akenside. [Edited by the Rt. Hon. Jeremiah Dyson.] pp. xii. 402. *J. Dodsley & M. Cooper : London,* 1772. 8°. 671. b. 9.

—— [Another copy.] L.P. 83. l. 25.

—— [Another edition.] pp. vii. 208. *J. Balfour & W. Creech : Edinburgh,* 1773. 8°. [*British Poets.* vol. 40.] 11604. a. 40.

—— [Another edition.] [With a portrait.] pp. 368. *C. Bathurst, etc. : London,* 1779. 8°. [*JOHNSON* (Samuel) LL.D. The Works of the English Poets, *etc.* vol. 55.] 11601. cc. 15.

—— [Another edition.] [With a portrait.] 2 vol. *Apollo Press : Edinburg,* 1781. 12°. [*Bell's Edition. The Poets of Great Britain, etc.* vol. 85, 86.] 1066. c. 1.

—— [Another edition.] [With the life by Johnson.] 1790. *See* JOHNSON (Samuel) LL.D. The Works of the English Poets, *etc.* vol. 6, 63, 64. 1790, *etc.* 8°. 237. d. 6, 238. d. 24. & 25.

—— [Another edition.] 1794. *See* ANDERSON (Robert) *M.D.* A Complete Edition of the Poets of Great Britain. vol. 9. 1793, *etc.* 8°. 11607. f. 9.

—— [Another edition.] With the life of the author. [With a portrait, and other engraved plates.] pp. 263. *C. Cooke : London,* 1795. 12°. 11632. aa. 1.
With an additional titlepage, engraved.

—— [Another edition.] pp. 263. *C. Cooke: London,* 1800. 12°. 991. c. 1.
The " Life " is different from that in the preceding edition.

—— [Another edition.] 2 vol. *Charles Whittingham: London,* 1805. 16°. [*PARK* (Thomas) *F.S.A.* The Works of the British Poets. vol. 25.] 1066. c. 37.

—— Additions to the Poems. 1809. *See* PARK (Thomas) *F.S.A.* The Works of the British Poets . . . Supplement, *etc.* vol. 6. 1808, *etc.* 16°. 1066. d. 16.

—— [Another edition.] The Poems of Mark Akinside . . . With his life, a fac-simile of his hand-writing, and an essay on the first poem, by Mrs. Barbauld. 2 vol. *John Garnett : New-Brunswick,* 1808. 12°. 11631. b. 4, 5.

—— [Another edition.] [With the life by Johnson.] *See* CHALMERS (Alexander) *F.S.A.* The Works of the English Poets, *etc.* vol. 14. 1810. 8°. 2041. f.

—— [Another edition.] The Poems of Mark Akenside (The Life of Mark Akenside by Dr. Johnson.—The Poems of John Dyer.) 2 vol. *C. Whittingham : Chiswick,* 1822. 12°. [*British Poets.* vol. 52, 53.] 11603. aa.

—— [Another edition.] With a biographical sketch of the author (by Dr. Johnson). pp. xv. 223. *Jones & Co. : London,* 1823. 32°. 11604. a. 52.
With an additional titlepage, engraved.

A page from GK II.

ment of the new series. With the idea that the accession entries might be used in a future, updated edition of the catalogue, or in a supplement to it, produced by photolithography, all entries in the new series were printed with their heading on a separate line and the rest of the entry indented and preceded by a dash, not, as previously, run on with the heading, so that if the headings were removed the entries would conform exactly in style to those (other than the first under each heading) in the catalogue itself.

In November 1932 the subscription list for the catalogue was closed, and a discount of 10 per cent to booksellers was fixed for copies sold to non-subscribers at £4 a volume. The decision to issue important headings as excerpts was made in May 1933.

As in the case of the earlier edition, copies of each volume as it appeared, printed on one side of the paper, were cut up and mounted to form new volumes of the laid-down catalogue.

The discussions that must have taken place among senior members of the Department before Sharp's proposal was drafted are unfortunately unrecorded. It is difficult today to understand how the forecast of two volumes a month can have been arrived at, since it represents production at nearly five times the rate achieved by Garnett between 1881 and 1900, when revision of earlier cataloguing was excluded except where it was needed to clarify arrangement or to remove obvious errors. It was now proposed that the whole catalogue should be brought into line with the current rules. It was reasonable to assume that entries written since 1900, when the rules differed only slightly from those still in force, would require little alteration; but the vast majority of the older entries, numbering nearly two million and constituting two-thirds of the catalogue, would have to be substantially revised. In the main entries for all books catalogued before 1880, pagination and, for English books, publishers' names had to be supplied. The practice of cataloguing works forming parts of series by means of cross-references had continued until 1920: all these cross-references had to be converted into main entries. Both of these alterations required reference to the book itself in every case. Many thousands of other cross-references had to be put into up-to-date form, in many cases with additional information taken from the books. There is no evidence of any serious attempt to assess the amount of work involved.

Another surprising feature of the plan in all its stages of development is that it took no account of the effect, of which Garnett had been so acutely aware, of adding accessions to the catalogue during printing. Sharp's estimate of the number of volumes was based directly on the size of the earlier catalogue and the quantity of accessions printed down to the date of his report in 1928. Every year's accessions added the equivalent of approximately two volumes to the catalogue. Of the accession entries printed during its publication, about half would be incorporated in the volumes as they appeared; the other half, printed too late for inclusion in the appropriate volume, would appear only in the monthly lists unless and until published later in a supplement. Even at the rapid rate of 24 volumes a year, the material to be included would have grown by at least seven volumes while printing was in progress. If the point was considered, it may have been regarded as negligible as it would extend the period of publication by only a fraction of a year. But as the plan matured the expected rate of production gradually fell, and by the end of 1929 had been halved to 12 volumes a year. At this rate the catalogue would have been completed in 15 years and would have consisted not of 165 but of 180 volumes – or 195 volumes if a supplement similar to that of 1900–05 were to be added. However, the proposed advance subscription of £400 remained unchanged.

The results of over-hasty calculation and failure to benefit by earlier experience soon made themselves felt. At the end of 1929 Sharp retired and was succeeded by W. A. Marsden, the senior Deputy Keeper,[7] of whom Sharp, in recommending his appointment, had written: 'His familiarity with the Catalogue and his enthusiasm for its proper maintenance and improvement will be of great service when the work of the projected new edition of the General Catalogue is begun'. In his first report on the work of the Department, written within a month of his appointment, after stating that work on the new catalogue had begun and that the first batch of copy had already been sent to the printer he added, without committing himself to a more precise forecast, that 'Mr Marsden feels bound to express his opinion that the annual output will be less than the prospectus envisaged, certainly at the beginning of the undertaking, and probably throughout its course.' He had allocated the work of preparing copy to seven Assistant Keepers, of whom the two senior, L. C. Wharton and A. F. Johnson, would give it half their time. Wharton, who was to revise all the Slavonic entries, was also responsible, with one junior Assistant Keeper, for the acquisition and cataloguing of accessions in Slavonic languages, and Johnson also acted as 'Placer'. The other five were E. D. O. Lynam, A. G. Macfarlane, L. A. Sheppard, C. B. Oldman and F. C. Francis. All of them would have some other duties, but on average the catalogue work would occupy about three-quarters of their time. The senior Deputy Keeper, Henry Thomas, hoped to read all the final proofs before they were passed for press.

A year later, 30,000 entries had been revised, the first volume had been completed and was ready for publication, and half of the second was in proof. After making allowance for the largely experimental character of the first six months' work and for the relatively heavy demands for revision in the earliest volumes of the old edition, Marsden had to admit that, creditable as it was to the staff employed, in comparison with the forecast this was slow progress. He had now come to the conclusion that, with only six editors, the most that could be produced in a year was four volumes. Assuming that the Trustees would 'decline to contemplate the abandonment of a project which will confer so great a benefit upon the libraries of the world', and that a drastic lowering of the standard of revision would be unacceptable to subscribers, he saw only two alternatives: to accept the prospect that the catalogue would not be completed for at least 50 years, or to apply to the Treasury, which had not so far been asked to contribute, for additional staff. He pointed out that the staff of Assistant Keeper grade and above in the Department was 26, whereas in 1880, when the first printing of the catalogue was begun, there had been 40 in the corresponding grades, although the intake of books had then been far lower. A table of staff functions compiled early in 1931 shows that, in a staff of 22 Assistant Keepers, seven were fully occupied on duties unconnected with the General Catalogue – public service, acquisitions, the Map Room and Music Room – and there was one unfilled vacancy. Seven were engaged in cataloguing accessions, incorporating new entries in the catalogue and editing the Subject Index. Of the remaining seven available for work on the new catalogue, all to some extent combined catalogue work with other duties. The Trustees decided to ask for six more Assistant Keepers. The Treasury agreed to *three* additional posts, for the duration of the work on the catalogue, and these were immediately filled by appointing three of the applicants who had been considered for another vacancy earlier in the year.

Marsden's annual report on the year 1931 shows that, while the employment of the three new Assistant Keepers on current cataloguing as part of their training had made substantial inroads into the arrears built up by the increased flow of accessions since the war, it had so far had no effect on the new catalogue. Only two volumes had appeared in 1931 and the third would not be completed until March 1932. The transfer of more men to the work during the year would increase production, but the rate of four volumes a year, mentioned in the previous year's report, was still not in sight.

The catalogue's slow progress was already causing concern outside the Museum. In July 1931 the Standing Commission on Museums and Galleries, a new body which was preparing its first report, asked the Museum for an indication of the staff that would be needed to complete the work in 10 or 15 years. The Director replied that if the staff concerned (recently raised from six to nine) could be increased by another three at the end of the year, the work would take 25 years. The addition of three more Assistant Keepers every six months for two further years, bringing the staff to 24, would reduce the time to something between 10 and 15 years.[8] This enquiry was to bear fruit later, but not until after the publication of the Commission's report in 1933. Another enquiry, from W. W. Bishop, Librarian of the University of Michigan, asked whether the delay was due to lack of funds and suggested a fresh approach to the Rockefeller Foundation. Although the Trustees were willing to accept such help, the suggestion does not appear to have been pursued.

The expected increase of production was not achieved in 1932 because of 'an abnormal amount of illness'. Volumes 3 and 4 appeared during the year, and volume 5 was completed in April 1933. At this point a new factor was introduced by the report of the Standing Commission,[9] which emphasised the catalogue's worldwide importance as 'an instrument for learning' and urged that completion in about 15 years should be aimed at, adding that 'the undertaking should be dealt with on its merits as a unique activity deserving of special consideration, independently of the normal activities and finances of the Museum'. These views carried weight with the Treasury, and by October 1933 the Trustees had secured agreement to the creation of 20 additional posts, for which the qualifications would be similar to those for Assistant Keepers. They would be temporary and unestablished, and would continue for about 23 years, the period now estimated for completion of the catalogue at the rate of ten volumes a year. The additional staff, who were to be known as 'Assistant Cataloguers' and would receive a salary slightly below that of Assistant Keepers, were to be recruited at the rate of four every six months.

Recruitment proceeded successfully, and by August 1936 the complement of 20 had been reached. In the next three years five Assistant Cataloguers were appointed to replace members of the original team who had left for other employment or, in one case (Clutton, the first to arrive), had been promoted to Assistant Keeper. Of the total of 25, six were women – the first appearance of women among the staff of the Department. All 25 had good honours degrees but, since none had any previous experience of library work, their training absorbed much of the time of the experienced Assistant Keepers, so that the full effect of their presence on the catalogue's progress was not immediately felt. However, in the years 1934 to 1939 average production was four volumes a year, reaching five only in 1938. It was at the moment when their training was complete and a really large expansion of output could reasonably have been expected that, with revision having just reached the end of the letter *B*, the whole programme was rudely interrupted by the outbreak of the Second World War.

Notes and References
1. Board of Education, Public Libraries Committee. *Report on Public Libraries in England and Wales.* Cmd. 2868, 1927.
2. Standing Committee Minute, 10 December 1927. (B.M. Archives.)
3. The title 'Principal Librarian' was altered to 'Director and Principal Librarian' in 1898.
4. Note by Sharp in file of correspondence with Clowes, 1929–48, B.L. Archives (Printed Books).
5. Clowes file, 29 July and 10 February 1930.
6. *A new edition of the General Catalogue of Printed Books.* Prospectus, dated December 1929, B.L. Archives (Printed Books).
7. In 1920 the posts designated 'Assistant Keeper' and 'Assistant' had been renamed 'Deputy Keeper' and 'Assistant Keeper' respectively.
8. Trustee's Minute, 11 July 1931. (B.M. Archives.)
9. *Standing Commission on Museums and Galleries, First report.* HMSO, London, 1933, pp. 16–17.

12 Cataloguing in the 1930s

From the beginning of 1930 the time of the cataloguing staff was divided about equally between the two major tasks of cataloguing accessions and editing the new catalogue. Three Assistant Keepers who had been appointed in 1929 (R. A. Wilson, N. F. Sharp and myself) catalogued 'copyright' books (that is, British publications deposited under the Copyright Act) and other accessions in Western European languages; one (J. C. W. Horne), appointed five years earlier, catalogued books in Russian, Hungarian and other Eastern European languages. Every new entry had to be checked by one of the experienced cataloguers known as 'revisers', who also acted as instructors to the new recruits. Five of the seven Assistant Keepers allotted to the preparation of the new catalogue were also revisers and gave part of their time – on average about a quarter – to this work. The remaining two had some responsibilities in other areas; and one reviser (W. A. Smith) edited the quinquennial Subject Index and was not involved in the new catalogue. Each of the two cataloguing activities thus engaged the equivalent of between five and six full-time Assistant Keepers. The new catalogue, as an enterprise occupying a significant proportion of the staff and requiring a distinct organisation of its own, needed a short and convenient name, and soon became known among the staff as 'GK II' – 'GK' representing 'General Catalogue', the 'K' borrowed from the mark (derived from the Greek original of 'catalogue') chosen by Panizzi in 1839 to show, on the title page of a book, the heading under which it had been catalogued. The term soon came to denote not only the catalogue itself but also the whole of the activity involved in its production. Inevitably the earlier printed catalogue acquired the designation 'GK I', which was applied to it not only in its original form but also as enlarged and modified in the three laid-down copies.

The cataloguers of accessions worked in the Catalogue Room, the most easterly of the series of large rooms built about 1840 and forming the northern side of the rectangle within which the Reading Room and main book-stacks were constructed in the 1850s. In 1930 these rooms were still in their original form, equal in height to the neighbouring King's Library and, like it, with windows only in the upper half, around which ran a book-lined gallery. Along the whole of the lower half of the walls in the Catalogue Room ran four rows of shelves holding two copies of the working catalogue – in the upper two rows the red copy, used by the cataloguers, and in the lower two, below a projecting shelf on which volumes were laid while being consulted, the green copy, used for incorporation. Several large tables provided ample working-space for the cataloguers, and there were two desks for revisers, partly screened from the rest of the room by bookcases containing reference books. One table was occupied by the Incorporator, who needed space for the volume being marked and for boxes containing the title-slips of the current part of the accessions, older slips with alterations that had to be carried through into the working catalogue, slips altered by the Incorporator himself, and slips for the next part of the accessions in course of arrangement and numbering.

Books for cataloguing were brought to each cataloguer's place on flat-topped barrows, each carrying the equivalent of two or three shelves of books. A barrowload might contain a mixture of English 'copyright' books and books in various languages acquired by purchase or gift. The average daily output expected from each cataloguer was 30 'titles' – this term being used to cover all written slips, whether main entries or cross-references, so that the figure represents a rather smaller number of books. The quota may appear small if it is not appreciated that the writing of titles was far from being the whole of the cataloguer's task. This was not just to provide an accurate and adequate description of each book, but to ensure that it was properly related to the rest of the catalogue. This involved, first, looking up in the catalogue the name of the author and every other heading under which an entry for the book would be required, to determine whether it was already there and if so in what form, and whether any other edition of the same work had already been catalogued. If the volume of the red copy containing one of the headings was absent from the Catalogue Room, either for the incorporation of new entries or to replace a Reading Room volume undergoing the same process, the cataloguer had to go to the Reading Room to make the check. He had to satisfy himself that an identical name already appearing in the catalogue in fact represented the same person and, if this proved not to be the case, to provide distinguishing epithets for both. If a surname in the book was accompanied by initials only, the full name had to be found, if possible, by consulting such sources as biographical dictionaries, university calendars and membership lists of learned societies, a number of which were kept in the Catalogue Room.

New information in the book being catalogued might lead to alterations in entries already in the catalogue or to the writing of new ones, under the same or some other heading. If the work had an altered title or was a translation, the title of the original had to be noted – usually, if the original already appeared in the catalogue, not as part of the entry to be printed but in a pencil note for the benefit of the Incorporator. As an aid to the Placer, the pressmark of an earlier edition or, if the book was part of a series or work in progress, the pressmark already allotted to it and recorded in a special file kept in the Catalogue Room, also had to be given in a pencil note on the title-slip. If the book appeared to be a reissue or a duplicate of one already catalogued, the other book had to be sent for to verify this fact. All existing title-slips requiring alteration had to be sent for and corrected. Only new titles counted towards the quota of 30 and were recorded daily in an official diary which was submitted every month to the Keeper.

The young Assistant Keeper's training in cataloguing was completed by a period of work with the Incorporator, who shared with the revisers the responsibility for passing on the details of the system to newcomers. Throughout the 1930s this position was held by one of the most experienced Assistant Keepers, G. D. R. Tucker, a small, myopic, friendly man whose quiet conscientiousness and devotion to tradition qualified him admirably for his work but kept him from promotion to the wider responsibilities of a Deputy Keepership.

The work of preparing copy for GK II was allotted to the Assistant Keepers in portions corresponding to the content of single volumes of the laid-down catalogue. Each Assistant Keeper was supplied with the boxes containing the relevant part of the file of original manuscript titles and also with a copy of the laid-down volume. The titles, amended where necessary, were to be used as copy for the printer; the volume was needed to ensure the completeness of the copy, because titles might have been withdrawn from the file for alteration and, if not found, had to be rewritten. In dealing with any sequence of titles the cataloguer first had to list the pressmarks of those which lacked pagination, the publisher's name or any other essential information, or of which the accuracy seemed doubtful. The books were fetched from the shelves by one of the two Attendants specially employed for the work. The cataloguer compared the titles with the books and made any necessary additions and corrections. He then had to ensure that the titles were in the correct order and strike out repeated headings with a blue pencil. This always entailed some rearrangement, because the titles in the file were not arranged in catalogue order, but by date under each heading, so that the filing in the Title Room could be done by staff who had not been trained in the rather complex rules of arrangement.

We have already seen that this editorial method never achieved anything like the output originally expected, and that Marsden when he became Keeper was already conscious of the unrealistic character of the published estimate. He hoped to maximise output by issuing instructions limiting the amount of revision to be done. In a printed circular headed 'Memoranda for the compilers of the new edition of the General Catalogue',[1] after a mention of the two changes announced in the prospectus (separation of *I* from *J* and *U* from *V* and the abolition of ACADEMIES) he gave a list of 17 'minor additions and alterations' necessary for the sake of uniformity. Apart from the addition of pagination and publishers' names, the conversion of the older entries for books in series from cross-reference to main-title form and the addition of dates in some analytical cross-references, there is nothing in the instructions that appears to require research in sources outside the catalogue. They did not, however, succeed in entirely preventing this. Comparison of entries with the books, as one of the original editors later recalled, 'often revealed faults in transcription and other inadequacies and it was thought a pity not to take advantage of the opportunity to make those corrections as well'.[2] Cataloguers trained in the bibliographical standards observed in the cataloguing of accessions could not easily be persuaded to ignore doubts about dating or authorship or the relation of one work to another which could be resolved either by careful examination of the book or by consulting one of the large number of bibliographies and other reference books which had become available since the date of the original cataloguing. These indeed appear to have been regularly used in GK II from the beginning to expand names to their full form and to supply the names of authors of anonymous works. Another frequent cause of extra work was the discovery of inconsistencies in the application of the Rules, and particularly in the interpretation which had been put on one part of Panizzi's rules for anonymous books. An addition made in 1841 to his rule 17 reads: 'where a person is referred to in a title page by a description sufficiently clear to render his or her identity obvious, the proper name of such person to be adopted as a heading'. The difficulty arose not so much from this instruction in itself as from its extension in practice from persons to collective bodies and other entities that might have proper names.

Cataloguers did not always agree on whether a descriptive word or phrase made a particular identity obvious. Was it to be obvious from the title alone, or from the title in conjunction with other parts of the book? An interesting example is the treatment of the word 'Church'. 'The authority of the Church in matters of religion' appears in the old catalogue under CHURCH (1881), but reappears under ENGLAND. – *Church of England. [Appendix]*, printed in 1900. The title 'Church and King' similarly appears in both places, but in each for a different work bearing this title. 'Church versus Chapel' was catalogued in 1880 under CHURCH, but the heading ENGLAND. – *Church of England. [Appendix]* contains such titles as 'The Church and the People', 'The Church as it is' and 'Church? or Dissent?'. A song entitled 'The Church is our Guide' was entered under ROME, *Church of. [Appendix]*. The new edition brought all these entries together under CHURCH, treated like any other common noun. On the same principle two entries which had been made under CHRISTIAN CHURCH in the old catalogue – 'The Duty of the Church respecting Christian Missions' and 'Leading events in the history of the Church, for Children' – were moved to CHRISTIAN MISSIONS and EVENTS respectively. This type of recataloguing was not, however, carried out consistently. A few cross-references were made under CITY for titles containing this word which had been entered under LONDON. *[Appendix. – Miscellaneous]* and two entries under the latter were moved to the compound headings CITY MATRONS and CITY THOUGHTS, but the treatment of 'the City' as equivalent to an explicit mention of the City of London was allowed to continue. No attempt was made to re-locate any of the vast number of titles which appeared in the old catalogue in the various divisions of the appendix to ENGLAND although they did not include the name of the country: the presence, for instance, of entries for two copies of a poem entitled 'My Country', one under COUNTRY, the other under ENGLAND. *[Appendix. – Miscellaneous]*, passed unnoticed. On the other hand, several entries under ENGLAND. *[Church of England. – Archbishops and Bishops]* were transferred to BISHOPS, while numerous titles entered in the old catalogue under BISHOPS as a class-heading were moved elsewhere because 'Bishops' was not the first substantive. To all the complications of ensuring conformity to the current rules was added the further task of providing a system of subheadings for large headings not already subdivided.

Evidence of the involvement of proof-readers as well as copy editors in decisions on the exact form of entries is provided by an exchange of letters in October 1930 between the printer and the Keeper.[3] Clowes complained of excessive corrections in both galley and revise proofs and insisted that 'no alterations of phraseology or insertion of fresh entries' should be allowed in proof. Because some of the manuscript slips were not easily legible, he suggested that cut-up volumes of printed entries should be used as copy instead. Marsden rejected this suggestion as impracticable, but undertook that all copy prepared by one man would be revised by another before being sent for printing and that titles not easily legible would be rewritten. 'To some extent', he added, 'no doubt this will reduce the speed in the output of copy, but most of the time lost should be made up over the proof-reading of no more than a single revise.' This change, while helpful to the printer, only transferred some corrections from the proof to the revision stage, and did not reduce the total work to be done. The output of copy of each member of the team settled down at about 600 entries a month, not much higher than the output of an experienced cataloguer writing new entries for accessions. It may be thought to compare not too unfavourably with Roy's 1882 estimate of 1,000 for final revision of existing titles for incorporation in the amalgamated General Catalogue.[4] It was, however, only one-tenth of the rate of production estimated by Sharp in 1928.

The volumes of the catalogue were printed in a page size and a typographical style identical with those of the earlier edition, so that, as in 1881 to 1900, each volume as it appeared could replace the corresponding part of the working catalogue. Three copies, printed on one side of the paper only, were cut into separate columns and mounted. The conversion of a fourth copy into cards for the shelf-list was a somewhat laborious task, as the headings which had been omitted from individual entries had to be restored by hand. Another task which had to be undertaken urgently by staff from the Catalogue Shop, under the direction of one of its most experienced members, was the dispersal through the working catalogue of entries from ACADEMIES. The title-slips, with the word 'Academies' struck out, were re-filed under the following word – the name of the place – and the printed entries were taken up from the volumes and similarly redistributed and remounted.

Before the staff was enlarged by the addition of the Assistant Cataloguer grade, the accommodation occupied by the cataloguers, which would have been too small to take the increased number, was radically transformed. During 1932 and 1933 an upper floor was inserted in the Catalogue Room and in the equally lofty adjoining room (known as the Old Music Room), and the windows of the latter were extended almost to the old floor-level, so providing twice as much well-lit work space in

Cataloguing in the 1930s

rooms of half the height. Space for the books formerly stored in the Old Music Room and in the Gallery of the Catalogue Room was provided by dividing the two corresponding rooms at the western end of the northern range, known as the Supplementary Rooms, into four floors closely packed with metal bookcases. After about a year in a room in the southeastern corner of the Museum – previously the Newspaper Room, and now, after several more changes, the Students' Room of the British Museum's Department of Medieval and later Antiquities – the cataloguers returned to the ground floor of their own room and of the Old Music Room, re-equipped and refurnished and able to accommodate a much larger number. The upper part of the Catalogue Room was now occupied by the Title Room (containing the two files of manuscript titles and fourth-copy cards – about five million of each), transferred from the basement of the iron book-stack. The Catalogue Shop was also brought into proximity with other units concerned with the catalogue by being moved to the top floor of the three into which the Banksian Room, which adjoined the Old Music Room on its south side, had simultaneously been divided.

The need to preserve coherence in the new edition of the catalogue precluded any extensive revision of the 1927 Rules, but consultations among revisers to resolve problems encountered by cataloguers were still necessary. The increasing size of the cataloguing staff and its division between two distinct activities – accessions cataloguing and GK II – demanded an improved method of recording and communicating decisions. Typewriters were not used in the Department until after 1930 and notices could only be circulated in single handwritten copies or posted on noticeboards. The first surviving record of cataloguing decisions after 1925, when the last entry in the Black Book was made, is a set of typewritten notes, duplicated outside the Museum, copies of which were issued to all cataloguers at some point between 1930 and 1935 in loose-leaf covers bearing the title 'Memoranda for Cataloguers'[5] and supplemented during the same period by a second batch designed for insertion in the same covers. This collection was known, from the colour of the cover, as the 'Orange Book', and comprised 60 sheets, most of which were headed by the number of the rule to which they were related. The majority of the notes are clarifications of details of practice, and do not conflict with the 1927 Rules. Several, however, comprise substantial revisions of those rules: a new rule for publications of societies, providing for the disappearance of ACADEMIES and the entry of international organisations directly under their names; a revised rule for laws and public documents; and a new rule for treaties, absent from

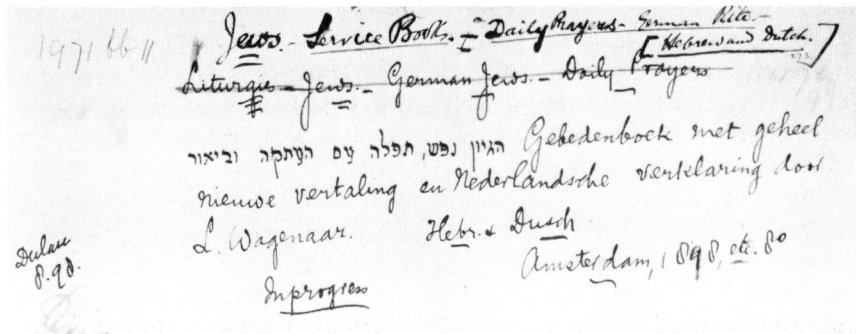

Title showing change of heading from LITURGIES. – *Jews*.

earlier printed editions of the Rules but repeating a decision recorded in the 'Abstract of additions' of 1847 and implemented in the catalogue ever since that date. Two important changes recorded in the Black Book but not in the 1927 Rules are included: the alteration of the rule on translations of anonymous works to exclude the use of the translator's name as the heading, and the exception for Dutch married women to the rule on compound surnames.[6] All these amendments represented practice adopted in GK II from its inception and were incorporated in a new edition of the Rules published in 1936. This was edited by Henry Thomas, with the help of a committee of revisers, among whom the three Assistant Keepers appointed in 1929 were now included. Thomas's interleaved copy of the 1927 Rules, containing his notes for the new edition, including several references to the Orange Book, has been preserved.[7]

One instruction appearing for the first time in the 1936 edition is not mentioned in either the Black Book or the Orange Book, but represents a practice adopted as far back as 1899: the entry of Jewish books of prayers under the heading JEWS. – *Service Books*. These were (and still are) treated as oriental works and not entered in the General Catalogue unless they contained material in a European language. The file of manuscript titles shows that between 1893 and 1899 a large number of entries for service books previously entered only in the Hebrew Catalogue were written for the General Catalogue under the heading LITURGIES. – *Jews*. These entries were excluded from LITURGIES when this heading was printed in 1899, but appear under JEWS. – *Service Books* in a volume of the supplement printed in 1903. A few of the associated cross-references to LITURGIES. – *Jews* are to be found in parts of the catalogue printed between 1894 and 1899, but the majority appeared only as references to the new heading in accession lists printed after 1900.

Neither the published rules nor the internally circulated memoranda contained any instructions on the order of entries in the catalogue. These continued to be handed down orally or by example by revisers and the Incorporator until 1939, when Tucker, shortly before his retirement, committed them to writing in a document which was printed in 1940.[8] This became known as the 'Rose List' because the explanation of the rather complex rules for arranging among themselves headings consisting of or beginning with a particular word[9] took the form of a set of hypothetical headings all beginning with 'ROSE', chosen as a word which could be plausibly represented as a common noun, a personal name, a surname or place-name, or the first part of a compound surname or place-name or of various other compound headings, or the first syllable of a longer word.

Notes and References

1. B.L. Archives, Acc. 233.
2. Francis, F. C., 'New Edition for British Museum Catalogue', *Library Journal*, vol. 82, 1957, p. 917.
3. Clowes file, 1929–48, 8 and 10 October 1930, B.L. Archives (Printed Books).
4. See p. 60.
5. B.L. Archives, Acc. 281.
6. See p. 100.
7. B.L. Archives, Acc. 281.
8. *Guide to the arrangement of headings and entries in the General Catalogue of Printed Books in the British Museum.* Printed by order of the Trustees, London, 1940.
9. See p. 89.

13 The last days of GK II

During the war activity was much reduced. Several Assistant Keepers Keepers and almost all the Assistant Cataloguers were called away to the armed forces or to other forms of war service. Between 1939 and 1941 the intake of new books and the number of new titles written and printed fell by more than half. The work on the new catalogue was kept going and in the six years from 1940 to 1945 nine volumes, covering the letter *C* as far as *COEN*, were published.

When a new Keeper, Henry Thomas, succeeded Marsden early in 1943, he quickly turned his attention to the Department's post-war prospects. In his report to the annual meeting, on 10 July, of the Trustees' Subcommittee on the Library Departments, he combined consideration of GK II's future progress with some more general thoughts on the staffing of the Department. He estimated that, if the pre-war arrangements for GK II were restored, production was unlikely to exceed four volumes a year, and at this rate it would take more than 60 years to complete the catalogue. He felt that this prospect removed the basis for the temporary character of the Assistant Cataloguer grade, which, he wrote, 'can hardly be expected to give of its best, especially when by so doing it is hastening the extinction of its source of employment'. He proposed that the grade be abolished and its members absorbed into the Assistant Keeper grade. This absorption, he added, 'would serve to emphasize the discrepancy between the Department of Printed Books and the other Museum Departments in the number of higher posts: in the smaller Departments an Assistant Keeper may look forward to becoming a Deputy Keeper, and then Keeper, sometimes at a relatively early age'. While the Department's full complement of staff in the relevant grades was one Keeper, three Deputy Keepers, 25 Assistant Keepers and 20 Temporary Assistant Cataloguers, the next largest department – the Manuscripts – had one Keeper, two Deputy Keepers and ten Assistant Keepers.

In the event, his proposals for the cataloguing staff were only partly realised. By the end of 1945, when the absent members of the staff had been released from their war service, 14 of the 20 Temporary Assistant Cataloguers had already been promoted, in most cases in their absence, to Assistant Keeper rank to fill vacancies caused by death or retirement, and four of these decided to take other jobs. All of the remaining six Temporary Assistant Cataloguers had either left during the war or taken up other employment on being released. The arrangement finally agreed by the Treasury in October 1947 was an increase of six Assistant Keepers, not 20 as Thomas had suggested, and the replacement of the vacant Temporary Assistant Cataloguer posts by a new permanent grade of Assistant Cataloguer to be filled by graduate entrants to the Executive class of the Civil Service – a lower qualification than had been required from the Temporary Assistant Cataloguers who had now become Assistant Keepers. Thomas's representations on the inferior promotion prospects of members of his department were acknowledged in a reorganisation which placed the head of the Department in a new grade of 'Principal Keeper', raised two of the three Deputy Keepers to the rank of Keeper, added one Deputy Keeper post and granted an allowance of £100 a year to five Assistant Keepers with special responsibilities.

During 1946 and 1947 nine new Assistant Keepers and ten Assistant Cataloguers were appointed, but cataloguing output grew only slowly while they were being trained. In the same two years efforts to acquire foreign books that had been unobtainable during the war and to replace books destroyed by bombing absorbed part of the increased strength of the staff and, combined with the revival of the publishing trade and the receipt from the Inter-Allied Book Centre of 20,000 books received from salvage drives, doubled the wartime volume of acquisitions needing to be catalogued. Only seven members of the staff could be assigned to GK II, and of these only two could devote their whole time to it.

The beginning of 1948 saw the beginning of a new phase in the development of the Department's organisation. Thomas (who had become Sir Henry in 1947) was succeeded as Principal Keeper by C. B. Oldman, who since Macfarlane's retirement in 1942 had combined with other responsibilities the general direction of both GK II and current cataloguing. R. A. Wilson was appointed editor of GK II with N. F. Sharp as assistant editor, and the supervision of current cataloguing devolved on me. F. C. Francis, who had been Secretary of the British Museum since 1946, returned to fill the Keeper post vacated by Oldman and exerted a strong influence on subsequent events. Wilson organised the

Top: Sir Frank Francis. *Below left*: C. B. Oldman. *Below right*: N. F. Sharp, with Reading Room catalogue.

staff preparing G K II copy in three 'groups', each consisting of one of the Assistant Keepers appointed after the war and one Assistant Cataloguer. The editor and assistant editor directed and checked their work, ensured the flow of copy to and from the printer, and shared the proof-reading with two other Assistant Keepers, of whom one worked also as a proof-reader of accessions and the other prepared copy in advance for particular complicated headings.

It was clear that a much enlarged staff would be needed to complete the catalogue in a reasonable time. Thomas, who had assumed that the whole staff of Assistant Cataloguers would be replaced by Assistant Keepers, had estimated that 35 Assistant Keepers, with a Deputy Keeper in charge, could produce ten volumes a year and complete the catalogue within 25 years. A calculation made by Francis and Sharp in April 1948 showed that to achieve the same result with the new combined groups would require at least 24 Assistant Keepers and 15 Assistant Cataloguers, with 12 clerks 'for sorting of copy and supply of books'. Room could be found immediately for only four or five of the 12 additional groups and even this partial solution would have to await a further increase in the staff of the Department.

Since 1945 the number of Assistant Keepers in the Department had been raised from 26 to 32 and the six Assistant Cataloguer posts converted to the Executive Officer class had been increased to 12, but the substantial improvement in the staffing of G K II that these increases had been intended to make possible had not taken place. By 1948 much of the new staff had been trained and the output of accessions cataloguing had returned to its pre-war level, but no progress had been made with the arrears accumulated during and immediately after the war – equivalent to nearly two years' cataloguing work at the current rate of between 50,000 and 60,000 titles a year. It was only after the recruitment of a further seven Assistant Keepers, bringing the total to 39, that the Principal Keeper was able to report in July 1950 that arrears of 'copyright' cataloguing had been overtaken and a year later that the work was 'now abreast of current intake' from all sources, though considerable arrears in cataloguing books presented to the Library in earlier years, including several large collections, still remained. With additions to the staff continuing to be absorbed by the urgent work of cataloguing accessions, G K II's rate of progress did not improve. Only one volume had been published in each of the three years 1946, 1947 and 1948; two were published in 1949 and two in 1950. Production of copy actually declined in 1950 by about 25 per cent. In his report for the year, Sharp (editor since December 1948 when Wilson became Superintendent of the Reading Room) attributed this to staff changes – two Assistant Keepers and two experienced Assistant Cataloguers had left during the year and their replacements were newcomers unfamiliar with the work – and to dislocation caused by having to vacate the main working-space (room A2, the upper part of the Old Music Room) while it was adapted to accommodate more staff. He had also come to the conclusion that the Assistant Cataloguers recruited from graduate entrants to the general Civil Service Executive class were not suitable for GK II work, and he recommended that all copy preparation should in future be carried out by Assistant Keepers, who would have a wider knowledge of languages and a more advanced academic background as well as more interest in the work.

This recommendation was accepted, and played a part in a reorganisation of the accessions cataloguing early in 1951. With the aim of making better use of the special qualifications of members of the staff, four 'sections' were created, one of which was manned by Executive-class cataloguers and dealt with 'copyright' accessions and official publications in English. Three of the Executive cataloguers had been regraded Higher Executive, for supervisory duties, and one of these was made head of this section. Another took charge of the incorporation. Three of the Executives were assigned to a new enquiry service for readers. Two sections, consisting of Assistant Keepers, were responsible for the cataloguing of material in two groups of foreign languages – Romance and Germanic – combined with the selection of acquisitions in these languages and replies to related enquiries received by post or referred from the Reading Room. The fourth section performed the same functions for all English material not falling to the first section, including purchases from abroad and books of earlier periods. These functions were modelled on the broad responsibility for books in Slavonic languages and the other languages of Eastern Europe which had already been exercised for many years by a special section.

It was in Oldman's annual report written in June 1950 that doubts about the feasibility of completing GK II first appeared in an official communication to the Trustees:

It may be thought that the whole project of revising and reprinting the General Catalogue was a mistaken one and should never have been undertaken, but it would be difficult to abandon it now without a serious loss of prestige and none of the alternative methods of publication that have so far been suggested, such as photographic or phototype reproduction of the existing working copy of the Catalogue, can be considered at all satisfactory. What is certain is that the longer its completion is delayed the longer will the Department be saddled with a burden that acts as a continual drag on all its other activities.

This paragraph reflects discussions in the Department which had been initiated by Francis not long after his return from his two-year spell as Secretary of the Museum. Perhaps partly because of this temporary absence, he took a wider view than most of his colleagues of the Museum's role, and in particular that of the Department of Printed Books, as a national library. He deplored the absorption of so large a proportion of the Library's staff by a single activity – cataloguing – and saw it as an obstacle to the development of new services of the type exemplified by the Library of Congress.

One desirable reform that remained impossible as long as the publication of GK II continued was the revision of the cataloguing rules to bring them nearer to the general practice of other libraries. This was a prerequisite for the effective participation of the Museum in any centralised or co-operative cataloguing system, and it was with this in mind that Barwick had unsuccessfully sought to initiate discussions ten years before GK II was started.[1] With the example of the Library of Congress card service before them, British librarians did not give up the idea; and it is an interesting example of discontinuity in the thinking of successive Keepers that Thomas, when asked about the Museum's position in 1944, suggested that, although anything like the Library of Congress card service was at that time impracticable, the Museum's accessions lists already offered a cheap and useful service of catalogue entries to those libraries which chose to buy them. He made no reference to the problem of divergent cataloguing rules.[2] In the more sanguine atmosphere of the post-war reconstruction period, the Library Association appointed a Committee on Central Cataloguing with Francis as its chairman in July 1947. The Committee recommended the production of a current national bibliography, to be issued weekly with annual cumulations and 'to be compiled in close connection with the copyright office of the British Museum'. The recommendation was accepted by the Library Association and the Trustees of the British Museum, and detailed planning was entrusted to a new committee on which publishers and booksellers were represented – again with Francis as chairman. Under his energetic guidance the new committee worked fast: early in 1949 the Council of the British National Bibliography (BNB) was created, and the first weekly issue of the Bibliography appeared on 4 January 1950.

Oldman, reporting to the Trustees on the project's progress wrote that 'its successful development is very largely due to the drive and initiative of Mr F. C. Francis, who was chairman of the original committee that examined the project and continues to preside over the bodies now established for its execution' (that is, the Council and its Executive Committee).

The Bibliography was compiled from the books deposited in the Copyright Office, and the small staff of seven were accommodated within the Museum. The entries, which were arranged according to the Dewey Decimal Classification, were designed as model catalogue entries, and, as was to be expected, followed the British version of the cataloguing rules issued in 1908 in slightly different forms by the British and American Library Associations.[3] While the British Museum Rules continued to have an influence in large academic libraries – they had been adopted, for instance, in the National Library of Scotland and, with some variations, in the London University Library – they could not compete seriously as a model for general use with the Anglo-American Rules, which were widely followed in the public libraries for whose benefit the Bibliography was mainly intended. In these rules the points included in the Library Association's earlier code under the influence of the British Museum[4] had been abandoned. The class-heading LITURGIES had disappeared; 'subject words' as headings for anonymous works had been rejected in favour of the first word; and English compound surnames were to be entered under the full form, not as previously under the last part. These changes added fresh differences in the choice of headings to those already existing in the treatment of periodical publications and the publications of societies and institutions.

The BNB was universally welcomed as a notable advance in the provision of bibliographical information and as an aid to cataloguing and book-selection, but in one respect it was an embarrassment to the Department of Printed Books. The books added day by day to the most comprehensive collection of new British publications were now passing through the hands of two distinct groups of trained cataloguers and were being meticulously catalogued twice under two largely incompatible systems. The wastefulness of this arrangement could not escape attention; but the British Museum system, with which the staff who operated it were becoming increasingly dissatisfied, could not be changed without destroying the coherence of the published catalogue.

An attempt to avoid some of the waste of labour was made during 1950. Cataloguers of 'copyright' accessions were supplied with slips on which entries cut from the BNB were pasted, and were asked to alter these by hand so that they would conform to British Museum rules. It was found, however, that the work of altering a considerable proportion of headings and all imprints and collations, with the writing of the cross-references which still had to be made, was such that no appreciable saving of time resulted, and the experiment was abandoned. Serious discussions about possible changes in the Rules were begun in the Department, but the difficulty of introducing into GK II during its publication the changed rules which were so clearly desirable strengthened the arguments for a quick solution of the GK II problem.

The solution proposed by Francis was based on the recent production in America of a photographic reproduction in 167 volumes of all the printed cards – numbering nearly two million – issued since 1901 by the Library of Congress.[5] This publication had been put together and printed in four years, and in spite of imperfections due to variations in cataloguing practice was enthusiastically welcomed by libraries both in the United States and elsewhere. Clearly a similar method of production offered the possibility of producing a complete British Museum catalogue in what would formerly have been thought an impossibly short time.

Francis proposed that the revision of the catalogue should be abandoned, and its publication completed by making a photolithographic reproduction of the remaining entries – enough to fill over 200 volumes – as they stood in the updated working copies maintained in the Library. The production process would be rather more complicated than in the case of the Library of Congress cards: the entries since 1900 in the form of accession-slips and those in columns from the earlier catalogue would have to be combined in a single alphabetical sequence in continuous columns, and the repetition of headings on individual accession entries would have to be eliminated. This would involve a laborious process of lifting entries from the pages of the laid-down volumes and reassembling them in double-column pages. The feasibility of such a process had already been proved in the Catalogue Shop when the entries under some existing headings had been reorganised, but additional staff would have to be engaged. Francis estimated that a catalogue produced in this fashion could be completed in about six years.

The proposal offered quick completion of the catalogue at the cost of a considerable sacrifice in quality. Nearly half the entries to be reproduced had been printed between 1881 and 1905, in some cases from copy written as far back as the 1840s, and failed in various ways to conform to the rules and standards embodied in the GK II volumes. Doubts about the value of reproducing this material unrevised, in view of the existence of a photographic reprint of the whole of the 1880–1905 catalogue produced in America in 1946,[6] were countered by pointing out that, since 1905, a number of important headings had been revised or rearranged,[7] and many individual entries had been corrected or amended in the light of later information and altered in manuscript or reprinted: all these improvements would appear in the photolithographic edition. The arrangement would also be improved by bringing together entries for a particular work, whether in the form of main entries or cross-references.

Oldman and the members of his staff most closely involved in GK II were reluctant to agree that the project in its existing form would have to be abandoned. In 1951 Oldman set out for the Trustees four alternative courses:

(1) to drop the whole scheme without providing any substitute for the unpublished volumes;
(2) to stop printing a revised edition, but to complete the work in photographic reproduction of the remaining volumes of the catalogue as it stands at present;
(3) to abandon the present standard of scholarship and print the rest of the catalogue as speedily as possible and with the minimum of revision; and
(4) to recruit the greatly increased staff that would be necessary to complete the work on the present basis in a reasonable space of time.

It had been estimated, he added, that a staff of just over fifty could finish it in 25 years. No action was taken immediately. The debate in the Department continued, and it was not until two years later that a full report was presented to the Trustees with a request for a decision. At the end of 1952, following the sudden death of F. G. Rendall, one of the two Keepers, R. A. Wilson was promoted to fill the vacancy and was succeeded as Deputy Keeper and Superintendent of the Reading Room by Noel Sharp, the editor of GK II. Sharp's responsibilities were transferred to me and as I was already in charge of current cataloguing and the maintenance of the existing working catalogue I thus assumed the direction of all work affecting the General Catalogue in both its forms, a responsibility recognised shortly afterwards by a Deputy Keepership. This change brought into sharper focus the conflict between the continuance of GK II and the need to devise a cataloguing system which would accommodate both the British Museum catalogue and the BNB. As Deputy Keeper in charge of cataloguing, I was asked to assist Francis in seeking a solution to these two related problems. Systematic discussions on possible changes in the cataloguing rules were started,[8] and at the same time detailed calculations of the implications of the alternatives for GK II were undertaken. On the basis of rough estimates that the part of the catalogue still unrevised would fill 200 volumes and that additions each year were equivalent to two further volumes, it was calculated that, at the existing rate of production (one and a half volumes a year) the catalogue would fill 650 volumes and would take 400 years to complete – an obvious absurdity. To complete it in 40 years and 290 volumes, six volumes must be produced each year and a staff of 26 Assistant Keepers and ten clerical officers would be needed. In contrast with these estimates, it was calculated that two Incorporators and 16 mounters could produce pasted-up copy in page form for the whole catalogue within seven years – a period which the Library of Congress catalogue of printed cards showed to be reasonable for the photolithographic printing of a catalogue of this size. These calculations, with a survey of the history of the GK II project and a discussion of the possible options, were included in a report by Oldman to the Subcommittee on the Library Departments in July 1953. The Subcommittee, feeling obliged to 'take note of the Government's declared policy to reduce the size of the Civil Service', thought it unlikely that a large increase of staff would be authorised and favoured a photographic reprint of the remainder of the catalogue, but asked that a more detailed report should be prepared for a meeting of the full Standing Committee later in the year.

In Oldman's report to the Standing Committee, which met on 13 November 1953, the estimates of the extent of the work to be done and thus of the time and staff needed for the completion of GK II were somewhat increased, and the timetable actually suggested was production at seven volumes a year for 45 years with completion by the end of the century. The staff required would be a Keeper, one Deputy Keeper, 26 Assistant Keepers, one Executive officer and 12 Clerical officers. The cost was estimated at £61,000 per annum (£40,000 for staff salaries and £21,000 for printing), giving a total of £2,745,000 over 45 years. The photolithographic edition, though greatly inferior in quality, could be produced in a short time and at a much lower cost, estimated at a total of £450,000. Oldman expressed his own recommendation as follows:

After carefully weighing all the considerations set out above, Mr. Oldman is still convinced that GK II is a work of great value to the Department as well as to the subscribers to it, and strongly recommends that it should be continued. He recommends that every effort should be made to induce the Treasury to provide the staff necessary to enable it to be continued roughly on its present lines and completed before the end of the century. Only if it is found that there is no hope whatever of obtaining this extra staff should the other courses mentioned be considered.

At the meeting of the Standing Committee, at which Oldman and I were present, the opinion was expressed that 'it would be unrealistic to approach the Treasury with a very costly scheme when an alternative involving the expenditure of much less public money might prove to be preferable'. The Committee decided in favour of the photolithographic edition, while expressing the hope that the publication of important headings in a revised form would continue. Detailed consideration of the method of preparing the copy for photography was begun, and it was decided that the reproduction would cover all books catalogued before the end of 1955, but no later accessions. Meanwhile, work on GK II was continued. Volume 50 was published in April 1954, and volume 51 (*DEO–DEZ*), the last to appear, though dated 1954 was not actually issued until March 1955.

Notes and References

1. See p. 97.
2. Thomas, H. 'The British Museum and centralized and co-operative cataloguing', *Proceedings of the British Society for International Bibliography*, vol. 6, part 2, 1944.
3. See p. 100, note 2.
4. See p. 73.
5. *A catalog of books represented by Library of Congress printed cards, issued to July 31, 1942.* Edwards Bros., Ann Arbor, 1942–46.
6. *The British Museum Catalogue of Printed Books, 1881–1900*, 58 vols. J. W. Edwards, Ann Arbor, 1946. Supplement, 1900–05, 10 vols. 1950.
7. See p. 95.
8. P.B. file, *C.P. 1, 1952–65*. 2 January 1953.

14 GK III: production

The production of the catalogue in its new form was delayed by a number of unexpected obstacles, and six years were to pass before any part of it was actually in print. The first step was to present the Trustees with a detailed plan of operation. This was done in June 1954. The estimate of the staff needed to remount the columns and accession-slips was increased from 16 to 30, and the possibility of entrusting this operation to the printers was mentioned as an alternative. The total cost, covering staff, materials, printing, binding and distribution was now estimated at 'not more than £500,000'. It was anticipated that the work could begin in 1956 and would be completed within six years. The Trustees deferred their decision until 21 January 1955, when their Standing Committee gave its approval to the plan.[1] No expenditure on it could be incurred, however, until two conditions were fulfilled: a favourable response from the subscribers to GK II and the consent of the Treasury.

The plan suffered its first setback in February 1956, when the Treasury refused to authorise any expenditure on it in the financial year 1956–57, so delaying for another year any action to engage staff for the project or to make an agreement with a printer. Consultation with the subscribers could, however, go ahead.

The announcement of the Trustees' intentions and the invitation to subscribe were embodied in three different circulars, one for GK II subscribers who were paying for each volume as it appeared, one for those who had made the advance payment of £400 for the whole catalogue, and one for possible new subscribers. The circulars asked for a statement of intention to subscribe and gave the probable cost as £8 a volume, but stated that precise terms would be announced when the number of probable subscriptions was known. The original subscribers of £400 for GK II were offered a full refund. It was at this stage that the decision was announced to begin the publication with volume 52 (starting at *DF*) since many probable subscribers already had the volumes of GK II (*A–DE*). These would be reprinted, with accessions to 1955, when the rest of the alphabet was completed. The circulars were in print and approved by the Trustees by October 1956, but their distribution was deferred pending a decision by the Rockefeller Foundation on the continuation of its support to American subscribers. In January 1957 the Foundation agreed to pay out the unexpended balance of its original grant, so allowing to the libraries which had benefited from it a reduction of £200 in their first year's subscription. On 31 January the Trustees made a public announcement of the project and an article on it by Francis appeared in *The Times*.[2] The circulars were immediately sent out to 2,000 libraries in all parts of the world.[3] Supporting publicity, mainly undertaken by Francis personally, took the form of articles in library periodicals published on both sides of the Atlantic.[4]

Discussions with Clowes about the method and cost of production of the catalogue had been going on since 1953, and it was on these discussions that the price suggested in the invitations to subscribe was based. By the end of 1955 consideration of the difficulties involved in the rapid recruitment and training within the Museum of a large force of mounters employed on conditions parallel with those of the Catalogue Shop had persuaded the Principal Keeper and his advisers that the physical preparation of the copy, after appropriate marking by library staff, should be undertaken by the printer. Comparative estimates for producing the catalogue, including this operation, were obtained from Clowes and several other printers in 1956. It was expected that Clowes would receive the contract, but formal tenders were not invited until after the Trustees' announcement of January 1957.

This announcement and the public invitation to tender for the work resulted in an approach from a printing firm with which the Museum had not previously had any contact, Messrs Balding and Mansell, who proposed an entirely new method of preparing the copy for the press. They suggested that, instead of the laborious process of detaching the entries from the pages of the catalogue and rearranging them in continuous columns, the individual entries and blocks of entries could be photographed directly from the existing pages but in the order required in the reprint. This would be achieved by using a specially designed camera which could photograph each entry or continuous group of entries separately, exposing in each case only the exact length of film required. The continuous film so produced, cut into column lengths, could then be used to make the lithographic plates. The staff required would be much smaller than for the pasting-up operation and the work could proceed more rapidly.[5]

When the tenders were received and examined in April it was found that this combination of arrangement and photography in a single operation had enabled Balding and Mansell to quote a price well below any of those based on the remounting of entries, and indeed little more than half the quotation submitted on that basis by Clowes. The Trustees referred the tenders to a special subcommittee, which, on 13 April 1957 after questioning representatives of the firm about their proposal and receiving the information that a trial camera had been constructed and could produce specimens by the end of the month, recommended that Balding and Mansell's tender should be accepted subject to the production of satisfactory specimens and the negotiation of a mutually acceptable contract. The scheme was approved by the Treasury in June, and on 13 July Oldman reported that the marking of entries had begun in the Department; that subscriptions for 395 copies had already been promised; that the photography could be started in September; and that the printing of the first volume might be expected to be complete in January 1958. In October, when the number of subscriptions had risen to 420, it was decided that 750 copies should be printed.

Up to this point plans and forecasts had been based on the assumption that, once the method of production had been settled and a printer chosen, work could begin almost at once. The conclusion of an agreement with the printer was not expected to cause any significant delay. In fact, however, this operation faced the project with another serious obstacle. Difficulties arose partly from the novelty of the technical processes involved and partly from the involvement in the negotiations of a third party – the Treasury. A draft 'commissioning letter' embodying the standard terms of agreement for Government printing contracts was sent to the printer at the end of July. As it stood, this was not acceptable to Balding and Mansell, who had not previously undertaken work for the Government. Discussions on various points continued during August and September, and led to the decision that the special nature of the project required a specially drafted contract. This was to be negotiated between the Treasury Solicitor, acting for the Museum, and Balding and Mansell's solicitors. Several months were consumed in an unsuccessful attempt by a member of the Treasury Solicitor's staff, in consultation with the Deputy Keeper in charge of cataloguing, to define unambiguously the technical requirements of the work to be done. This was abandoned on representations from Francis that there was complete agreement between the Department of Printed Books and the printer and that minute specification in the contract was unnecessary.[6] However, negotiations on other points, such as the inclusion of a 'break' clause, continued between the solicitors for the greater part of 1958, and the agreement was not signed until December. Meanwhile, the printer, who had begun to recruit operators for the photographic work in July 1957, had felt obliged to disband them and recruitment now had to begin again.[7] It was agreed that, in addition to the staff needed for the photographic work, the printer would employ a group of temporary workers to mark the entries in the copy and add the cost to his bill. In this way a request to the Treasury for an addition to the British Museum's staff complement could be avoided. The markers, mainly recent graduates with a knowledge of foreign languages, were selected in consultation with the Department of Printed Books. They worked within the Department, under the supervision of members of the Department's staff.

The method and organisation of work on what now became known as 'GK III' had to meet the requirements imposed by the nature of the photographic process and by the proposed rate of production. The camera, designed for Balding and Mansell by the Williamson Manufacturing Company, was known as the Williamson Abstractor. Six of these were produced and installed in premises not far from the Museum. When a sheet of copy was placed in the base of the camera, a light shining through the lens onto the copy could be controlled by an adjustable mask so that it illuminated exactly the space occupied by the lines to be copied, within a range from one line to fifteen lines. This mask was mechanically connected to another which restricted to the same measurement the length of film that could be exposed. Another mechanical link to the film-feed mechanism ensured that, after exposure, the film was advanced by the same distance. It was possible for the operator to vary the exposure time and so take account of the varying colour and contrast of entries printed at different times over a period of 75 years. Because the text was to be made up into double-columned pages of a predetermined size – the same as that of GK II – the camera was also fitted with a device which showed how much of the normal column length remained to be filled after each exposure. A tolerance of about half an inch either way made it possible, except in very rare instances, to avoid dividing the entry for one book between two columns.[8]

The chief elements in the preparation of the copy for photography were the marking of the entries to show their correct catalogue order, the merging of the parallel sequences of 'column' and 'accessions', and the amending of the order where errors of incorporation were found or the existing arrangement did not accord with current practice.

The reproduction was made from the red copy of the working catalogue – the one which had served as replacement for volumes temporarily removed from the Reading Room copy for updating. Before the entries could be marked, some preliminary work had to be done. The numerous additions and corrections that had been made in manuscript in the printed entries were checked and, if not clearly legible or if extending outside the limits of the printed column, were covered and rewritten. Where they were unusually extensive or untidy, the whole entry was reprinted and inserted in the copy and, from February 1961, all pressmarks with manuscript alterations were retyped on narrow gummed strips and superimposed. Long series of entries under particular headings, where the system of arrangement was confused or not easily understood, were examined in advance by Assistant Keepers, who indicated the correct order and any subheadings that should be introduced. Slips bearing the new subheadings were printed and inserted before the copy was marked. As the leaves of the copy were to be separated before being photographed, the pages were numbered consecutively from the beginning of each letter of the main alphabetical sequence of the catalogue. The need for these preparations emphasised the importance of beginning work on a volume several months before it would be required for photography. Fortunately the delay in settling the contract had given time for the marking of the first 99 volumes of copy, equivalent to 25 of the new printed volumes, and production was never delayed by shortage of copy for the photographers.

The method of marking was to number the entries in each volume of copy in their correct catalogue order in successive sequences from 1 to 99. The number was written in black ink immediately to the right of each entry. When the next entry to be photographed was to be found on another page this fact was signalled by a pencil note; entries already marked as part of an earlier sequence were distinguished by drawing a line round the number. When, after the completion of a sequence of 99 entries, one which should have been included was found at a later point, it was given the same number as the entry that was to precede it, the two being distinguished by adding 'A' and 'B'. When a volume of the copy ended (as it usually did) with an incomplete sequence, the number 99 was added below the number of the last entry, to indicate that the next to be photographed would start a new sequence.

The copy so prepared was photographed by the abstractor on con-

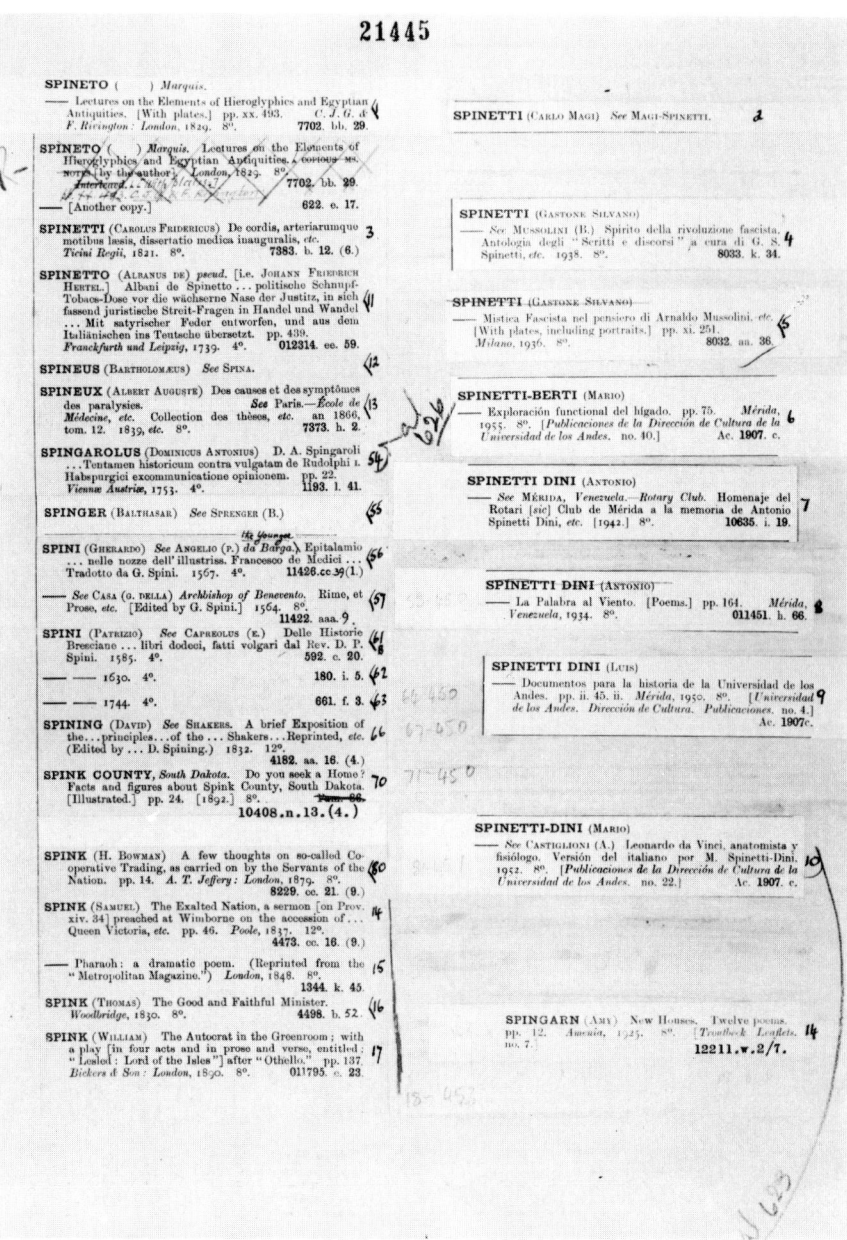

A page of laid-down catalogue marked for photography for GK III.

SPINGARN (JOEL ELIAS)
—— [Another copy.] A History of Literary Criticism in the Renaissance... Fifth impression. *New York*, 1925. 8°.
011840. a. 58.

—— La Critica letteraria nel Rinascimento ... Traduzione italiana del Dr A. Fusco. Con correzioni e aggiunte dell' autore e prefazione di B. Croce. pp. xii. 358. *Bari*, 1905. 8°.
11825. d. 25.

—— Jacobean and Caroline Criticism. 1911. *See* WARD (Adolphus W.) and WALLER (A. R.) The Cambridge History of English Literature. vol. 7. 1907, *etc.* 8°. **11870.g.1.**

—— The New Criticism. A lecture, *etc.* pp. v. 35. *Columbia University Press : New York*, 1911. 8°. **11840. pp. 32.**

—— The New Hesperides. A poem, *etc.* pp. 14. *Laurentian Press : New York*, 1901. 8°. **11650. h. 27.**

—— The New Hesperides, and other poems. pp. 60. *Sturgis & Walton Co. : New York*, 1911. 8°. **11688. l. 50.**

—— [Another copy.] The New Hesperides, *etc.* 1911. 8°. 011686. eee. **45.**

—— A Note on Dramatic Criticism. 1913. *See* London.—*English Association*. Essays and Studies, *etc.* vol. 4. 1910, *etc.* 8°. Ac. 2664/4.

—— Poems. pp. iv. 143. *Harcourt, Brace & Co. : New York*, 1924. 8°.
011686. c. 72.
No. 39 of 40 copies printed for private distribution.

—— Poetry and Religion. Six poems. *Privately printed at the Troutbeck Press : Amenia*, 1924. 8°. [Troutbeck Leaflets. no. 1.]
One of an edition of 40 copies. **12211.w.2/1.**

—— A Question of Academic Freedom : being the official correspondence between N. M. Butler, President of Columbia University, and J. E. Spingarn...1910–1911, with other documents. [Edited by J. E. Spingarn.] pp. 53. *New York*, 1911. 8°. **8306. de. 37. (4.)**

—— Two Notes on Clematis ... Reprinted from the Bulletin of the Garden Club of America, *etc.* [*New York*, 1935.] 8°. 07028. aa. 47.

—— The Younger Generation. A new manifesto. (Reprinted from the Freeman.) pp. 9. *Privately printed at the Troutbeck Press : Amenia*, 1925. 8°. [Troutbeck Leaflets. no. 4.]
12211.w.2/4.

—— A Spingarn Enchiridion. Being passages from the writings of J. E. Spingarn in reply to Paul Elmer More's charge that he has taught that " criticism is no impression," collected by Alain T. Peters. *Minaret Press : New York*, 1929. 8°. **11859. b. 2.**

SPINGARN (LAWRENCE PERRY)
—— The Lost River. Poems. pp. ix. 85. *William Heinemann : London*, 1951. 8°. 11658. g. 135.

SPINGAROLUS (DOMINICUS ANTONIUS) D. A. Spingaroli ...Tentamen historicum contra vulgatam de Rudolfo i. Habspurgici excommunicatione opinionem. pp. 22. *Viennæ Austriæ*, 1753. 4°. **1193. l. 41.**

SPINGER (BALTHASAR) *See* SPRENGER (B.)

SPINI (GHERARDO) *See* ANGELIO (P.) da Barga, *the Younger*. Epitalami. ... nelle nozze dell' illustriss. Francesco de Medici ... Tradotto da G. Spini. 1567. 4°. 11426.cc.39(1.)

—— *See* CASA (G. DELLA) *Archbishop of Benevent*... Rime, et Prose, *etc.* [Edited by G. Spini.] 1564. 8°.
11422. aaa. 9

SPINI (GIORGIO)
—— La Congiura degli Spagnoli contro Venezia del 1618. *In*: Archivio storico italiano. anno 107, 108. 1950. 8°.
P.P. 3557.

—— Cosimo I de' Medici e la indipendenza del principato mediceo. pp. 287. *Firenze*, 1945. 8°. 9168. p. 16.

—— Ricerca dei libertini. La teoria dell'impostura delle religioni nel Seicento italiano. [With special reference to Ferrante Pallavicino.] pp. 346. *Roma*, 1950. 8°.
4606. m. 4.

—— Tra rinascimento e riforma. Antonio Brucioli. pp. 248. *Firenze*, 1940. 8°. **10633. s. 55.**

SPINI (PATRIZIO) *See* CAPREOLUS (E.) Delle Historie Bresciane ... libri dodeci, fatti volgari dal Rev. D. P. Spini. 1585. 4°. **592. c. 20.**

—— —— 1630. 4°. 180. i. 5.

—— —— 1744. 4°. 661. f. 3.

SPINIFEX, *pseud.* [i.e. DAVID MARTIN.] *See also* MARTIN (David) *Writer of Verse*.

—— Rob the Robber. His life and vindication. By Spinifex. [A lampoon on the Right Hon. R. G. Menzies. In verse.] pp. iii. 45. *Joseph Waters : Melbourne*, 1954. obl. 8°.
Cup. 1246. bb. 19.

SPINING (DAVID) *See* SHAKERS. A brief Exposition of the ... principles ... of the ... Shakers ... Reprinted, *etc.* (Edited by ... D. Spining.) 1832. 12°.
4182. aa. 16. (4.)

SPINK AND SON.
—— Artistic Coronation Medals of Their Majesties King Edward VII. and Queen Alexandra. Designed and struck by Spink & Son. [With illustrations.] pp. 11. *London*, [1902.] 12°. 1703. c. 1. (16.)

—— Hints to Collectors of Coins and Medals. *London*, [1898.] 8°. 7756. *e.* 50

—— Loan Exhibition. The treasure of the Cathedral of Mainz. Catalogue, with introduction and notes by Professor Tancred Borenius. pp. 10. *Spink & Son : London*, 1932. 8°. 7817. c. 41.

SPINK COUNTY, *South Dakota*. Do you seek a Home? Facts and figures about Spink County, South Dakota. [Illustrated.] pp. 24. [1892.] 8°.
10408.n.13.(4.)

SPINK (ALEXANDER M.) and TAYLOR (P. S.)
—— " The African World " Egyptian Company Manual : a handy guide to investors in Egyptian securities, dealing authoritatively with the English and other limited liability companies established in Egypt, *etc.* pp. 96. *African World : London*, 1908. 8°. 08228. ff. 62.

tinuous rolls of film. Besides photographing the entries in the correct order, which often meant taking successive items from different, and sometimes widely separated, pages of the copy, the operator had another responsibility. In all accession entries printed before 1932 (perhaps a quarter of the whole catalogue) the headings had been aligned to the same margin as the rest of the entry, not projecting to the left as in the original catalogue and in GK II. Whenever one of these was the first or only entry under a heading, the heading had to be photographed separately, before the rest of the entry, and aligned to the same margin as the headings in the columns. In photographing entries where the heading was already on a separate line, headings struck out were omitted and the exposure began with the first line of the title. When material under a heading ran over from one column to the next, the heading had to be rephotographed at the head of the new column.

The first proof took the form of a bromide print from the film. In this the numbers and the crossings-out of headings sharing a line with titles remained visible, and the proof-reader's primary task was to check that all the numbered sequences were complete and in the correct order and that no headings had been wrongly excluded or repeated. The time available for checking – only one week for each volume of nearly 1,000 columns – did not permit careful reading of the text or comparison with the copy, except where conspicuous errors were noticed. A film embodying the proof-reader's corrections and with the numbers and unwanted headings painted out was submitted as a second proof, and some corrections could still be made at this stage. The finally corrected film, cut into columns and made up into pages, was used to make the lithographic plates from which the volumes were printed. Page proofs were checked for correct numbering and sequence of columns and for quality of reproduction.

Photography from the marked copy already in hand was begun early in 1959, and in May of that year R. A. Wilson, who had become Principal Keeper on Oldman's retirement in April, was able to report that complete photographic proofs of the first volume had been received and the distribution of the first eight volumes might be expected early in 1960. On this basis a subscription agreement form was sent out to prospective subscribers. Batches of eight volumes were to be despatched every two months, and the price for each volume was fixed at £6.10s, almost 20 per cent lower than that suggested in the earlier prospectus. But once more there was an unexpected delay, due to 'technical difficulties at the photographic and plate-making stages'. Only the first volume had been completed by April 1960, and the first consignment of eight was not ready for despatch until October. The planned rate of four volumes a month was reached in December 1960 and thereafter was steadily maintained.

Early in 1963 the marking of copy was approaching the end of the alphabet, and attention was turned to the reprinting, with accessions to 1955, of the 51 volumes of GK II. Subscribers who had received these in their original form were asked whether they wished to subscribe also for the updated reprint; the majority decided to do so. A problem now arose about the numbering of the volumes. The first of the GK III volumes already published had borne the number 52, but it was found that GK II enlarged by its accumulated accessions would fill 64 volumes of similar size. It was initially suggested that the subscribers be offered 64 volumes, at the existing price of £6.10s each, but that the continuous numeration of the volumes be preserved by treating the three volumes of BIBLE as one volume in three parts and by issuing 22 of the remaining volumes as parts of two-part volumes: for example, 12(I), 12(II). This proposal, however, did not commend itself to the Subcommittee on Publications, which decided in favour of 51 larger-sized volumes, charged if necessary at a higher price.[9] As the total payments received from subscribers for the volumes already published considerably exceeded the cost of their production, it was not found necessary to increase the price, and the 51 volumes, each about 25 per cent larger than those in the rest of GK III, were issued at the slower rate of about three a month instead of four, and publication of the whole catalogue in 263 volumes was completed in July 1966. Thus, although after the initial decision to produce it six years had been spent on overcoming difficulties from sources outside the control of the Department of Printed Books, the period of actual production was very close to the six years originally estimated. The whole edition of 750 copies had been exhausted and transatlantic sales had brought in more than a million US dollars.[10]

Notes and References
1. Standing Committee Minute, 12 February 1955. (B.M. Archives.)
2. Francis, F. C. 'New British Museum Catalogue', *The Times*, 31 January 1957.
3. *Liaison*, February 1957.
4. *Library Journal*, 1 April 1957; *Library Review*, Spring 1957; *Unesco Bulletin for Libraries*, October 1957.
5. P.B. file, L.1/3/4.
6. P.B. file, 'GK III correspondence', 26 June 1958.
7. P.B. file, L.1/3/4.

8. Commander, J. 'The abstracting process and the British Museum Catalogue of Printed Books', *Penrose Annual*, 1968, pp. 216–23.
9. Subcommittee on Publications Minute, 1 May 1954. (B.M. Archives.)
10. Press notice, 5 October 1966. P.B. file, L.1/3/8.
    Francis, Sir Frank. 'The New B.M. Catalogue', *The Times Literary Supplement*, 6 October 1966.

15 GK III: characteristics

The completion of GK III was hailed as a notable publishing achievement, both because of the size of the catalogue – larger than any single publication previously in existence – and because of the speed of its production. General satisfaction that a virtually complete record of the printed books in the British Museum was now available to the world reduced to insignificance any comment on its bibliographical deficiencies. The decision to reproduce without revision was fully vindicated. Even before the last volumes appeared plans were being prepared in the United States for producing a microcard edition, but the Trustees refused permission for this to be undertaken until at least one year after the whole catalogue had been published.[1] In the event the Readex Microprint Corporation issued in 1967 a 'compact edition', not on microcards but in a reduced facsimile just legible to the naked eye, displaying on each page four pages of the original and filling 27 volumes of about 1,200 pages each.[2]

The 51 volumes of GK II, reproduced in their entirety in GK III and its compact edition, now ceased to have any value except as a historical record. They constitute nevertheless a monument to British Museum cataloguing at its best. The large double-columned pages reproduce faithfully the general appearance of Garnett's 1881–1900 catalogue and preserve its typographical merits of bold eye-catching headings and entries clearly marked off from one another, but in the arrangement of entries under each heading and the content of individual entries GK II is vastly superior. Striking a careful balance between the summary brevity of a mere finding-list and the elaborate detail appropriate to a full bibliography, while taking account of the latest available bibliographical information, the entries follow a system which had remained remarkably consistent since the beginning of the century and apart from the abolition of two large class-headings – ACADEMIES in 1929 and CONGRESSES in 1946 – was virtually unchanged during the production of the 51 volumes. Some features of the cataloguing rules, such as the treatment of periodicals and anonymous books, although acknowledged in the post-war years to be undesirable, were left unchanged in order to preserve the coherence of the catalogue.

The virtues of GK II are preserved almost intact in volumes 1–51 of GK III, printed from GK II columns and (with a few exceptions in the first two or three volumes) from the accession entries printed after 1931, which had been designed to merge with those of GK II in any future reprint. The same applies to volume 52 and the first 41 columns of volume 53, based on the galley proofs of the material prepared and typeset in 1955 for GK II's unpublished fifty-second volume. This includes the important heading DICKENS (Charles), meticulously revised by David Foxon and introducing an innovation not incorporated in the Rules until after the completion of GK III – the provision of full main entries under the author's name, instead of cross-references, for books published anonymously. This heading, like a number of important headings in GK II, was also issued separately as an excerpt. (The only heading in GK III thought worthy of separate issue in its unrevised form was SHAKESPEARE, printed in 1964.) This part of GKIII, from *A* to *DIOM*, although textually up to GK II standards, exhibits in some respects a visual inferiority resulting from the method of production. The paper used, which had been specially chosen and tested for durability as well as suitability for the photolithographic process, formed when folded pages which, while of the same height as those of GK I and GK II, were somewhat narrower. The columns, reproduced from strips of film, were printed with a slightly wider space between them than in the typeset catalogues, and without the central dividing rule. The result is a noticeable reduction in the width of the inner and outer margins. There is also some unevenness in the length of columns, due to adjustments made to avoid splitting an entry between them.

The rest of the catalogue, from *DION* to *Z*, shows the full effect of the sacrifices, both visual and bibliographical, imposed by the photographic reproduction of existing material. To the visual imperfections already mentioned, two more are added. The first of these is irregularity in the layout of entries. In a large proportion of entries, the deletion of a repeated heading from the beginning of a line leaves a title starting an inch or more away from the left-hand margin and sometimes almost at the end of the line. Where subheadings have been used, further irregularities appear. A subheading may follow a blank space (where a heading has been deleted) and may continue on the next line; in other cases it may begin at the margin and be followed on the same line by the beginning of a title; or it may be placed centrally in the column on an entirely separate line, and may be in bold type, in small capitals, or in italic. When entries under a subheading continue from one page to the next, the subheading is not as a rule repeated. The voluminous heading PERIODICAL PUBLICATIONS presents a special difficulty of its own: in the original (1899–1900) edition the title of each periodical was printed in bold type and projected to the left of the remainder of the entry in the same way as headings in the rest of the catalogue. Periodical titles printed later as accessions were in the typeface normally used for other titles and like them were indented, following a dash. Where the two forms of entry are combined, the original GK I titles present at first sight the appearance of headings to which the succeeding entries, representing entirely distinct publications, seem to be subordinate. All these anomalies are obstacles to the sure and rapid finding of entries. The second imperfection is irregularity of impression. While the legibility of the catalogue is generally good, the efforts of the camera operators to adjust exposure to different states of the copy have not always been successful. Fine broken lines in some entries and thick blurred ones in others have made some entries difficult to read.

In bibliographical description, measured by GK II standards, deficiencies are numerous and pervasive. The most obvious is the absence (except in some important headings revised during and after the printing of GK I) of pagination and publishers' names from the entries for books catalogued before 1880. Other practices surviving from the nineteenth century are the entries in cross-reference form for works published as parts of series and the special form of cross-reference devised in Panizzi's time for the subjects of biographical works. On such matters as attributions of authorship and the relations between one work or edition and another, much information that a GK II revision would have provided is absent.

In all these respects, however, GK III is to some extent an improvement on GK I. In the interval between the two printings a number of important headings were revised and brought up to date. Several of these, including VOLTAIRE (transferred from AROUET) and SWIFT, appeared in the 1901–05 supplement; others, including DISRAELI and KEATS, were revised and reprinted later. Thousands of individual entries were corrected in manuscript or reprinted in a revised form.

One defect, which cannot be regarded as negligible, is attributable not to the photographic method itself but to the decision to maintain a fixed and rapid rate of production. This was the accidental omission of entries or deletion of headings which should have been retained. This meant, in

279

PERIODICAL PUBLICATIONS.—*London*.

Periodical publications not found under this heading may be entered either in the Catalogue of Newspapers or under the heading appropriate to the issuing body.

—— The Empire Commercial Guide and Empire Year Book, *etc*. London, [1925– .] 8°. **P.P. 2501.** ecu

—— Empire Foods. A journal of household hints and practical recipes, *etc*. London, 1930– . 8°. **P.P. 1524.** fu.

The Empire Journal. *See infra*: PRESTON.

—— Empire Library. [Tales.] vol. 1. no. 1–36. 19 Feb.–22 Oct. 1910. London, 1910. fol. **P.P. 5993.** ran. *Wanting no. 8–15.*

The Empire Magazine. London, 1885. no.1 8°. **P.P. 5987.** id.

The Empire Magazine. no. 1. July, 1895. London, [1895.] *s. sh.* 8°. **1866.** c. 3. *No more published.*

—— Empire Opinion. London, 1947– . 8°. **P.P. 3610.** fml.

—— The Empire Review. Edited by C. Kinloch Cooke. vol. 1. no. 1–vol. 77. no. 505. Feb. 1901–June 1943. London, 1901–43. 8°.
[Continued as:]
Commonwealth and Empire Review. vol. 77. no. 506–vol. 85. no. 535. Sept. 1943–Jan. 1951, April, Autumn, 1951. London, 1943–51. 8°. **P.P. 3773.** gb.

—— Empire Youth Annual, 1946(–52). *London*, [1946–51.] 4°. *The annual for 1949 was not published.*
[Continued as:]
Commonwealth and Empire Annual, 1953 (–*1957*). *London*, [1952– .] 4°.
[Continued as:]
Commonwealth Annual, 1958 [etc.]. *Watford*, [1957– .] 4°. **P.P. 6753.** ap.

The Employees' Gazette. Edited by J. David. A monthly journal of the employees of the drapery and kindred trades. Jan. 1893–Jan. 1894. London, [1893, 94.] fol. **Hendon**. *No more published.*

—— The Employer's Year Book. May, 1920, *etc*. London, 1920, *etc*. 8°. **P.P. 2501.** ecr.

Emporio Italiano. [Edited by A. Vera.] no. 1–7. London, 1857. fol. **Hendon**.

The Emporium of Literature, Science, and Belles Lettres. vol. 1. London, [1831.] 8°. **P.P. 5900.**

—— Empress Dainty novels. *See infra*: The Empress Novelette.

Empress Novelette and Diamond Jubilee Novelette. Edited by C. Shurey. ("Bow Bells Novelettes" incorporated.) vol. 1. no. 1–4. March 22–April 19, 1897. London, 1897. fol.
[Continued as:]
The Empress Novelette, with which is presented "The Diamond Jubilee Novelette." Edited by C. Shurey. no. 1–223. London, 1897–1901. fol.

280

PERIODICAL PUBLICATIONS.—*London*.

[Continued as:]
Empress Dainty Novels. no. 1–25. London, 1901–02. 8°.
[Continued as:]
Dainty Novels. no. 27–1214. London, 1902–24. 8°. **P.P. 6004.** cr.
After no. 1214, "Dainty Novels" was incorporated with "Smart Novels."

The "Encore" Annual. 1895, *etc*. London, [1895, *etc*.] 4°. **P.P. 6657.** e.

The Endeavour: a magazine of literature. Contributed by Members of the Lewisham Improvement Society. vol. 1, no. 1–6. London, [1865, 66.] 8°. **P.P. 5814.** ie.

—— Endeavour. A quarterly review designed to record the progress of the sciences in the service of mankind. London, 1942– . 4°. **P.P. 1447.** bbi.

—— Endeavour. Eine Vierteljahrs-Revue, *etc*. [A German edition of " Endeavour. A quarterly review."] *Imperial Chemical Industries*: London, 1942– . 4°. **P.P. 1447.** bbl.

—— Endeavour. Revue trimestrielle, *etc*. [A French edition of " Endeavour. A quarterly review."] *Londres*, 1942– . 4°. **P.P. 1447.** bbn.

—— Endeavour. Rivista trimestrale, *etc*. [An Italian edition of " Endeavour. A quarterly review."] vol. 7. no. 25, *etc*. genn. 1948, *etc*. Londra, 1948– . fol. **P.P. 1477.** bbq.

—— Endeavour. Трехмесячное обозрение посвященное развитию науки в услугу человечества. [A Russian edition of Endeavour. A quarterly review.] *Imperial Chemical Industries*: London, 1942–*45*. 4°. *tom.1. no.4 – tom.4. no.16.* **P.P. 1447.** bbo.

—— Endeavour. Una revista trimestral, *etc*. [A Spanish edition of " Endeavour. A quarterly review."] *Londres*, 1942– . 4°. **P.P. 1447.** bbm.

Endless Entertainment; or, comic, terrific and legendary tales, with. .cuts by J. Mark. vol. 1. [London,] 1825. 8°. **P.P. 5814.** q. *Imperfect; wanting no. 1, 2, and 18.*

—— The Enemy. A review of art and literature. Editor Wyndham Lewis. London, 1927– . fol. **P.P. 5938.** di.

—— [The Engineer.]

—— "The Engineer" Directory. (*The Engineer Buyers Guide*) London, [*1895*.] 8°. **P.P.2505.** sec.

The Engineer and Machinist, and Engineering and Scientific Review. (Edited by T. S. Browne.) 3 vol. London, Manchester printed, 1850, 51. 8°. **P.P. 1660.** b. *Wanting the titlepages and indices of vol. 1 and 2.*

The Engineer and Surveyor's Magazine, Railway Journal, and Monthly Register of Practical Science. no. 1, 2. London, 1839. 4°. **P.P. 1675.**

—— The Engineer Apprentice. London, 1947– . 8°. **P.P. 1660.** dp.

A page from GK III: Periodical Publications. Note the mixed typography and the inconspicuous appearance of Wyndham Lewis's *The Enemy*.

the former case, the disappearance from the catalogue of the record of a publication and, in the latter, the apparent attribution of one or more works to the wrong author. Such errors if detected at the proof stage could be corrected by rephotographing the columns affected, but in the severely limited time available for checking a considerable number escaped notice. The concern of the staff directly involved was expressed at an early stage by C. E. N. Childs, Assistant Keeper in charge of the editorial operations, in a memorandum dated 13 May 1960,[3] but little could be done to reduce the risks of error without abandoning the promised rate of production. One particularly grave risk was that, in tracing a sequence of numbers that might be spread over several pages and overlap with another sequence, the photographer might move from one sequence to the other and so omit 99 entries. This did in fact occur, and in more than one case went uncorrected in published volumes. A conspicuous example was the heading WILLIAM I., *Prince of Orange, Stadholder of the Netherlands*. Ninety-nine entries, including all the cross-references for books about William which had been transferred in the marking from the beginning of the heading to an appendix at the end, were missed. They were printed in 1968, in a revised form, in the Ten-Year Supplement covering books catalogued from 1956 to 1965.[4] At about the same time the whole heading, supplied with subheadings and revised throughout, was reprinted separately for incorporation in the working catalogue.

A number of other errors and omissions noticed while publication was in progress were corrected in the Ten-Year Supplement, but the great majority were discovered later. When the work on the catalogue was finished, a small team drawn partly from Museum staff and partly from markers employed by Balding and Mansell was given the task of comparing the contents of GK III, entry by entry, with a copy of the working catalogue. The resulting corrections have never been published in a separate errata-list. Their ultimate treatment is described in chapter 18.[5]

Notes and References
1. Trustees' Committee on Publications Minute, 19 November 1965. (B.M. Archives.)
2. *British Museum General Catalogue of Printed Books to 1955*, compact edition, 27 vols. Readex Microprint Corporation, New York, 1967.
3. P.B. file, L.1/3/8.
4. See pp. 148, 149.
5. See p. 166.

16 Supplements to GK III

The decision to reproduce the content of one copy of the working catalogue as it stood at the end of 1955 led to a change in the treatment of accessions. To incorporate them in the two remaining copies would have been wasteful, as they would have had to be re-incorporated later in laid-down volumes of GK III. A record of additions was needed, however, for users of the Reading Room and also, in published form, for purchasers of the catalogue. In 1957 it was decided that this record should be kept in the form of cards, which could provide both a cumulative card-catalogue for use in the Library and the copy for photographically produced supplementary volumes.[1]

At first the cards were made by mounting slips from the monthly accession-lists, but, in the expectation that these would be replaced by annual lists produced from the cards, their publication was stopped in February 1958 and printing of accessions continued, for use in the Library only, in the form of single-column corrected galleys. From August 1959 printed cards were produced from the same type as the paper slips. While the paper copies were stored for future incorporation in laid-down volumes, the cards were used to build up two alphabetical files, one for the staff and the other housed in a large card-cabinet which took the place of one of the double lines of readers' desks in the Reading Room and which had originally been installed in 1951 to hold BNB cards as a supplementary source of information about recently acquired books.

By 1960, when volumes of GK III began to appear, each file contained over 300,000 cards, and three copies of each entry on paper – in all nearly a million slips – had been accumulated. As soon as each volume of the catalogue was printed, three sets of the sheets, printed for this purpose on one side only, were mounted on stouter paper to form the three working copies. In these, the leaves were held together in strong loose-leaf covers, instead of being bound in the traditional way. Initially a whole page of the catalogue was mounted on each leaf, leaving a blank facing page for accessions, but in the later volumes, from N onward, mounting in single columns became normal, with whole pages used only in places where few accessions were expected.

Each printed GK III volume was thus expanded into at least five looseleaf volumes of about 100 leaves and in three copies of each of these the appropriate portion of the accumulated accession-slips had to be pasted by hand. This was a formidable task: for each published volume, over 1,000 entries (that is, 3,000 individual slips) were awaiting incorporation before the operation began, and, as the work proceeded, the printing of new entries steadily raised the number to be inserted in each new volume and the number of earlier volumes to which fresh entries had to be added. This meant an increase in the entries due for incorporation in each year from about 50,000 in the first year to about 120,000 in the fourth, a burden which, when added to the laying-down each year of 48,000 columns of the printed catalogue, was beyond the capacity of the Catalogue Shop, which was geared to an annual incorporation of about 60,000 entries and could not be augmented quickly. By the end of 1965, when the published catalogue had reached Z and only volumes 1–51 (reproducing and supplementing GK II) remained to be printed, incorporation in laid-down volumes had only reached the end of O: more than half the work still remained to be done. It was decided that there should be no more incorporation of slips cut from galleys, and that for the rest of the laid-down catalogue, from P to Z and A to DE, the accession entries would be taken from sheets of the Ten-Year Supplement which was to be produced from the cards and was expected to be published in 1966 or 1967. The laborious task of cutting out and arranging in alphabetical order thousands of small paper slips received in small batches from the printer would thus be eliminated; the entries in the supplement would already be in the required order, and where several accession entries referred to the same page or column of the catalogue they could be handled as a single unit.

It had been intended from the outset that the cards should be used to produce not only a supplement covering the ten years 1956–65 but also annual lists of accessions. The printing of photolithographic lists from the cards could not be begun, however, before the completion, at the end of 1959, of the arrangements for printing the catalogue itself. There was then a further delay while the precise method of production was considered. Should the cards be laid down for photography in complete pages (as at the Library of Congress) or should they be photographed one by one with Balding and Mansell's abstractor? The decision was in favour of using the abstractor, and the first annual list produced was for the year 1963: the cards destined for the staff file were kept apart during that year until they had been photographed, and were then incorporated in the main file, which was to be used later for the Ten-Year Supplement.[2] The 1963 list was published in 1964 in five volumes of the same size as those of GK III, and was followed by similar lists for 1964, in seven volumes, and 1965, in six. In 1965 the idea of producing a seven-year supplement to fill the gap between 1955 and 1963 was considered, but was dismissed on the ground that its preparation would disrupt the work already in progress on the Ten-Year Supplement which had already been announced and which would contain all the missing material.[3]

The production of the Ten-Year Supplement was not simply a matter of reproducing the file of cards. As the cataloguing of new accessions proceeded during the ten years, many entries already in the file were altered to correct misprints, to add new information about authors or particular works, or to record the completion of publications in progress. All these alterations had to be embodied in the copy used for photography – in manuscript when the alteration was only small but in most cases by reprinting the entry. Changed pressmarks were dealt with, as in GK III, by pasting new typewritten pressmarks over the old ones. The copy actually used to produce the supplement did not consist entirely of cards. The filing of cards, like the incorporation of paper slips, had fallen behind, and the addition of cards for which the corresponding slips had already been incorporated in the laid-down volumes would have been of no value to readers or staff. Fortunately the abstractor camera could be used with both cards and laid-down slips, and the copy for the supplement was therefore completed by adding accession entries up to the end of 1965 to the volumes already laid down and completing the card file only for the remaining parts of the catalogue. The supplement was thus a reproduction of cards from *A* to *DE* and *P* to *Z* and of accession entries pasted in volumes from *DF* to *O*. Despite careful planning by Peter Brown,[4] who had succeeded me as Deputy Keeper in charge of cataloguing in 1960, the first batch of copy was not ready by the time photography for GK III was finished – in February 1966. This was mainly due to a partial withdrawal of labour by the Catalogue Shop staff in a dispute, not with the Museum but with the Treasury, over a pay increase, to which they believed they were entitled, to maintain parity with pay scales in the Stationery Office bindery from which the Catalogue Shop had been separated in 1930. If Balding and Mansell's photographic staff were to be held in readiness to produce the supplement, work had to be found in the interim for the abstractor staff, who were employed exclusively for the British Museum work. The gap, from March to October 1966, was partly but not entirely filled by photography for the six volumes of the 1965 list of accessions and for a 15-volume photolithographic edition of the 'Catalogue of printed maps, charts and plans'. Some reduction in the photographic staff had been unavoidable, and the 50 volumes of the supplement consequently took two years to produce instead of one and were completed in the autumn of 1968.

Consideration of the terms on which the Ten-Year Supplement should be supplied to GK III subscribers revived a question that had been hotly debated before the printing of GK III itself began. The subscription price had been calculated to ensure that the production costs would be covered by 400 subscriptions, and no expenditure had been authorised by the Trustees until this number was assured. The probability that more than 400 copies would be sold therefore offered the prospect of a considerable surplus of income, and in 1957 and 1958 Francis, in a series of letters and memoranda, argued strongly that, since the catalogue was financed by payments made in advance by subscribers, not by funds provided by the Treasury, any surplus should not accrue to the general funds of the Treasury but should be held in a separate fund at the Trustees' disposal, and should be either refunded to the subscribers, perhaps by a reduction in the price of the later volumes, or used to finance future publications.[5] The Trustees agreed to take up the question with the Treasury, but were unable to obtain any variation of the established procedure by which expenditure was authorised by a Parliamentary vote and receipts were recorded as 'appropriations in aid'.

In an explanatory note to Francis, the Director (Sir Thomas Kendrick) wrote: 'The GK III copy (i.e. our Reading Room Catalogue) is produced at public expense by established civil servants. Under no circumstances could the Trustees trade any reproduction of the copy in a private enterprise.'[6] In spite of further protests from Francis, the position remained unchanged until 1965 when, in response to renewed representations, the Treasury agreed that the Ten-Year Supplement should be issued free to GK III subscribers, subject to the condition – which was fulfilled without difficulty – that the cost should not exceed half of the total net surplus.[7]

In 1969 a reduced reproduction of the Ten-Year Supplement was added to the Readex Microprint compact edition of the catalogue. Two other supplements followed, each covering a five-year period – 1966–70, published in 1972, and 1971–75, published in 1978–79. Both were reproduced from printed cards but, in the second, in a reduced size with three columns to a page instead of two, so that the whole was contained in 13 volumes (still of the same overall dimensions), whereas the 1966–70 supplement had filled 26. 'Compact' editions of these supplements were produced by Readex in 1974 and 1980 respectively. The content of the supplements was not confined to books published after 1955, or even to those received by the Museum after that date. They included a considerable number of entries for material which had been in the Department long before 1955 but had not been entered in the General Catalogue. Two important categories were 'Private Case' books[8] and a section of the French Revolution tracts.

Notes and References

1. P.B. file, C.P. 1, 'Proposed method of maintaining the General Catalogue during the printing of GK III', 8 July 1957.
2. P.B. file, C.P. 3/1, 'Production of annual volumes of accessions'.
3. P.B. file, C.P. 3/1, Memorandum by Peter Brown, 17 May 1965.
4. Later Keeper of Catalogues at the Bodleian Library and then Librarian of Trinity College, Dublin.
5. P.B. files, 'GK III correspondence' and L.1/3/9.
6. P.B. file, L.1/3/9, 20 May 1958.
7. Publications Committee Minute, 19 November 1965. (B.M. Archives.)
8. Books segregated from the general stock on grounds of obscenity. They were not entered in the General Catalogue and were issued only on the personal authority of the Keeper for the purpose of serious research. In 1964 the Trustees authorised the entry of Private Case books in the General Catalogue.

17 Post-war cataloguing developments

The recording of decisions in the Orange Book was not continued after the publication of the 1936 edition of the Rules, and there is no record of any decisions made during the war years. The resumption of normal working on GK II in 1946 was quickly followed by an important change: the abolition of the class-heading CONGRESSES. The international conferences entered there were to be treated in future like other international organisations: that is, entered under their names. This introduced an inconsistency in GK II, in that numerous cross-references in the volumes published before 1946 led to the old heading. The necessary alterations were made before those volumes were reprinted in GK III. Another decision made during the production of GK II, in 1948, was intended to remove a curious and rarely mentioned anomaly in GK I – the prohibition of the use of the word 'God' as a heading. This product of mid-Victorian religious scruples apparently dates from about 1865. Original title-slips for books received in that year were written with the heading GOD in one case ('God's Love in Chastisement') but not in another ('God's Sovereign Electing Grace'). In the printed catalogue the entries appear under LOVE and GRACE respectively. The heading GOD was used in the earlier British Museum catalogues of 1787 and 1813–19, and in the catalogue of English books to 1640 which was printed in 1884 from titles written earlier for the General Catalogue. No ban on its use was observed in other important nineteenth-century catalogues, and GK I itself contains entries under DEUS, DIEU, GOTT, and also under JEHOVAH. A typewritten note, dated '2.12.48' by N. F. Sharp and preserved in a file of 'Catalogue notices' kept by him as editor of GK II,[1] reads as follows:

In the cataloguing of anonymous books the words GOD and DEVIL and their equivalents in other languages are to be treated as common nouns.

The effect on GK II was to remove from the heading DEVIL a number of

A title showing the removal of the heading GOD, and (below) the same title as transcribed for incorporation.

entries in which the word had been treated as a proper name and was not the first substantive. The heading GOD duly appeared in volume 87 of GK III (1961), but showed only a few new or supplementary entries written between 1948 and 1955. The number of entries in the laid-down volume grew as material from the supplements was incorporated, but no systematic effort was made to transfer entries from other headings, and – to take one example – several titles beginning 'God is Love' or 'God's Love' were still to be found only under LOVE in 1987.

During the period 1948–52, when work on the General Catalogue was organised in two parallel units – GKI (mainly the cataloguing of accessions) and GK II, under the direction of myself and Sharp respectively – a new series of numbered 'Catalogue notes', designed for insertion in loose-leaf binders, was issued to both units. A binder kept for the use of GK II staff has been preserved:[2] it contains a set of notices, not quite complete, extending from 1950/1 to 1959/3 and comprising altogether about 50 notices. Most of them are refinements or interpretations of the existing rules, or deal with questions of procedure. The only one that makes a substantial change in the headings under which books are entered is no. 1955/1 (April 1955), which records the decision to abolish the class-heading DICTIONARIES. The anonymous dictionaries so far entered under it were to be recatalogued according to the general rule for anonymous books, but with a cross-reference under DICTIONARY or an equivalent word in English or a foreign language if it was the first substantive but not the heading for the main entry. The example given was 'Dictionnaire nouveau de la langue française': this would have its main entry under FRENCH LANGUAGE, with a cross-reference under DICTIONNAIRE. The decision was taken during the preparation of volume 52, in which DICTIONARIES would have appeared. This volume was not published as part of GK II but appeared in 1959, with additions, in the first two volumes of GK III. A significant but less conspicuous change, which had in fact been carried out in GK II at least since 1939,[3] was announced in cataloguing note 1951/10. This permitted separate entries ('main-title cross-references') under an author for works issued under a pseudonym, if editions had appeared also under his real name. It amended the previous unsatisfactory practice by which the pseudonymous editions had been covered only by a single general cross-reference from the author's name to the pseudonym.

GK III itself, although in principle merely a reproduction of the existing working catalogue, was not entirely immune to changes of headings during its production. One of these affected only the order of their arrangement in the catalogue. The separation of *I* from *J* and *U* from *V* had been carried out throughout GK II, but not in the unrevised part of the catalogue. It was not until 1961, when 29 volumes of GK III had been printed and the letter *G* had been reached, that the separation was begun in the marking of copy, so that volumes 52 to 80, from *DF* to *GA*, are inconsistent in this respect with those produced later.

A more substantial alteration was the transfer, also in 1961, of all the entries under SAINT PETERSBURG to LENINGRAD. In application of a general policy to enter places under the current English name or form of name, the heading AGRAM, used in GK I and GK II, had been altered to ZAGREB before production of GK III began, but several other less-used names were left in GK III and still in 1987 appear in the catalogue – for example, AIX-LA-CHAPELLE for 'Aachen'; KLAUSENBURG instead of either 'Kolozsvar' or 'Cluj'; and a form only rarely used at any time in English, LEOPOL, for the town originally entered in GK I under LEMBERG, and also known as 'Loewenberg' as well as 'Lwów' (in Polish), 'L'vov' (in Russian) and 'L'viv' (in Ukrainian). LEOPOL (an English form derived from the Latin name 'Leopolis') was chosen in 1930 by L. C. Wharton, the Department's Slavonic specialist, as 'being neutral on all hands and accepted universally'.[4]

In 1962 the entries under POQUELIN DE MOLIÈRE were moved to MOLIÈRE, following the precedent set in 1900 by the change from AROUET to VOLTAIRE. Cross-references in volumes printed before volume 155 (*MASP–MAURIA*), and also in the early part of that volume, lead to the old heading. A similar change made later, the removal of Leonardo da Vinci from VINCI to LEONARDO, had a different result. As the decision was made after *L* had been passed, the whole heading, fully revised by GK II standards, appeared as VINCI (Leonardo da) in volume 249 of GK III and was then reprinted separately under LEONARDO, *da Vinci*, for incorporation in the new laid-down catalogue.

The decision, in 1953, to hasten the completion of the catalogue offered the prospect that a radical revision of the Rules might soon be possible. A series of cataloguers' meetings was inaugurated, at which desirable changes were discussed. The general aim was to remove features of the catalogue which had been found to be unhelpful to readers or were markedly inconsistent with general contemporary practice. Proposals which found general acceptance were the entry of anonymous works under the first word of the title; main entry for periodicals under their title rather than under the special heading PERIODICAL PUBLICATIONS; main entry under the name of a person for works of which he was known to be the author, though published anonymously; and the entry of corporate or collective bodies – or at least those with distinctive names – under their names rather than under a place.[5] All these were to be large-scale changes envisaged as part of a comprehensive revision to be undertaken later. One change of some significance was, however, introduced in 1955. This was the abandonment of the practice of entering Asian authors under transliterated forms supplied by the Department of Oriental Printed Books and Manuscripts and used there in cataloguing works in the original languages. This had resulted in the entry of numerous works under forms that were unrecognisable to Western readers – for example 'Mukhopādhyāya' for the name commonly written 'Mukerji'. The new rule was that headings for the General Catalogue should be based on forms of names appearing in books published in European languages, a part of the name apparently used as a surname in the European manner being placed first, and that, in cases where a single original name appeared in various forms (for example, 'Dutt' and 'Datta'), the author's own preference should be followed.[6] Entries following this rule occur in the three supplements to GK III, but only for names appearing in the catalogue for the first time after 1955.

The use of a card-index for recording accessions after 1955 led to a new instruction designed to facilitate correct filing of the cards by clerks who were not experienced cataloguers. The required arrangement of titles under a heading was not uniformly alphabetical. All editions and translations of a work were kept together, in an order determined by date and language, regardless of differences of title, collections were entered before single works (in chronological, not alphabetical order) and entries for anonymous works about an author came after all those for his own work. Cross-references to other headings for related publications (for example, criticisms or replies) were incorporated below the entries for the work itself, not in the main series of cross-references. The need for such special treatment was not indicated in the printed accessions entries: it was the business of the Incorporator, aided where necessary by pencil notes written on the title-slips by cataloguers, to maintain the proper order in the laid-down volumes. To ensure its observance in the card file, cataloguers were instructed to insert before the title, in all cases requiring such non-alphabetical arrangement, either a 'filing title' (the original or most used title of the work) or one of the appropriate subheadings such as *Collections* or *Appendix*, previously used only under extensive headings.[7]

Notes and References

1. B.L. Archives, Acc. 281.
2. Ibid.
3. For example, under BRONTË (Charlotte).
4. MS note on original title-slip of cross-reference 'LEMBERG, *in Galicia. See* Leopol'.
5. Chaplin, A.H. 'A reconsideration of the British Museum rules for compiling the catalogue of printed books – II', in Mary Piggott, ed., *Cataloguing Rules and Principles.* Library Association, London, 1954.
6. P.B. file, C.P. 2, note by A.H. Chaplin, 7 May 1955.
7. Catalogue notes 1959/1, 1959/2. (B.L. Archives.)

18 The final phase

The end of the Panizzi Rules
The impulse towards radical change in the Rules, accepted as an objective since 1950, was strengthened by developments outside the British Museum. To the need for co-ordination with the British National Bibliography was added the influence of a general post-war movement towards uniformity in cataloguing systems.

In 1957, the Library Association's Cataloguing Rules Sub-Committee, dormant during the war, renewed its co-operation with the Cataloguing Rules Committee of the American Library Association in producing a new Anglo-American code. The British Museum was represented on the Sub-Committee by Sharp (who became its chairman in 1961) and myself, but neither of us felt the need, as Bullen and Garnett had in 1880, to press for the recognition of practices peculiar to the Museum. On all major points of difference, opinion in the Department of Printed Books already favoured change in the direction of the Anglo-American position.[1]

Before the British and American committees had completed their work, the possibility of a wider international agreement was discussed at the International Conference on Cataloguing Principles (ICCP). This was sponsored by the International Federation of Library Associations and brought together delegations from 53 countries and 12 international organisations in the Unesco building in Paris in 1961. The British Museum played a prominent part in the organisation of this conference. Francis (who had now become Director of the Museum) was its president and I acted as executive secretary and chairman of the organising committee. American, French, German and Russian librarians also took an active part in the preparatory work. The conference confined its attention to principles governing the choice and form of headings and entry words in alphabetical author and title catalogues, the class to which the British Museum's General Catalogue and the principal catalogues of many other large libraries belonged. It adopted a 'Statement of Principles',[2] which showed clear signs of the influence of Seymour Lubetzky, of the Library of Congress, who had published in 1953 under the title *Cataloging Rules and Principles*[3] a penetrating critique of the rules then current in the United States[4] and who in 1956 was appointed editor of the proposed new Anglo-American code.

The Statement approved several practices which were already part of the British Museum system – notably main entry under the name of a corporate body for works which were 'the expression of the collective thought or activity' of the body, and the use of a single form of each author's name and a single 'uniform title' of each work to assemble the works of the author and editions of the work at one place in the catalogue despite variations in the books themselves. It rejected British Museum practice by requiring that the main entry for every work known to have been written by an author, including those published anonymously, should be made under his name; that corporate bodies should be entered directly under their names, not under geographical headings (which were reserved for 'states and other territorial authorities'); and that periodicals and works of unknown authorship should have their main entries under their titles, not under a special class-heading or under a significant word selected from the title.

These differences, as we have seen, were acceptable in principle to the British Museum and, shortly after the conference, the drafting of new rules, in which the choice and form of headings were to be based on the 'Statement of Principles', was begun under the direction of Peter Brown. He suggested that a number of the resulting changes could be introduced immediately, some would require only minor alterations in existing entries, while some would have to wait for the opportunity to make major changes, which would occur after the completion of GK III and the incorporation of the accumulated accessions, possibly in 1967.[5]

By 1967 GK III itself was complete, but the incorporation of the accumulated accessions was not. In that year, however, the situation was changed again by the publication of the new Anglo-American Rules (commonly referred to as AACR 67).[6] These rules followed the ICCP principles for headings but gave much more precise and detailed instructions and included rules for the descriptive elements of the entries (title, imprint, collation, notes) based on the practice of the Library of Congress. The British National Bibliography adopted the new rules in January 1968, and at the same time the decision was taken in the Department of Printed Books to abandon the drafting of new British

Museum rules and make AACR 67 the basis of its own future cataloguing.

It was not intended, however, that the old catalogue should be wound up and a new one begun. The radical reform projected since 1953, like other changes made earlier, was not regarded simply as an adaptation of current cataloguing to generally accepted practices but as an improvement to be applied to the catalogue as a whole. A single integrated catalogue of the whole collection of printed books was a much prized asset, and it was felt to be a grave disservice to readers to require them to search a new and separate catalogue for works by authors already established in the old one or for new editions of works already entered there, in both cases possibly under new headings. Such treatment did not seem necessary. Headings for individual authors, constituting the greater part of the catalogue, would be so similar under the old and new rules as to blend without difficulty in one alphabetical sequence, and the variations between one system and the other in the form and order of items of descriptive information were not such as to cause inconvenience to readers. The distribution of entries under PERIODICAL PUBLICATIONS to headings beginning with the first word of the title would be a mechanical operation similar to the breaking up of ACADEMIES in 1930, and would be aided by the presence in the existing catalogue of the required new headings in the guise of cross-references from titles. The transfer of entries for anonymous books to the first word of the title and those for corporate bodies from place-name to the names of the bodies would take time, but would not make a heavy call on the labour of skilled cataloguers. These operations could not begin, however, until the catalogue had been brought up to date by the issue of supplements to GK III and the incorporation of their contents in the laid-down volumes.

Meanwhile, in the cataloguing of accessions, a partial and provisional application of AACR was adopted under the direction of a new Head of the Catalogue Division, R. S. Pine-Coffin, assisted by Ann O'Donovan. In all new main entries AACR 67 was to be followed in the 'description' – that is, the part of the entry beginning with the title of a work and including imprint, collation and notes. Additional entries, which under the British Museum Rules would have taken the form of 'main-title cross-references' (consisting of an abridged main entry followed by a reference to the main-entry heading), were to be replaced by full added entries, repeating the whole description from the main entry but distinguished from it by the addition of '[Added entry]' as a footnote.

Headings were to be chosen in such a way as to avoid conflict with entries already in the catalogue. Existing headings for particular authors and corporate bodies would be retained unchanged, and new entries for works already recorded in the catalogue would be made under the headings already used; but works by authors (personal or corporate) whose names did not already appear as headings and previously unrecorded works not requiring author headings (for example, periodicals and works of unknown authorship) would be catalogued according to AACR 67. Where both sets of rules required a main entry under one heading and a full added entry under another (for example, under a person and a corporate body, or under author and title) AACR would determine which was to be the main entry.

Where entry under title was required, the common practice of making the entries directly under the title as a whole, without a separate heading, was rejected as incompatible with earlier entries in which heading and title were always distinct elements. Each title would be entered under a heading of the kind already established for cross-references from the titles of periodicals. While such a heading would begin with the first word of the title (other than an article) and might consist of that word only, it might include other words also. This would occur whenever the title began with an expression consisting of a noun preceded by one or more adjectives or other nouns qualifying it: in these cases the whole expression would form the heading. This preserved consistency with earlier headings, but resulted in separate sequences under the first word by itself and under various combinations with other words, so that the alphabetical order of the complete titles was not observed. The result is illustrated by the following examples:

CHILD
– The child at school
– The child in care
– A child of the Revolution
CHILD ADOPTION
– Child adoption. The journal of . . .
CHILD CARE
– Child care. The papers of the seminars
– Child care, health and development
CHILD CARE NEWS
– Child care news. Published by the Association of Child Care Officers
CHILD LABOUR
– Child labour and education

FIRST
— First and last
— The first of seven general letters on religion
FIRST AID
— First aid in the house
FIRST CORNISH ANTHOLOGY
— A first Cornish anthology.

The decision to adopt the AACR form for all parts of the entry after the heading considerably facilitated co-operation with the BNB. Earlier attempts to use BNB entries as copy for accessions to the General Catalogue had failed because the number of alterations required to comply with British Museum practice had precluded any significant saving of cataloguers' time. It was now possible to reproduce the greater part of each entry unaltered. From May 1968 entries printed on British Museum title-slips from linotype slugs used in producing the BNB were amended by hand by British Museum cataloguers to conform with the special requirements described above, and were then reprinted for inclusion in the General Catalogue. Books not covered by the British National Bibliography (mainly foreign books and older English books) were catalogued on the same principles by the various language sections of the Cataloguing Division. Entries of the new type appeared in the 1966–70 supplement to GK III, and are normal in the later supplement covering the years 1971–75.

This pronounced move away from traditional British Museum practice was the first step towards a decisive break in the process which, in spite of gradual changes in form and content, had preserved the General Catalogue for over a century as a single continuously developing organism. The change was precipitated by a combination of two factors: the advent of computer-based catalogue production and the creation of the British Library.

Since the early 1960s the application of computers to the storage and manipulation of bibliographical data had been seen as likely to have a profound effect on the future of the General Catalogue. In 1967 the report of a two-year study by two Assistant Keepers, John Jolliffe and A. M. Cain,[7] recommended *inter alia* using computer-controlled phototypesetting to produce accession lists which could be cumulated mechanically, and also, as the only means by which the full benefits of a computer system could be realised, the conversion as soon as possible of the whole of the General Catalogue to machine-readable form. It was suggested that, as part of this operation, old headings could be revised to conform to the new rules and past and future cataloguing could thus be combined in a single integrated and constantly updated record from which a great deal of information, obtainable from the old catalogue only at great expense in time and labour, could be rapidly extracted by the computer.

Implementation of this scheme was deferred to allow consideration of its possible extension to other institutions, such as the BNB and the other copyright libraries – a decision that was soon reinforced by the appointment early in 1968 of the National Libraries Committee (the 'Dainton Committee'), which in 1969 recommended the creation of a new organisation uniting the library departments of the British Museum with the BNB, the National Central Library and the National Lending Library of Science and Technology. The result was the constitution in 1973 of the British Library, in which the Department of Printed Books and the British National Bibliography formed the principal components of the Reference Division and the Bibliographic Services Division respectively. A study of the possible uses of computers in this combination of institutions, carried out under the direction of Maurice Line in 1970 and 1971, had resulted in strong recommendations (1) that entries for the BNB and catalogue entries for the Department of Printed Books should both be produced, as a single joint operation, on magnetic tapes for a computer system, and (2) that, as earlier recommended by Jolliffe and Cain, the whole of the existing General Catalogue should be converted to machine-readable form, with the headings (but not the other parts of the entries) altered where necessary to conform to AACR.[8]

On the formation of the British Library, these recommendations were accepted in principle but were not put into effect immediately. Since January 1971 the BNB had been printed by computer-operated phototypesetting from tapes compiled according to the MARC system – a machine-readable format embodying the Anglo-American Rules and devised jointly in 1967 by the BNB and the Library of Congress. The corresponding entries for the General Catalogue continued, however, to be printed separately, using as copy BNB entries amended in the manner described above (page 161). This procedure was followed until August 1975, by which time the Printed Books staff engaged in foreign-language cataloguing had been fully trained in the methods required by the MARC system. From that date all new entries for books published after 1970 were made in machine-readable form on magnetic tape. These entries, conforming entirely to AACR and no longer available in print on paper, could not be incorporated in the old catalogue. They constituted therefore the beginning of an entirely new catalogue of books published after 1970, made available to users by computer output on microfilm, at first in the form of 16mm film in cassettes and from 1977 onward of 105mm microfiches, each carrying about 2,500 entries, of which a number of copies, with the necessary reading-machines, were placed in the Reading Room. The decision, so long resisted, to abandon the single integrated catalogue had at last been taken.

This did not mean, however, that the old printed General Catalogue was finally closed and ceased to grow. Each year about 30,000 entries, for books published before 1971 and either still uncatalogued in 1975 or newly acquired, continued to be printed in accession lists and incorporated in the laid-down volumes.

The last printed edition
In 1979 one more edition of this still growing catalogue was begun. This time the British Library did not itself undertake the production of the catalogue, as the British Museum had done, but entrusted it to independent publishers, Clive Bingley and K. G. Saur. The principle of photo-reproduction of existing material, as in GK III, was maintained, but the method was different.

The working catalogue then in use consisted of the columns of GK III (replaced here and there by sections that had been revised and reprinted since 1966), with entries cut from the first two supplements (1956–65 and 1966–70) or printed after 1975 pasted beside them, and with whole pages of the third supplement (1971–75), which had been printed in smaller type, inserted in a separate sequence at the end of each of the laid-down volumes. To produce the new edition, photocopies of complete pages of the main sequence, combining columns and accessions, were cut into individual entries or blocks of consecutive entries, and similar copy for the content of the 1971–75 supplement was made not from the supplement itself but from the cards (typographically uniform with the main catalogue) from which it had been produced. The entries were then arranged in a continuous sequence and mounted in columns which were rephotographed at a slightly reduced size to form the double-columned pages of the new edition. The result is a reproduction of GK III combined with its three supplements, but with certain modifications and additions.

Each volume reproduces the content of the corresponding portion of the working catalogue as it was when it was photocopied. The volumes therefore include a varying but substantial number of entries which have been revised or corrected since their earlier appearance and a much larger number which have been added to the catalogue after 1975.

The most important examples of the former category are headings which have been entirely revised. When the Trustees agreed in November 1953 to the reproduction of the existing catalogue without revision, they expressed the wish that revised editions of important sections of the catalogue should continue to be produced. After the completion of GK III in 1966 the revision of selected headings was resumed, and in the next 16 years about 30 headings, mainly for English authors, were brought into line with current cataloguing standards and reprinted. Eleven of them were issued as separate publications in 1974. All were substituted for the corresponding parts of GK III in the working catalogue but did not appear in the published supplements, and it is in their revised form (with the addition of a few more recent entries) that they appear in the Bingley–Saur edition. Scattered throughout the catalogue, there are also a large number of other entries which have been amended since they were printed in GK III and its supplements.

Additions to the content of the catalogue are of three kinds: entries for books published before 1971 which were acquired after 1975; entries for books which had been in the Library for a considerable time but had not yet been catalogued; and entries formerly in the catalogue which had been accidentally omitted from GK III. Of these additional entries (amounting to 120,000 when the new edition was begun and increasing by as many as 30,000 each year) the first group is by far the most numerous, and examples of it occur on almost every page. The second group represents the result of efforts to overcome the long-standing problem of cataloguing arrears, particularly affecting collections acquired in bulk many years earlier but catalogued in detail only gradually as time could be spared from recording the main stream of accessions. Outstanding among these were the three collections of French Revolution tracts, acquired from or with the help of John Wilson Croker in 1817, 1831 and 1856. Although the cataloguing of the tracts had been begun by Panizzi as a new Assistant in the early 1830s,[9] only the first collection (pressmarked 'F') and about half of the second (pressmarked 'F.R.') had been catalogued by 1899, in time to be included in the first General Catalogue and its supplement.[10] The remainder of the 'F.R.' collection and about half of the third (pressmarked 'R') were included in GK III or in its Ten-Year Supplement. Several thousand entries covering the remainder of the 'R' collection, some of which had been written before 1966 but not printed, were revised or written between 1971 and 1976 by Audrey Brodhurst, the head of the French language section (partly as a personal contribution to the catalogue after

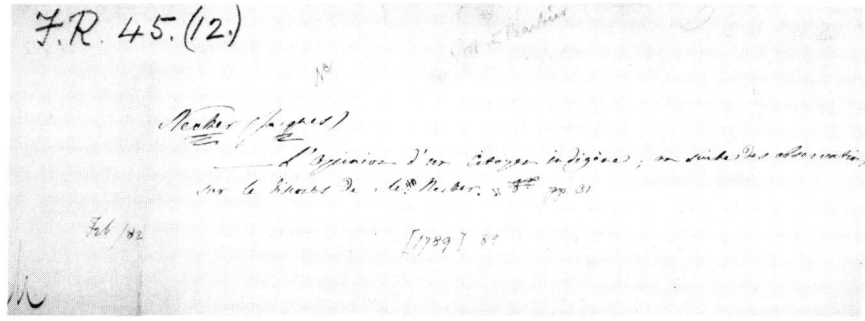

A title written by Panizzi as a young Assistant (pagination, date and pressmark added later).

her retirement), and appeared for the first time as part of a published catalogue in the Bingley–Saur edition.

The third group of additions has at last remedied a defect in the published volumes of GK III, by supplying entries accidentally omitted during its production and correcting other errors, such as the appearance of entries under the wrong heading.[11] Since 1965, a complete check of the printed volumes against a copy of the old working catalogue to discover 'misplaced or omitted headings and entries' had been under way with the intention that a list of errata and addenda should be issued to subscribers. Over 3,000 errors and omissions were discovered, but the consequent amendment of the working catalogue and production of an errata list were postponed pending a review by an experienced member of the British Museum staff, James Etherington, who had supervised much of the preparatory marking. It was found that a number of the missing entries had been omitted deliberately as not being required by current cataloguing practice. Gradually copies of the rest were located, photocopied or reprinted, and incorporated in the new laid-down volumes. This work, continued by Etherington after his official retirement, was still not completed by 1979 when the printing of the Bingley–Saur edition began. This publication, however, provided an opportunity to make good the errors and omissions, and the insertion in the working catalogue of copies of the missing entries in the later part of the alphabet was continued so that all could be included in the published volumes.

With almost half the volumes of the new edition printed, each giving a slightly more up-to-date record than its predecessor, a new development at the end of 1982 fixed a final limit to its content.

The technical preparation for converting the whole catalogue to machine-readable form had reached the stage where the start of actual conversion seemed imminent. No entries for books received in the Library since the beginning of 1983 have therefore been printed in the traditional form. Since that date, books published before 1971 have been catalogued, like later books, on MARC-format tapes, but in a separate record, known as 'GK MARC', in which conformity with existing headings is preserved. These may later be merged with the tapes for the whole catalogue which were originally expected to be produced by an 'optical character recognition' system from the pages of GK III and its supplements.[12] This project has, however, been abandoned as unlikely to achieve its purpose within the time proposed and the financial resources available. In August 1986, tenders were invited for the conversion of the catalogue.

The edition of the catalogue now in production, although entitled *The*

British Library Catalogue of Printed Books to 1975, would be more accurately described as a complete catalogue of books published before 1971 which were catalogued in the Department of Printed Books before the end of 1982, together with those books published in the period 1971 to 1975 which were catalogued in time to be included in the 1971–75 supplement. (Entries for 1971–75 books catalogued later are to be found only in the microfiche catalogue produced from computer tape.) This description will apply to the working catalogue when all the accession slips written before the end of 1982 have been incorporated, and to the published edition when it has reached the end of the alphabet and if it is then completed by a supplement of some 75,000 entries for books catalogued before the end of 1982 but too late for inclusion in the volumes as they appeared.

As a further safeguard against misapprehension, the user of the catalogue must be reminded of those important categories of printed matter that have never been included in it: books in oriental languages, maps and atlases, music (including texts accompanied by musical notes) and the whole contents of the Newspaper Library (which comprise not only 'most daily and weekly periodicals' as stated in the 'Notes for readers' issued in the Reading Room, but also a large number of monthly and even quarterly publications – mainly trade journals and magazines devoted to specialised professional, sporting and recreational interests). Even when these exclusions are taken into account, the claim in the introduction to the new edition that the catalogue is 'the official record for all books published in the United Kingdom up to 1970' needs to be qualified by mentioning the omission of a large number of British scientific and technical publications deposited in the Copyright Receipt Office since 1966 which have been transmitted not to the main collection but to the Science Reference Library, which from 1966 to 1973 (under its earlier name of National Reference Library of Science and Invention) was a division of the Department of Printed Books.

The catalogue in its fullest and final form (whether embodied in the published edition or in the laid-down volumes in the Reading Room) is not the coherent and carefully edited work that GK II aspired to be. Like a landscape variegated by outcrops of geological strata of different ages, it presents on its surface evidence of the process by which it was formed. To the peculiarities of GK III resulting from the reproduction of unrevised earlier entries[13] it adds some new features of its own, due to the introduction in the 1970s of the AACR system. Of these, the one most likely to mislead is the use of the first word of the title to enter works for which the heading under the old rules would have been some other word. Where entries for editions of one work have been made under each of the two systems, a linking reference or note has usually, but by no means always, been made. Different works with identical or similar titles are to be found divided between two headings—usually with no link, although some adjustments have been made, as, for instance, in the reprinting in volume 149 under HISTORY of a number of titles beginning 'The history of England' which had already appeared in volume 100 under ENGLAND. [*Appendix. – History and Politics. – General.*] The searcher for anonymous books clearly needs a knowledge of both the old and the new rules if he is not to miss his quarry: but even this will hardly suffice without awareness also of some surprising interpretations of the Rules in the older parts of the catalogue. For example, the entry: 'The General Election, 1874: biographical sketches of the Metropolitan Candidates' is entered under LONDON. [*Appendix. – Miscellaneous*], although some entries for other titles beginning 'The General Election' appear under ELECTION and some under GENERAL ELECTION.

These deficiencies, though not insignificant, will not seriously inconvenience the great majority of users. Searches under the names of authors or of persons who are the subjects of books will present little difficulty. At least until the complete machine-readable catalogue is available, the General Catalogue will continue to be used as a key to the contents of the national library and as a source of general bibliographical information. Its long undisputed primacy as the most comprehensive single record of books printed in European languages was lost with the publication in 1968–80 of the 685 volumes of the American *National Union Catalog: pre-1956 imprints*, which greatly exceeds it in size and surpasses it in completeness even in some categories of books published in the United Kingdom. It still, however, makes its own indispensable contribution to the unattained and probably unattainable ideal of a universal bibliography.

Its history illustrates the extreme difficulty, so clearly seen by Panizzi, of producing a complete, accurate and up-to-date *published* catalogue of a very large and constantly growing library. In its several attempts to get as near as possible to this goal, the British Museum at first adopted the method of including in each part, as it was prepared for the press, the latest available entries coming within its scope. In the 1881–1900 printing this followed naturally from the fact that, at its inception, the aim of converting the working catalogue from manuscript to printed form took precedence over that of producing a published edition. The deficiencies inherent in the method were to be remedied by a supplement bringing the whole catalogue down to a uniform date – the end of 1899. When a new catalogue with revised entries was started in 1930 the same procedure was followed, but in this case proved fatal to the project because the achieved rate of revision and printing hardly exceeded the rate of growth of the collection, so that completion receded indefinitely into the future.

This situation led to the adoption of a different strategy: the fixing of a uniform closing date for the content of all the volumes, combined with the abandonment of any further revision and the reproduction of the existing entries as they stood by a rapid photographic process. Again a supplement was required, containing the entries written while printing was in progress.

There is a curious parallel between the histories of the two complete editions. Each was preceded by a false start: Panizzi's single volume of 1841 and the more substantial achievement of GK II spread over 25 years but still covering only a fifth of the ground. In both cases the failure was due to a false estimate of the magnitude of the task – in 1839 by the Trustees, who did not appreciate the need felt by Panizzi for greatly improved bibliographical standards, and in 1929 by the Keeper of Printed Books and his advisers, who underestimated the effect of attempting to apply the standards of the 1930s to a nineteenth-century catalogue. In each case the successful completion of a printed catalogue which, in combination with its supplement, was only a few years out of date was due to the insistence of one man that speed in production must override the application of the latest standards, in spite of the doubts and hesitations of the practitioners and guardians of those standards. The role of Garnett in the eighteen eighties and nineties was paralleled by that of Francis in the nineteen fifties and sixties.

Their pragmatic approach found its justification in the reception accorded to the two catalogues. Both were hailed by librarians and the world of learning generally as notable achievements. GK I was out of print by 1918 and a photographic facsimile of it was successfully launched in 1946, when 39 volumes of a slowly progressing revised edition (GK II) had already been published. All copies of GK III were sold before printing was completed, and a photographic reprint was put on the market in the following year. Only 12 years later, still another edition, embodying most of the deficiencies of earlier ones, was found to be a commercially viable proposition. The strength of the demand for a complete, or nearly complete, catalogue of the contents of the Department of Printed Books (whether of the British Museum or the British Library) has regularly reduced to relative insignificance any concern for the unevenness of its bibliographical quality. Indeed, this unevenness is interesting in itself as evidence of the development over 140 years of the practices and standards, often taken as a model elsewhere, of several generations of scholarly and conscientious cataloguers, to whose efforts the General Catalogue will be an enduring memorial.

Notes and References
1. See pp. 154, 155.
2. *International Conference on Cataloguing Principles, Report.* London, 1963, pp. 91–6.
3. Lubetzky, S. *Cataloging Rules and Principles: a critique of the ALA rules for entry.* Library of Congress, Washington, 1953.
4. *ALA Catalog rules: author and title entries.* Chicago, 1941.
5. P.B. file, C.P. 118, 'The preparation of revised rules for the cataloguing of printed books' (undated).
6. *Anglo-American cataloguing rules ... British text.* Library Association, London, 1967.
7. *Report on the feasibility of using automatic data processing in the British Museum, principally in the Department of Printed Books.* Issued April 1967.
8. *The scope of automatic data processing in the British Library.* HMSO, London, 1972, paras. 185–203.
9. Esdaile, Arundell. *The British Museum Library.* George Allen and Unwin, London, 1946, p. 77.
10. Preface by Richard Garnett to *List of contents of the three collections of books pamphlets and journals in the British Museum relating to the French Revolution,* compiled by G. K. Fortescue. Printed by order of the Trustees, 1899.
11. See p. 145.
12. Clements, D. W. G. 'Conversion of the General Catalogue of Printed Books to machine-readable form', *Journal of Librarianship*, 15(3) July 1983, p. 206.
13. See pp. 142, 143.

Index

AACR 67, *see* Anglo-American Cataloguing Rules (1967)
Aberdeen, Earl of 7
Abstractor camera 133, 134, 147, 148
Academies 13, 34, 35, 45
   scope and arrangement 21–23
   change of rule, 1873 46
   abolition of heading 103, 116
Accessions
   addition to catalogue 3, 39
   annual lists (1836–38) 5, 20
   annual lists (1983–85) 147, 148
   card file 1955–80 146, 155
   printing 47–9, 52
   use by other libraries 96
   inclusion in printed parts of catalogue 63, 106, 107, 163, 168
Acts of Parliament 82
Added entries 159, 160
Adjectives in headings 26, 27, 80, 99
Advocates' Library, Edinburgh 68
Aldrich, S. J. 57
Alphabetical author and title catalogues 157
Alphabetical order, departures from 88, 89, 90
Alterations by cataloguers 95
American libraries
   subscriptions for GK II 102, 103
American Library Association 71
   Committee on co-operation 1877 71
   Rules, 1878 72
   Cataloging Rules Committee 157
   Catalog Rules, 1941 158
Anglo-American Rules (1908) 97, 126

Anglo-American Cataloguing Rules (1967) 158–60, 162, 167
Anonymous books
   rules for 19, 79, 80
   cross-references under authors 75, 76
   compromise over entry 19
   entry under first substantive 19, 35
   entry under first word 38, 154, 159
   entry under 'leading' word 4, 5, 10
   entry under name in title 12, 19
   main entry under author 68, 69, 142, 154
Anonymous classics 80
Appendix to Report of the Royal Commission, *see* Royal Commission, Report, Appendix
Aristotle 13, 28, 62, 63, 86
Arrangement
   of headings 28, 29, 71, 89, 90, 119
   of entries under a heading 20, 21, 25, 28, 30, 70, 85–9
   letter-by-letter, word-by-word 29, 30, 89
Arrears of cataloguing 39, 40, 121, 123, 164
Assistant Cataloguers 109, 120–24
Assistant Keepers 110n, 120–24
Athenaeum 50
Audiffredi, Giovanni Battista
   catalogue of Biblioteca Casanatense 8

Baber, H. H. 1–5
   rules 10, 11, 15, 16, 19
Balding and Mansell 132, 133, 134, 147, 148
Bandinel, B. 67

Index

Banks, Sir Joseph
  catalogue of collection 2
Banksian Room 117
Barwick, G. F. 97, 125
Bible 21, 67, 70
Biblioteca Casanatense 8
Bingley, Clive 163
Biographies, anonymous, entry under subject 69
Bishop, W. W. 109
Bishops 45
'Black Book' 99, 100, 117, 118
Blackstone, F. E. 59, 60, 81
Blades, William 48
Bodleian Library
  catalogue, 1674 8
  catalogue, 1845–51 67
Bond, E. A. 52, 53, 54, 59, 60, 81
British Library 162, 163
British Library Catalogue of Printed Books to 1975, The 163, 167
British Museum, Trustees, *see* Trustees of the British Museum
British National Bibliography 125, 126, 128, 158, 161, 162
Brodhurst, Audrey 164
Brown, Peter 148, 158
Brown University
  catalogue by C. C. Jewett 68
Bullen, George 48, 49, 50, 51, 53, 54, 59, 60, 62, 63, 77

Cain, A. M. 161
Cambridge University Library 47, 73
Carlyle, Thomas 38
Cary, H. F. 2
Catalogue
  plans for a new catalogue 1834–41 2–5, 7, 8
  question of printing 6–9
Catalogue, in manuscript, 1841–1880 42
  revision for, unsatisfactory progress 59, 60
Catalogue, printed editions
  1813–19, *see* Octavo catalogue
  1841, vol 1 completed 14
    description 26–32
  1880–1905, *see* GK I
  1930–1955, *see* GK II
  1961–1966, *see* GK III
  1979–1987, *see British Library Catalogue of Printed Books to 1975*
Catalogue Room 111–13, 116, 117
Catalogue Shop 93, 94, 95, 116, 117, 147, 148
Cataloguers, notes for
  Notes respecting the General Catalogue, 1920–25 (the Black Book) 99, 100, 117, 118
  Memoranda for cataloguers 1930–35 (the Orange Book) 117, 118
  Catalogue notes, 1950–59 153
Catalogues, cataloguing of 23, 82
Catalogues, special, of parts of the Library 6, 50, 51
Cataloguing
  organisation 124, 153
  procedure 112–14
  general movement towards uniformity 157, 158
Cathedrals 79
Centralised cataloguing 97, 101, 125
Central Library for Students 101
Cervantes 95
Change of name 70, 73
Chaplin, A. H. 111, 128, 129, 130, 153, 156, 157
Childs, C. E. N. 145
Civil Service Inquiry Commission 47
Class-headings 16, 23, 24, 68, 70, 73, 92, 97
Clowes, William, & Sons 54, 58, 115, 116, 132, 133
Cluj 154
Clutton, Sir George L. 109
Collections, works published in
  entry by cross-reference 76
Collier, John Payne 38
Committee on Public Libraries, 1927 101
Commissioners appointed to inquire into the constitution and management of the British Museum, *see* Royal Commission
Compound surnames 89
  French 70, 92
  English and Dutch 100
  Dutch married women 100, 118

Index

Computer-operated typesetting 161, 162
Computer output on microfilm 163
Computers, application of 161
Conference of Librarians, Edinburgh, 1877 50, 71
Conference of Librarians, Philadelphia, 1876 71
Congresses 97, 151
Conversion to machine-readable form 161, 162, 166
Cooley, W. D. 57, 68
Copyists, as substitutes for Transcribers 53
Copyright Libraries 97
Corporate authorship 69
Corporate bodies 16, 26, 69, 83, 98
Courtney, W. P. 92
Croker, John Wilson 38, 41, 47, 164
Cross-references 9, 10
Cutter, C. A. 70–72

Dainton Committee, *see* National Libraries Committee
De Morgan, Augustus 37, 38
Department of Printed Books staff 108, 120, 121, 123
Devil, as heading 151, 152
Dickens, Charles 142
Dictionaries 153
Dilke, Charles Wentworth (1789–1864) 50
Directories 81, 82
Douglas, R. K. 56

Eccles, G. W. 62
Edinburgh Review 92
Edwards, Edward 11, 12, 38
Ellesmere, Earl of 38
Ellis, Sir Henry 2–7, 10, 35–7
England (heading) 64, 88
English books, definition 83, 98
English books to 1640, British Museum Catalogue of 51, 53
Etherington, S. J. 166
Excerpts 106, 130, 142
Executive Grade cataloguers 121, 123, 124

Filing titles 99, 155

Five-year supplements 149
Format 16, 18
Fortescue, G. K. 65, 66, 95, 96
Forshall, J. 6, 7, 8, 10, 38
Fourth copies 42, 43, 94, 117
Foxon, David 142
Francis, Sir Frank C. 107, 121, 123, 125, 126, 127, 128, 133, 157, 169
French Revolution tracts 65, 164

GK I
  title 111
  first printed part 58
  printing in alphabetical order 59, 62
  typography 91, 92
  photographic reprint, 1946 128
  question of new edition 65, 96, 101, 102
GK I and GK III
  parallel histories 169
GK II
  proposal 101, 102
  prospectus 102
  title 111
  bibliographical standards 114
  editorial method 113–15
  inconsistencies 151
  organisation 111, 121–24
  rate of production 102, 106–10, 114, 116, 123, 124
  staff and time needed for completion 108, 109, 120, 123, 128, 129
GK III
  proposals for photolithographic production 124, 127–31
  estimates of cost and time 127, 129, 131
  cut-off date 130
  print run 133
  price 131, 138
  subscriptions 131–33, 138, 139
  contract with printer 133, 134
  preparation of copy 132–35
  proofs 138
  distribution 138, 139
  inclusion of GK II volumes 139
  completion 139
  compact edition 141, 145

GK III *cont.*
  comparison with GK II 142
  bibliographical information 143
  cataloguing changes during
    production 153, 154
  errors and omissions 143, 145, 164, 165
  supplements 147–50
  supplements – finance 149
Garnett, Richard, Assistant Keeper 1838–50 10
Garnett, Richard, Keeper 1890–99 48, 49, 51–54, 59, 60, 62–6
General Catalogue
  amalgamation of pre- and post-1839 entries 46
  title 90
  exclusions 90–91
General Catalogue of English Literature 50
Geneva, Public Library, catalogue 8
German modified vowels 72, 73, 78
Germany 88
Glover, J. H. 4
God, as heading 151
Government publications 91
Gray, G. R. 38
Great Britain (heading) 64, 65

Hamilton, W. R. 37, 38
Headings
  based on information in the book 18, 82, 83
  parts of 91
  single word or compound 89
Horace 64, 86
Horne, J. C. W. 111
Horne, T. H. 4, 18, 22
Hyde, Thomas 8
Hymnals 97

I and *J*, *U* and *V* 64, 92, 96, 154
ICCP Statement of Principles 158
IFLA 157
Imprints
  order of items 70, 72, 74
Incorporation 10, 94, 95
  arrears 147

Incorporator 40, 94, 95, 112, 113, 118
Index of matters 5
Indexes of subheadings and titles 89
Inglis, Sir Robert 37, 38
Initials, entry under 18, 45
International Conference on Cataloguing Principles, 1961 157
  see also ICCP
International Federation of Library Associations, *see* IFLA

Jewett, Charles Coffin 57, 68–70
Jewish prayers 118, 119
Johnson, A. F. 107
Joint authorship 24, 83, 98
Jolliffe, John 161, 162
Jones, John Winter 11, 12, 43, 44, 51
Junior Assistants, *see* Transcribers

King's Library 2, 4, 9, 40
  catalogue 21, 22, 32
  pamphlets 2, 40
Klausenburg 154

Laid-down volumes
  three copy system 42
  of GK I 93
  of GK II 106
  of GK III 146, 147
Language sections 124, 161
Lardner, L. J. 40
Latin
  use of in headings 67
    in King's Library catalogue 21, 22
    for Greek authors' names 27
  priority in arranging translations 20
Leonardo da Vinci 154
Leopol 154
Library Association (of Great Britain) 50, 51, 56, 71
  Cataloguing rules, 1879 72
  Committee on title entries 72
  Cataloguing Rules Sub-Committee 157
Library Journal 72
Library of Congress 97, 125, 127, 158
Line, Maurice 162
Liturgies 64, 70, 73, 83
Liturgies.–Jews 118

Index

London University Library   126
Lubetzky, Seymour   158
L'vov   154
Lynam, E. D. O.   107

Macfarlane, A. G.   107, 121
Mahon, Viscount   38
Maitland, S. R.   38
Major, R. H.   42
Maps   42, 91
  catalogue   82, 149
MARC   162
Marsden, W. A.   107, 108, 116
Martineau, Russell   60, 64
  draft code of rules   77–82, 99
Meyer, H. H. B.   101
Miller, A. W. K.   59, 60, 64, 96, 97
Miller, Edward
  biography of Panizzi   1
Molière   154
Movable title-slips   41
Music   42, 82, 91, 167

Names
  in English form   17, 27
  in titles of anonymous books   19
National Lending Library of Science and Technology   162
National Libraries Committee   162
National Library of Scotland   126
National Union Catalog (US)   168
Newspaper Library   167
Newspapers   91, 167
Newton, C. T.   51, 52
Nicolas, Sir Harris   34, 35
Noblemen
  entry under title or family name   69, 70, 71

Octavo catalogue   2
  as basis for new catalogue   7
  mounted and interleaved copies   2, 5, 39
O'Donovan, Ann   159
Old Music Room   117, 124
Oldman, C. B.   77, 107
  report on GK II (1950)   124
  report on GK II (1951)   128
  report on GK II (1953)   129, 130

Oliphant, Thomas   42
'Orange Book'   117, 118, 151
Oriental books   17, 167
Oriental names   155

Pagination   69, 72, 74
Panizzi, Sir Anthony   1–14, 33–43, 164
  see also Rules (Panizzi, 1839)
Paper used for GK III   142
Parry, John Humffreys   12
Periodical Publications   23, 64, 143
  not to include official organs of societies etc.   98
  entry under title   159
Photolithographic edition, *see* GK III
Pine-Coffin, R. S.   159
Pollard, A. W.   64, 97
Pollard, A. W., and Redgrave, G. R.
  Short-title Catalogue   51
Popes   45, 88
Porter, G. W.   45, 48
Principal Keeper
  new grade   121
Printing suspended, 1846–47   34, 38
Printing, 1880–1900
  of accessions and older untranscribed titles   54, 59
  of over-full volumes   52, 57
  of whole catalogue   59, 62
  rate of production   62–4
Pseudonyms   19, 99, 153
Public libraries
  free copies of GK I   59
  reduced price for GK II   103
Publisher's name
  inclusion in imprint   74, 83

Quérard, J. M.   11, 12

Readex Microprint Corporation   141
Revisers   111–13
Revision of important headings   95, 164
Revision of pre-1839 entries   46
Rockefeller Foundation   102, 109
Rome   88
'Rose List'   119

Index

Roy, E. A.
  on movable slips 41
  on printing 48, 49
  on rate of revision 60
Royal Commission, 1847–1850 1, 38
  Report 38
  Appendix to report 1
  Minutes of evidence 14, 41, 47, 57, 66
Rules (Baber, 1834) 10, 11
  comparison with Panizzi's 15–19
Rules (Panizzi, 1839)
  drafts, March–June 1839 12
  approval by Trustees 13
  printed versions 24
  content and comparison with Baber's 16–24
  influence 67, 68–70, 72, 73
  amendments and additions 44–6, 75
Rules (extended draft, 1886) 77–81
Rules (printed editions)
  1897 (provisional) 82
  1900 83
  consultation with Oxford and Cambridge, 1920 97
  1920 97, 98
  changes and additions 99, 100
  1927 100
  changes and additions 117, 118
  1936 118
  changes considered, 1953–55 154
  influence of ICCP 158
  influence of AACR 67, 158–60
  use by other libraries 126
Rye, W. B. 44, 47, 48

Saint (Sainte), headings beginning with 89, 90
Saint Petersburg 154
Saur, K. G. 163
Science Reference Library 167
Select Committee, 1835–36 5
Series footnote 76, 98
Settled queries 95
Series title, cross-references from 100
Shakespeare 86, 142
Sharp, N. F. 111, 121, 123, 128
  editor of GK II 124, 151, 153
  chairman L A Cataloguing Rules Sub-Committee 157

Sharp, R. F. 97, 98
  proposal for new edition of catalogue, 1928 101, 102, 106, 107
Shelf-by-shelf cataloguing 4, 38, 39, 46
Sheppard, L. A. 107
Size, *see* Format
Smith, W. A. 111
Society of Arts 50, 51
Standing Commission on Museums and Galleries 109
State Papers, *see* Government publications
Stereotyping 57, 68
Stevens, Henry 68
Subheadings
  in 1841 volume 27, 28
  in GK I 86–8
  in GK II 142, 143
Supplement to GK I 65, 66
Surnames
  with prefixes 11, 12
  compound, *see* Compound surnames
Swift, Jonathan 143

Temporary Assistant Cataloguers, *see* Assistant Cataloguers
Ten-Year Supplement 145, 147–50
Thomas, Sir Henry 107, 118, 120, 121, 125
Thomason tracts 65
Title entries 160
Title page, heading to be based on 18
Title Room 94, 117
Titles
  cataloguers' additions 71
Todd, J. H. 67
Transcribers 40
  grading of their work 47
Translations 19, 20, 68, 99, 100, 118
Treasury 131, 134, 149
Treasury Solicitor 133
Treaties 45, 117, 118
Trinity College, Dublin
  catalogue 67, 68
Trustees of the British Museum 1–16, 24, 33–40, 42, 51, 53, 54, 57, 58, 65, 66, 96, 101–103, 108, 109, 120, 124, 125, 128–30, 132, 133, 139, 149
Tucker, G. D. R. 113, 119

Index

Tuckett, Charles, jun. 41
Twentieth Century Catalogue 96, 97
Typography
  of 1841 volume 32
  of GK I 91, 92
  of GK II 141, 142, 143

U and V, see I and J
Universal Catalogue 50, 51

Vaucher, Louis 8
Virgilius Maro 59
Voltaire, heading for 35, 70, 92, 143, 154

Volumes, number of 17, 18

Watts, Thomas 44, 46
  on printing of title-slips 47
Wedgwood, Ralph
  manifold writer 42, 43n
Wharton, L. C. 107, 154
William I, Prince of Orange 145
Williamson Abstractor, see Abstractor camera
Wilson, R. A. 111
  editor of GK II 121, 123, 128
  Principal Keeper 138
Wright, W. Aldis 47, 48